Latino Politics in the United States

Race, Ethnicity, Class, and Gender in the Mexican American and Puerto Rican Experience

Victor M. Rodriguez
California State University, Long Beach

KENDALL/HUNT PUBLISHING COMPANY
4050 Westmark Drive   Dubuque, Iowa 52002

• • • Contents • • •

● ● ● **Preface** ● ● ●

The book that my dear colleague and friend Victor Rodriguez has
written, and that you are about to read, was sorely needed. It is a work
that combines theory with empirics; history, political science and
sociology; case studies and firm generalizations. It is accessible.
Perhaps most importantly it compares and contrasts the racialized
experiences of Mexican-Americans and Puerto Ricans in the United
States, making the kind of comparisons among Latino experiences
that are so rare in academic books.

The work begins, in the first chapter, by addressing one of the least
studied aspects of the experience of Latin American migrants to the
United States. That is to say, the ways in which their cultural and
national differences are erased upon settling in this country, and their
subsequent pigeonholing into pre-established, uniquely American,
racial categories. Victor Rodriguez shows us the similarities and the
differences between Chicanos and Boricuas in the paths they took
into the racialized American space. The following chapters, full of
interesting historical events and empirical details, build on the theorizing of the first. The urban explosion of Los Angeles in 1992, following the acquittal of police officers in the brutal beating of Rodney
King, Rodriguez explains, was perhaps the first example of a
"multicultural" uprising in the United States. The author presents to
us a complex web: the social, economic and racial matrix that has
turned our urban cores into economic "badlands," providing the
explosive mixture that ignited in the 1992 Los Angeles events. The
book covers much ground literally and figuratively. We find out how
Boricuas and friends worked to build the movement towards Puerto
Rican independence in the West Coast of the United States from the
sixties to the eighties. Also in the West Coast we are treated to a
wonderful case study of the struggle against racism and marginalization in California. In affluent Orange County, a conservative Anglo
minority had for decades ruled unchallenged over an area that included one of the largest Mexican American urban centers in the
United States, the city of Santa Ana, California. We learn how Latinos,
organizing from the bottom up, brought about an end to what was in
effect a quasi-apartheid system. The book ends on a high and hopeful
note, at the other end of the Chicano-Boricua geographical span in
Vieques. We learn of the inspiring effort that brought world attention

and the unity of the most diverse political groups to end decades of naval bombardment of the Puerto Rican island of Vieques.

This book is about understanding oppression, but it is also, and for the most part, about resistance and victory. I think that's why I enjoyed reading it as I think you will too.

Raul A. Fernandez,
School of Social Science, University of California, Irvine[1]

---

[1] His most recent books are *Latin Jazz: The Perfect Combination*. Washington, D.C.: Smithsonian Institution, 2002 and co-author with Gilbert G. Gonzalez, *A Century of Chicano History: Empire, Nations and Migration*. New York: Routledge, 2003.

• • • **Acknowledgments** • • •

"Every victory is tinged by past defeats. It's never a total defeat if it helps us to see what road we should follow."

—Paco Ramos, in *The Vanquished* novel
by Cesar Andreu Iglesias

Every human effort has a history, even when it seems a spontaneous act. Every drama has various characters who provide perspectives about human action. It is important to remember that every human achievement occurs within a social context, even the seemingly individual act of writing a book. This book has a history, characters and an important social context. The ideas and experiences that are told in this book are an attempt to affirm, respect and understand the journey for empowerment of Mexican Americans and Puerto Ricans in the United States and Puerto Rico. The historical background for this book is my own involvement in some of these struggles, especially in the pro-independence movement of Puerto Rico, the liberation movement of Vieques and the island's trade union movement. All of these experiences shaped my world view and sense of social justice.

I also owe much to the people in my everyday life who supported and encouraged me, despite the fact that this project at times took me away, both geographically and emotionally, from my loved ones. Thanks to my beloved wife Laura Rodriguez, who trusted me enough to know I needed to tell these stories. Thanks to my children who already have their own children, Joseph, Arlene and Carlina, who have always been my inspiration. Thanks to my beloved parents, Rev. Victor M. Rodriguez and Sara Rodriguez, for always being there for me. Thanks to my friends and mentors, Raul Fernandez, Gilbert Gonzalez, Juan Manuel Carrion, Ivan Gutierrez, Luis Arroyo, Maria Merrill Ramirez, Maria I. Reinat Pumarejo, Doris Pizarro, Nestor Nazario, Ismael Guadalupe and others from whom I have learned so much. To them my deepest gratitude and my apologies for any misinterpretations of what I learned from them.

Finally, I want to thank Amanda Smith, Project Coordinator and Janice M. Samuells, Senior Editor, Kendall/Hunt, for their professionalism and the support they provided to this project. I also want to thank the anonymous editorial editors who made my prose read so much better than when I initially wrote these sentences.

Victor M. Rodriguez
Irvine, California
April 18, 2005

● ● ● ● ● ● ● ● ● ● ● ● ● ● ● ● ● ●

The Racialization of Mexican Americans and Puerto Ricans: 1890s-1930s[1]

Abstract

A theoretical framework that describes the basic processes of racialization is proposed by analyzing how Mexican Americans and Puerto Ricans were racialized during the first decades of the twentieth century. This was a significant time when the rise and saliency of the ideologies of scientific racism and imperialism became part of the popular culture and a time when Puerto Ricans and Mexicans were being colonized both in their nations of origin and in their diasporic homelands. While there is some significant descriptive work on contemporary racialization in the Chicano and Boricua experience, very little comparative and theoretical work underpins these efforts. By looking at the patterns that emerge in the process of subordinating, controlling, and classifying Mexican Americans and Puerto Ricans, we gain perspective of the role of colonialism (both internal and external), the role of class, and the role of gender in racialization, and we begin to create the basis for a theoretically grounded perspective on racialization.

Introduction

Understanding the process of the racialization of Latinos in the United States is a necessary task to clarify the dynamics and role of race and racism in this country. Clara Rodríguez (2000) said that the study of Latinos serves as a good illustration of the "social constructedness" of race in the United States.[2] However, although there is a significant literature that has focused on specific aspects of this process, very little comparative work is available on the similarities and differences between the racialization process of the various "Latino" groups.[3] We will have a better grasp of the process of racialization if we understand the particularities and similarities of racialization within various ethnic components of the Latino community.

Flores (2000) reminded us in his article, "Pan-Latino/Trans-Latino":

> "The adequacy of the embattled "Latino" or "Hispanic" concept hinges on its inclusiveness toward the full range of social experiences and identities, and particularly its bridging of the divergence within the contemporary configuration between recent "Latino immigrant" populations and, for want of a better term, the "resident minority" Chicano and Puerto Rican communities." (Flores, 2000:164).

The homogenization of differences among people of Latin American origin in the United States is part of the process of racialization.[4] An important constituent of pigeonholing groups into a racial taxonomy is the erasure of the distinctive qualities that humanize them. Those "rough edges" are erased in the process of categorizing. This makes the "fit" within the cells more precise. These individualizing characteristics, which become faded in the process, are the historical, cultural, and political differences among and within Latin American immigrants. To racialize Latin Americans is to provide them with a new encasement, with the kinds of racialized characteristics that will tightly fit them into the carefully constructed racial grids that constitute the racial architecture of the United States.

A strategic way of demystifying and revealing the fissures of this process requires the use of a comparative model, in order to examine the role and history of the racialization experience of Latinos. By comparing these groups we can highlight the salient features and patterns of the process of incorporating people of Latin American origin into the nation's racial grid. It seems strategic then, to focus on the experience of the two Latino groups who have become, to use Flores' term, the "resident minority" groups among Latinos in the United States. Many Latinos who have arrived in the United States, particularly after 1965, are racialized in the context of the preceding and accumulated racialization

experience of Boricuas and Chicanos. Their past experience becomes the foundation for the present pattern of becoming racialized "Latinos/ Hispanics" for many people of Latin American origin.[5]

To demystify racialization, we must theoretically delineate some of the salient features of the process of racialization by examining some basic historical texts. These salient features in turn will provide the contours for a framework that will help understand the particularities of racialization. Re-reading these texts within this theoretical framework serves to illustrate the need and benefits of further comparative work between Chicanos and Boricuas and their comparison with the racialization experience of other groups.

Racialization is part of a dialectical process where the groups in the process of being subordinated also challenge, contest, and contribute to the racialization of themselves and others. Since racialization is a process that includes the socialization into a culture signified by race, individuals internalize patterns of behavior and thought that contribute to their own subordination and to the perpetuation of the system.

Scope and Concepts

Renato Rosaldo (1987) developed the useful notion of "cultural citizenship." This idea is central to how we understand racialization. For Rosaldo, racialization is challenged by a whole range of strategies and practices, which allows a group to establish a contested territory or "social space" where Latinos can challenge and survive subordination. This process of creating a social space is what he calls "cultural citizenship." Part of those efforts to challenge racialization include resisting the polarized and bifurcated system of racial categories in the United States.

A recent attempt to utilize his theoretical concept is found in William V. Flores and Rita Benmayor (1997). However, while these narratives serve as data for work on the comparative dialectic of racialization, they do not include within them a comparative approach. In the United States, racial categories are constructed in binary opposition to each other; they become part of a comparative taxonomy of white/black where racialization occurs in the context of comparison and categorization with an "other." It is precisely in this process of comparison where meaning is constructed by creating categories that are cognitively intelligible. It is for this reason that to understand racialization, which is at its core a process of creating meaning, one must use a comparative approach.

Early work on the racialization of African Americans was conducted by W. E. B. Du Bois in his classical treatise *The Souls of Black Folks* (1903). Here, he introduced the concept of "double consciousness" as a pivotal component of racialization.[6] However, while much can be gleamed from the African American experience, the choreography of the dialectic of

racialization of a group like people of Latin American origin, requires a historically specific and comparative approach.

First, the racialization of Africans occurred in a comparative taxonomy that included whites as the "non-other." As Haney Lopez (1996) has revealed, the legal process of determining which immigrants were "white" (in order to be able to naturalize as U.S. citizen) implicitly recognized the dialectic of racialization:

> "No court offered a complete typology listing the characteristics of Whiteness against which to compare the petitioner. Instead, the courts defined "white" through a process of negation, systemically identifying who was non-White." (Haney Lopez, 1996:27)

Obviously, the courts assumed that a person was "white" if that person was not, "non-white." This double negative reveals an understanding that racialization implies a process where the incorporation of individuals and groups occurs into a system of racial categories that are not absolute, instead, they are "comparative taxonomies of relative difference." (Haney Lopez, 1996:27)

What this means is that if we are to understand racialization we must do it in a comparative way so that we can see the striking similarities and differences that occur in the racialization of groups. In the United States, the "black/white" relationship was foundational for the construction of the racial grid of the United States. But the experience of people of Latin American origin is so significantly different that it requires a different framework.

Second, people of Latin American origin become incorporated into the racial grid in more diverse ways. Some came from nations or regions that were conquered and colonized as the United States expanded, and others came as immigrants from nations with varying degrees of neo-colonial relationships with the United States. Thirdly, people of Latin American origin did not come as "tabula rasa" with respect to race, they came from countries that had already developed different systems of racial hierarchies. So the process of racializing people of Latin American origin into "Latino/Hispanic" is built upon the foundation of the mode of incorporation and the previous memory of racial hierarchies' immigrants or conquered peoples brought with them.[7]

For Mexicans and Puerto Ricans, their homelands (or fractions thereof) were conquered, and this conquest was followed by a process of "voluntary" emigration to the new metropolis. This meant that their relationship with the United States was similar, yet not the same, as that of European immigrants.[8] The trauma of the African middle passage and the holocaust of enslavement was not part of their historical memory as a group. Many persons of Latin American origin came with a strongly

held belief in the myth of the "American Dream." There was no possible "American Dream" for enslaved Africans.

Another factor that makes the racialization of people of Latin American origin quite distinct is that they arrived, particularly Puerto Ricans and Mexicans, from countries where miscegenation was common and where the ideology and practice of *mestizaje* was part of nation-building efforts (Klor de Alva, 1999). Furthermore, their racial hierarchies, contrary to the polarized system of the United States, had intermediate racial categories that allowed people not be "black." (Guerra, 1998; Bonilla-Silva and Glover 2005). In Mexico, the indigenous led rebellion against Porfirio Diaz' regime (1876-1911) used "mestizaje" to aid the coalescing of forces against the dictator. In practice, this meant, erasing the African category from any relevance in the racial hierarchy of Mexico. Earlier, the way the elite treated Afro-Mexican patriot Vicente Guerrero in contrast to right and left opponents indicates a strong anti-African undercurrent in Mexican colonial culture.[9] In Benedict Anderson's terms (1991) Mexico "imagined itself" as a mestizo nation, and incorporated Mexicans of African descent into mestizaje. Therefore, the *tercera raiz* (African) is conspicuously absent from the Mexican imaginary.

In Puerto Rico, since the racial system was not a bifurcated system of categories (black/white), moving from one racial category to a more prestigious status was easier than in the United States.[10] This racial hierarchy was not based on an either/or framework but a series of racial categories lined along a less rigid continuum. Each intermediate category was a composite of color and physical features, on one end white, and black at the other end of the continuum. The closer the cluster of physical characteristics resembled whites, the more social status the person could have. What this meant was that is was feasible to move into whiter categories, in the United States, "passing" was only possible in exceptional circumstances.[11] In Latin America, the "whitening" process was formalized, the Spanish King Carlos III in 1783 issued a decree by which a person of mixed, Spanish and African heritage could receive a *cedula de gracias al sacar* (Guerra, 1998:215). This *cedula* would grant the status of "white" to the recipient.

The extensive experience of miscegenation among Latinos has led to a strong challenge of this "othering" process, at least at the level of the bureaucratic racializing of the U.S. Census Bureau. In recent decades, and especially in the last Census (2000), Latinos, when asked to choose race, 42.2% have chosen "other," instead of black, white, or American Indian.[12] Ironically, among Boricuas in Puerto Rico, racialization and colonization have had quite a distinct impact. More than 80.5% of Puerto Ricans in the island chose "white" when confronted with the racial categories question for the first time since 1950.[13] Meanwhile, only 46.4% of Puerto Ricans in the mainland chose white, while 38.2% chose "other" (IUPLR, 2002). This is a trend that, according to Duany (2002),

signifies a gap in the outcome of the racialization experience between Boricuas in Puerto Rico and in the United States. Now, that Puerto Ricans in the United States are as numerous as those in the island (2003, 3,855,608 mainland and 3,878,532 in the island) it remains to be seen how the different racial consciousness will impact race relations in Puerto Rico (Falcon, 2004).

Historical Scope

This comparative look at racialization for Puerto Ricans focuses on the period after the Spanish-American War of 1898 and until the 1930s for a number of reasons. While Puerto Ricans had engaged in significant trade relations with the United States during the latter part of the nineteenth century, it is not until the conquest and occupation of the island when Puerto Ricans as a collective were significantly drawn into a quite distinct process of racialization. It is in this period, when racialization pivots on a matrix of bifurcated racial categories and a biological ideology that ascribes differences to immutable biological characteristics. A qualitative change in racialization took place between the Spanish and Anglo-Saxon periods in the island. After the abolition of slavery in 1873 in Puerto Rico, Puerto Ricans of African descent experienced a relative rise in social status. In Puerto Rico, intermarriage was more common, and the skills acquired by enslaved Africans in the plantation economy, and the existence of a significantly large population of free Blacks eased their gradual, although subordinated, integration into Puerto Rico's society. However, this period needs more research in order to delineate more precisely the process of racialization under Spain.

Meanwhile, the United States' influence in the island, especially its racial paradigm was not as pervasive as in Cuba. Compared to Cuba, Puerto Rico was not in the public imagination of the United States. The end of the "Splendid Little War" brought Puerto Rico to a more visible place in the United States' imagination as the issue of citizenship and future political status became part of the political discourse (Cabranes, 1979). It also brought Puerto Rican culture into direct contact with the racial paradigm of the United States. It is in this period where racialization in Puerto Rico begins to pivot more and more on the bifurcated racial system of the United States. A system where biological differences are signified and encoded in ways that shaped how Puerto Ricans are racialized.

However, within the island, Puerto Ricans were better able to challenge racialization than in the mainland. The relatively small number of Puerto Ricans living in the United States during this period also limited their ability to challenge racialization effectively. By the late 1930s, significant political and cultural changes were taking place in the United States and Puerto Rico that began to give rise to a new context for

racialization. Within the social sciences, more culturally based perspectives began to challenge biological and evolutionary frameworks, the rise of radical politics in the United States and nationalism in Puerto Rico also serve to contest racialization (Duany, 2002:264). This transition needs further exploration and analysis, especially the intensification of racialization that occurs after this transitional period in the United States.

The racialization process of Mexicans in the first two-thirds of the nineteenth century was qualitatively distinct to the one that developed in the late nineteenth and early twentieth century. As Tomas Almaguer (1994:45) argues, "white immigrants actually assigned Mexicans an intermediate location in the new society they imposed in the region." In other words, in the racial hierarchy constructed by white settlers in the newly conquered southwest, Mexicans, because they were Christians, mestizo, and still had a significant landed elite who mediated between Anglo whites and Mexicans, were not entirely racialized in the process. As a social group, Mexicans became an ethnic group akin to European immigrants in the sense that the basic process of differentiation was rooted in culture, not race as a biologically defined and culturally meaningful construct. During this period, the "otherness" of Mexicans was rooted in culture rather than on some assumed biological difference.[14] This more "biological racialization" begins to occur at the end of the nineteenth century and particularly during the twentieth century.

Traditional Chicano scholars have represented Chicano history as a seamless narrative that begins with the Mexican-American War and continues until today. As other Chicano/Latino scholars begin to look at the social and economic structures being developed after the conquest a more nuanced historical perspective is beginning to arise. Gonzalez and Fernandez (1998:83) argue that in order for Chicano history to achieve its place within U.S. mainstream history, there is a need to "break down barriers to historical understanding among the various groups that comprise the United States." One way that Gonzalez and Fernandez suggest achieving this is by engaging in comparative research and understanding that "capitalism did not come to every region (of the United States) at the same time nor on the same terms" (1998:83). In order to accomplish this, the political economy of the region must also be examined. Throughout the Southwest, the expansion of capitalism and the building of the railroads increased the demand for labor and contributed to effect significant demographic changes. Because of the growth of the white population, by the 1890s, Santa Barbara, California, the last politically significant Mexican enclave, lost its ability to influence and mediate with the white political system (Gonzalez, 1999:88-89). In Los Angeles, the arrival of the railroad had increased the Anglo population and by the 1880s had placed Mexicans in a minority status by the end of the century. In Arizona, it was also around the 1880s when

End to the mexican Resistance..

lost #'s

Mexicans lost control of local politics (Gonzalez, 1999:93). During that decade, the last members of the landed elite lost their lands and Mexicans lost their numerical majority. In Los Angeles, for example, in 1850, 60% of Mexicans owned some property; by 1870 less than 24% owned any property (Acuña, 1988:127). The political control of the city was transferred to the rising Anglo elite, closing a chapter of significant resistance to racialization in Mexican American political history and the beginning of another chapter signified by subordination.

With some exceptions, specifically in New Mexico, Mexicans become racialized subjects rather than a conquered nation struggling to resist political domination. In New Mexico, the process of subordinating and racializing the Mexican population took a while longer. Until the 1890s, New Mexicans were able to maintain a degree of local control even after significant Anglo immigration in the 1890s. One indicator of their ability to maintain a critical mass that could leverage some political protection was their substantial bilingual educational system. The system was maintained despite significant criticism from whites that it was a symptom that New Mexicans were not sufficiently "American." This was one reason used by members of Congress for not admitting New Mexico as a state until 1912 (Nieto-Phillips, 1999:56). From 1848 to 1880, throughout the Southwest, the nature of resistance against Anglo encroachment and domination took the character of an anti colonial struggle. The prevalence of insurrectionary efforts like Juan Nepomuceno (Cheno) Cortina in Texas, the "Gorras Blancas" in New Mexico, and social bandits like Juan Flores and Joaquin Murietta in California and later, Gregorio Cortez in Texas, begins to fade away as the Mexican American population is racialized and pigeonholed into its new racial identity.

"Mexican" then becomes a racial category rather than an ethnic descriptor. This process of racialization of Mexicans was quite advanced in Southern California by the end of the century, on August 20, 1892, Francisco Torres accidentally killed the foreman of a ranch in Modjeska Canyon (Orange County, California) where he was a ranch hand. A "posse" was organized, Torres was captured and lynched with a sign hung around his dead body saying "change of venue." This reference was in response to efforts to have him tried elsewhere. The *Santa Ana Standard* wrote:

> "Torres was a low type of Mexican race, and was evidently more Indian than white. True to his savage nature he had no more regard for human life than for the merest trifle.... He belongs to a class of outlaws in southern California and old Mexico." (Acuña, 1988:129)

By the 1890s, Mexicans had reached the status of a racial group in the United States, their previously held intermediate position in the racial hierarchy was giving rise to a new more modern form of subordination. In Puerto Rico, however, while Puerto Ricans had been racialized, they still did not achieve a fully racialized status like Mexican Americans in the United States. For Puerto Ricans in the mainland, their racialization was more intensive than for those in the island but less intensive than for Mexican Americans.

Social Theory, Racialization and Popular Culture

Clara Rodríguez (2000:ix) recently argued that much work in the area of racialization is not theoretically rigorous. It is necessary to contribute to that process of theoretical grounding and clarification. Not only because it makes a scholarly contribution, but also because it clarifies how "theory" insinuated itself into popular culture. No project can achieve this without having an awareness of the history of this process. It is unfortunate that until very recently sociologists and other social scientists failed to de-construct the racialized character of the content and context of the origins of social science. The period in which sociology developed its fundamental character in the United States is also the period in which scientific racism and imperialist ideology developed, crystallized, and perhaps more importantly, permeated the popular culture of the West. This "blind spot" in social theory is very illustrative of how steeped U.S. culture is in racist ideology.

Before we can begin to understand the nature and character of racialization of Puerto Ricans and Mexicans, we must contextualize it by looking at the origins of scientific racism. Scientific racism provided, at the level of popular culture, the ideological support for the shift in the process of racialization of these two groups. Scientific racism is based on the notion of biological continuity through biological evolution. While ascribed to Charles Darwin in his *Origin of the Species* (1859), evolutionary thought was quite common during this period. Throughout this period most macro and micro thinking about society was influenced by this basic mode of thinking. The world view that science can solve social problems, is a product of these intellectual efforts, and is accompanied by strong racializing influences, particularly in the marriage of biology and statistics.

Underlying all of these efforts is a Western cultural teleology where there is a need to find or impose order in chaos. In other words, part of the paradigm of western mode of thought is its need to organize, to classify, to pigeonhole, this need makes taxonomy a basic tool of science in this period. Taxonomy organizes the raw facts arising out of experience,

making them intelligible on the basis of a framework. Newton gave us order in the physical world, and Darwin gave us a taxonomical system for the biological world. We needed one for the social world. While Carolus Linnaeus, Johann Blumenbach, Immanuel Kant, and others contributed the fabric for the racial taxonomies, others contributed to the legitimation of race-based thinking in popular culture and in the academy.

Herbert Spencer (1820-1903) was a renaissance thinker who had a vast knowledge of many disciplines. One of the areas of knowledge he chose to focus a major portion of his work was social theory. He was an engineer by profession but unlike others who dabbled in social theory he was not wealthy, nor did he have a patron who would subsidize his work. In order to make a living he depended on a rising market for printed materials. A gifted writer, Spencer was able to make a living selling articles for popular science magazines like *Contemporary Review* in England and *Popular Science Monthly* in the United States. This was a time in which a growing middle-class reading audience in Great Britain and the United States provided a market for novel scientific thinking. Spencer was the one who coined and popularized the phrase associated with evolution that many ascribe to Darwin, "the survival of the fittest" (Collins and Makowski, 1998).

Spencer, who is the person most recognized for the development of social Darwinism utilized his popular writings to acquaint his middle-class audience with evolutionism and *laissez-faire* or free market ideologies. He provided his readers with a common sense way of appropriating and popularizing these concepts. His basic idea was that society was part of the natural order and could not function contrary to the laws of nature. Using a biological analogy, he described society like an organism, with specialization and division of labor (from simple to complex). Some human beings within this organism are destined to be on top, some on the bottom. He gave an elegant, rational justification for social stratification. In his framework it was useless to try and civilize the natives in the colonies. They can be trained but they will only reach a certain stage.[15] Spencer questioned the value of a universal education. He believed that before women are given suffrage their psychology should be studied, which in those days meant that the innate qualities of women should be studied to determine whether they deserved the suffrage. Spencer began to lay the infrastructure for the ideologically grounded sexist and misogynist thinking of his days.

But popular culture was not only influenced by academic social theory, it was also shaped by other sources that provided a content to the construction of these racial taxonomies. During these years numerous travel books, popular ethnographic descriptions of Captain Cook travels in the South Seas, Dr. Livingstone's experiences in Africa, or the numerous Caribbean travelogues became popular with the growing

reading masses in the United States. These contributed to providing a context to the racialization of the "other" in the United States. These "lay ethnographies" created a consumer public who vicariously experienced these travels while at the same time internalizing notions of difference that could not be easily integrated into their worldview. Why the differences? These exotic descriptions were finally provided with a taxonomical system that helped make sense of this raw information (Matos Rodriguez, 1999). These frameworks and taxonomies contributed to racialize, to give racial/biological meaning to cultural differences. It gave that "disorder" of information a way to become orderly and racially meaningful.

That is why Spencer is crucial at this juncture, his extensive work probably reached a wider audience than any other sociologist of his time, especially in the United States. He completed a twelve volume compendium of sociological analysis of every major area of knowledge, from psychology to ethics, from biology to philosophy. Carnegie, the United States millionaire, brought Spencer to the United States where he became very popular on the lecture circuit. The Carnegie Foundation was a very prominent contributor to the development of the eugenics movement in the United States.[16]

Interacting and mutually supporting each other, the strong anti-immigrant, nativistic movement and the popularization of pseudo-scientific racist thinking became part of mainstream discourse in the United States. It becomes part of congressional debates, pedagogical practice, and public discourse. Whites, as products of a socializing process that normalized racial thinking and transformed it into "common sense" brought to their relationships with Puerto Ricans and Mexicans a racial paradigm steeped in this culture. As white people, they were socialized into the culture and acquired paradigms they never questioned. These hidden paradigms helped them explain and classify social phenomena while also legitimating their lives of privilege in a world of inequality. White supremacy was efficiently and scientifically rooted in the basic institutional cultures of the United States. Racialized thinking became so embedded in U.S. core culture that it became unseen and unquestioned, an example of Rosaldo's concept of "cultural invisibility" (Rosaldo, 1989).[17]

The Racialization of Mexican Americans and Puerto Ricans

Racialization, in the sense that Omi and Winant use it, means "to signify the extension of racial meaning to a previously racially unclassified relationship, social practice or group" (1986:64). Racialization, is also an ideological process, and a historically specific one that assigns ethnic

groups, a racial identity, and status. "Racial ideology is constructed from pre-existing conceptual (or if one prefers, discursive) elements and emerges from the struggles of competing political projects and ideas seeking to articulate similar elements differently" (1986:64). A more descriptive way of talking about racialization is:

> "Racialization is the social and historical process of assigning individuals and groups a socially constructed racial identity and status. As populations compete for land, status and resources they build hierarchies based on clusters of phenotypical biological factors which are then assumed to represent archetypes for members of a particular racial group. Those who become the dominant group interpret those presumed phenotypical biological differences as indicators of essential differences and assign a negative meaning to them, subordinating the contending group and limiting their access to those things their society values. The process of racialization in modern societies, is historically specific, and is carried out by its basic social institutions: economy, education, family, religion, government, criminal justice system, media etc." (Rodríguez 2002a:7).

I situate my preliminary project within what Omi and Winant call the need for accounts of "racialization processes that avoids the pitfalls of U.S. ethnic history," which they argue need to be written (1986: 64). In other words, how has this subject been constituted in the social sciences and popular culture? I will illustrate this model with historical events in the racialization of Puerto Ricans and Mexicans.

The historical context of this process of racialization occurs as the United States becomes an empire and its economy transitions from competitive capitalism to the capitalism of trusts and corporations. During this period, at the end of the nineteenth century, the U.S. popular sense of Manifest Destiny clearly becomes global in character and projection (Rodríguez, 1988). Racialization, then, occurs within a nation defining itself politically and economically as an empire, and racialization, domestically and abroad, becomes a way of managing the "natives" and/or "subalterns," foreign and domestic, by placing them within racialized hierarchies of power.

Historical Processes of Racialization

There are at least four identifiable processes or "moments" in the racialization process (Rodríguez, 2002a:9). The four processes of racialization:

Primary Processes	Consequences
Limiting access and control of land	Imposition and Subordination
Ideology and Cultural Racism	Institutional arrangements
Negotiation/Contestation Acceptance and participation in discrimination by ethnic groups	Placement in racial system and hierarchy
Assimilation/Americanization, homogenization ("lumping"), internalized racist oppression etc.	Crystallization of a racialized identity

Rather than being dichotomous and mutually exclusive, these processes overlap each other and do not necessarily follow a specific sequence. Each of these stages contributes to the social construction of a "cultural" group (in Rosaldo's terms) a group that becomes a racial group in the perception and experience of the dominant white power structure and in the group's own sense of self.

Imposition and Subordination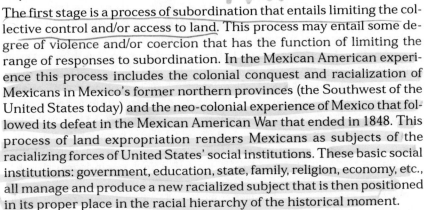

The first stage is a process of subordination that entails limiting the collective control and/or access to land. This process may entail some degree of violence and/or coercion that has the function of limiting the range of responses to subordination. In the Mexican American experience this process includes the colonial conquest and racialization of Mexicans in Mexico's former northern provinces (the Southwest of the United States today) and the neo-colonial experience of Mexico that followed its defeat in the Mexican American War that ended in 1848. This process of land expropriation renders Mexicans as subjects of the racializing forces of United States' social institutions. These basic social institutions: government, education, state, family, religion, economy, etc., all manage and produce a new racialized subject that is then positioned in its proper place in the racial hierarchy of the historical moment.

This process also sets the scene for the migration of millions of Mexicans who are then transformed into racialized subjects in the United States. These series of events excluded millions of Mexicans from having control or/and access to land, both in their homeland and in the

Mexicans

How?

diaspora. In the Southwest, this process included the legal and illegal ways in which the white/Anglo power structure took control of the millions of acres of lands that were in the hands of the Mexican landed elite (Acuña, 1988; Almaguer, 1994; Menchaca, 1995). These ways included laws that eased the expropriation of the landed elite, outright theft (squatters) and through the intermarriage between Anglo men and the daughters of the landed and lighter skinned Mexican elite (Acuña 1988:89).[18] Although the United States signed the Treaty of Guadalupe Hidalgo with Mexico (1848), which included protection for the religious, civil, and land rights of the Mexican community in the United States, U.S. legal institutions did not impede the almost complete expropriation of the Mexican community. By the 1880s, the Mexican American community was transformed from a community with a diverse social stratification system with a landed elite, to a community of proletarians. In the words of Mexican American historian Griswold del Castillo: "The promises the U.S. government made with respect to the conquered Mexican populations, however, have remained largely unfulfilled" (Griswold del Castillo, 1990:173).

This first moment of racialization not only led to the expropriation of Mexicans in the newly conquered territories of the Southwest, but it also extended itself, geographically, to the interior of the Mexican nation. In a recent manuscript by Gilbert Gonzalez and Raul Fernandez (2002) they explain how the expansion of U.S. imperial hegemony inserted itself into Mexico creating "...internal migration movements, mass population concentration along the border, the bracero program, low wage maquila plants, Mexico's agricultural crisis, and more important, a century of migrations to the United States" (2002:42). These are the dynamics in Mexico that run parallel to institutional changes taking place in the Southwest, which in the late nineteenth and twentieth centuries, led to the later crystallization of a Mexican American racial group.

If political, economic, and cultural dynamics are examined, rather than limiting the focus on a cultural model, like traditional Chicano historians, the history of the Mexican American/Chicano community is not a continuous history beginning in 1848, but a discontinuous process with an early phase of expropriation, disenfranchisement, and conquest leading to a second phase where a racialized Chicano population is formed. While it was true that the racialization process began earlier, it did not "produce" a racialized subject until this last period described by Gonzalez and Fernandez (1998).

This distinction is crucial because it underlies a distinct periodization of the racialization process, quite different from traditional Chicano historiography. It provides a beginning framework to understand the forms of resistance against racialization during the early process of expropriation and the latter when a racialized Mexican American subject arises. During the period preceding the late nineteenth century, the resistance to racialization had an insurrectionist character, akin to an anti-colonial

struggle.[19] As the racializing process crystallizes during the late nineteenth century and early twentieth centuries, resistance to racialization revolves around some community-based, legal, "civil rights," mode of attempting insertion into the excluding society. In other words, during the early stage of racialization (pre-twentieth century), the resistance is from the "outside" while in the latter stage the resistance is from the "inside."

During this latter period, resistance to racialization takes the form of *mutualistas* (mutual aid societies), labor unions, and community cultural groups. While other forms of resisting racialization do not disappear entirely, they are no longer as prevalent as in the following period after 1848. While the Mexican American population is being expropriated it is also gradually being proletarianized. The mode of integration of Mexicans into the social and economic structure of the United States, particularly in the later decades of the nineteenth century, is rooted in their transformation into proletarians, workers within the expanding industrial capitalist economy of the United States. It is within this process that race, class and gender become woven together in the Mexican American experience. This is the economic context for their racialization and what begins to shape the forms of resistance.

This distinction also serves to highlight the social, economic and political forces unleashed by the United States as it becomes a modern empire. It was in Mexico that the first full-scale imperial model of control, which Gonzalez and Fernandez (2002) call the "transnational mode of economic domination," was implemented.

This neo-colonial process in Mexico began in earnest during the 1870s. John Kenneth Turner described the process in his classic book *Barbarous Mexico* (1911). "The partnership of Diaz and American capital," he argued, "has wrecked Mexico as a national entity. The United States government, as long as it represents American capital...will have a deciding voice in Mexican affairs" (1906:256-257). The United States allied itself as a senior partner with the Mexican elite and particularly with their representative, President Porfirio Diaz. During his regime, called the *Porfiriato*, (1876-1911) the United States, using threats of military intervention invested heavily in railroads, mining, cattle farming, and cotton production (Gonzalez & Fernandez, 2002:3). By 1902, U.S. investments in Mexican railroads rose to 281 million dollars, in fact 80% of all investment in railroads in Mexico came from U.S. sources (2002:17).

> "Foreign investments (almost entirely of U.S. origin) was on the order of two thirds of the total for the decade 1900-1910, foreign ownership by 1910 has been estimated at half the national wealth" (2002:18).

This was a model that allowed the United States to control economically an entire nation without having to control it militarily. After the Spanish American War of 1898, Puerto Rico and Cuba, however, experienced a different model. In Puerto Rico, a "classic colonial" model was imposed, the island was directly controlled by the United States. In Cuba's case, a more intense model of neo-colonial control was implemented under the facade of a formally independent country with U.S. investment and the Platt amendment.[20] As U.S. Secretary of State, John Foster Dulles, would later say in the 1950s in reference to Guatemala and Iran: "...there (are) two ways of dominating a foreign nation, invading it militarily or controlling it financially" (Gonzalez & Fernandez, 2002:3). Cuba was controlled using both methods of neo-colonial control.

In summary, by the end of the nineteenth century the United States had extended its imperial hegemony over Mexico, although at the same time completing the subordination and racialization of Mexican Americans in the Southwest. The Mexicans, displaced by the dislocating forces of U.S. capital in Mexico ended up migrating into the racialized space of the Southwest. These newly arrived Mexicans constitute the material out of which a racialized Mexican American population was constructed.

Puerto Ricans

For Puerto Ricans, this first stage in the process of racialization occurs later, as the island becomes a "possession" of the United States after Spain, the colonial power for 400 years, is defeated during the Spanish-American War. In the island, the colonization process (economic, political, social, cultural) of Puerto Rico by the United States, is led by sugar, tobacco, textile, and other U.S. corporate interests. It is within this historical context that Puerto Ricans are racialized in this first stage. These forces and interests gave rise to the forces that created the process of migration and the beginning of the Puerto Rican diaspora.

During this stage Puerto Ricans were racialized in the diaspora and in the island with distinct consequences. In Puerto Rico, the Puerto Rican landed elite was not entirely expropriated like in the U.S. Southwest; instead, it was integrated into the sugar plantation complex controlled by major U. S. sugar corporations and interests. This integration of the landed elite took place in the form of central sugar mill owners or as *colonos*, who were small and medium farmers who cultivated sugar cane for the sugar mills. A significant part of the Puerto Rican elite were able to develop and maintain their own sugar mills and control a significant amount of agricultural land. In fact, during the 1920s, Puerto Rican producers were in control of 58% of the sugar output in the island. This percentage was even higher than the percentage under the control of the Cuban bourgeoisie for that time.[21]

differences.

The Puerto Rican elite, served as a mediating force between the colonial institutions and the Puerto Rican population. This mediation was much more complex because of two basic factors: a) contrary to the Mexican landed elite in the Southwest (who not only was expropriated of its land but was also integrated by marriage into the Anglo population) some members of the Puerto Rican elite supported forces that were in some degree of opposition to the colonial nature of Puerto Rico, b) although only 100,000 Mexicans lived in the conquered Southwest, close to 1 million Puerto Ricans lived in the island when the United States conquered it. These two factors made the process of racialization more complex and its outcome more diverse than in the Southwest.

While this process is developing in Puerto Rico, thousands of Puerto Ricans found themselves thrown into the migratory outflows created by economic and colonial policies. The collapse of the coffee industry, hurricanes, and labor brokers from Hawaiian sugar plantations all contributed to a process of out-migration that involved more coercion than the exercise of free will.[22] The coffee industry did not receive the same tariff protection sugar did, and was unable to compete in the U.S. market vis a vis cheaper coffees from Latin America. Puerto Rican immigrants in the United States, particularly before U.S. citizenship was imposed on Puerto Ricans, found themselves in a vulnerable status. They were "stateless" in the sense that they were citizens of a colony with no international standing, and did not have the protection of a consulate or an embassy in the United States. They did not speak English and a significant number of the migrants were black or mulatto.

As Bernardo Vega, one of the early Puerto Rican immigrants recalls in his memoirs, "We came from a colony and had no citizenship of our own" (Vega, 1984:xiii). The colonization process of Puerto Rico had rendered Puerto Ricans even more subordinated in the diaspora. In Puerto Rico the landed elite served as a cushion against racialization, but in the metropolis, racialization was more intense. For Bernardo Vega, "forced migration of colonial peoples was just another way of holding them in bondage" (1984:x). Puerto Ricans were excluded from trade unions despite the fact that many of them were militant socialists and were steeped in trade union struggles in Puerto Rico.

In conclusion, limiting the access and control of a people to land begins a process of subordination and of cultural change. Most of the island's political and economic institutions were in the hands of the military (1898-1901) and later U.S.-appointed civilian authorities. The process of subordination is aided because lack of access and control to the land places limits and shapes/limits contestation of the racialization process. While the Puerto Rican landed elite had some economic power, its economic foundation was based on the fact that the United States included Puerto Rico within its tariff structure. Its ability to sell its product, sugar, was dependent on the state policies of the empire. But, like

Mexicans, Puerto Ricans also underwent a process of proletarianiza-
tion both in the homeland and in the diaspora. Former peasants and
small agricultural producers become integrated into the growing and
expanding sugar plantation complex under the hegemony of U.S. capitalist investment. In the metropolis, Puerto Ricans become part of the
rising industrial working class in cities like New York. It is predominantly as proletarians, that Puerto Ricans and Mexicans experience the
process of racialization during this period. For both Mexicans and Puerto
Ricans, migration to the United States just changed the context of
racialization, not its consequences.

Ideology and Institutional Arrangements

The second stage of racialization is what Karenga (2002) calls the process in which "institutional arrangements" are constructed and supported with an ideology that gives legitimacy, stability, and continuity to
a system of exploitation based on class, race, ethnicity, and gender. These
institutional arrangements are the systems and social institutions that
ensure the continued subordination of the racialized subjects. They contribute to perpetuate subordination but without the same degree of coercion that marks the first stage. The arrangements include clusters of
norms such as slavery and Jim Crow Laws in the African American experience, reservations and federal laws in the American Indian experience, and dual wage systems, school segregation, and "Americanization"
programs in the Chicano and Boricua experience. "Americanization" as
an ideology legitimates institutional arrangements that lead to a process of cultural racism that distorts, trivializes the indigenous culture,
and imposes a different way of life on the subjects. Among the most
strategic institutional arrangements is education, the organization of
production, and the ideologies that support their role and function. The
educational system and the organization of production will be briefly
examined in their roles in both the Puerto Rican and Mexican American contexts.

In the Mexican American experience, both in Mexico and the conquered Southwest, "...a widely promulgated imperial ideology appeared
highlighting a pathological Mexican culture that concluded that a 'Mexican Problem' existed for foreigners, especially Americans, to resolve"
(Gonzalez, 2000: 1). This "Mexican Problem" ideology was constructed
on the basis of writings of travelers, Protestant missionaries, journal-
ists, academics, businessmen, and engineers who went to Mexico during the late nineteen and early twentieth century. These writings shaped
a popular culture "understanding" of who Mexicans were—a group that
had to be colonized and racialized both in Mexico and within the United
States. The United States had a "civilizing" mission and Mexicans, domestic and abroad, were to be the subjects of these efforts. The follow-

ing quote captures the racialized content of the civilizing mission, F. E. Prendergast wrote in page 276 of the July 1881 edition of *Harper's New Monthly Magazine*:

> "Now it is evident that any progress in Mexico must come through colonization by some higher and more progressive race, or by the introduction of capital in large amounts to develop her natural resources by the aid of native races who are generally peaceful and industrious" (Gonzalez, 2000:2).

This ideology, just like in Puerto Rico later in the twentieth century, led to the export to Mexico of racializing social economic practices like the dual wage system (whites and Mexicans received unequal wages for the same work), and the segregation of Mexican workers from U.S. personnel and their families. In mining, oil, and railroad camps, U.S. companies kept separate quarters for their Mexican and U.S. employees. The "civilizing" efforts never had the objective of "equalizing" colonizer and colonized, they merely had as an objective to teach the Mexican his/her proper place in the racialized order.

Also, this ideology assumed a biological content as it crystallized into a way of understanding the differences between Mexicans and U.S. whites. One writer, Chester Lloyd Jones, says: "...it must be confessed that (mestizos) often exhibit the well-known tendency to follow the vices and weaknesses of both sides of their ancestry rather than the virtues" (Gonzalez, 2000:10).

This ideology is then applied in the United States to the education of Mexican Americans as they are transformed into racialized proletarians. This racialized worker is seen as childish, brutish, and highly sexual. Wallace Thompson in his *The Mexican Mind: A Study in National Psychology* (1922) argues that Mexicans have compulsive sex drives and "...it seems to have a child's or savage's unwavering grasp of the details of desire..." and these negative representations are related to the fact that Mexicans were a product of miscegenation (Gonzalez, 2000:16).

This ideology is implemented in the development of an educational policy that justified segregation and the "Americanizing" of Mexicans into racialized "Mexican Americans." This racialized subject would be domesticated into the docile and obedient labor force that the various sectors of the U.S. economy needed. This racialized product was already anticipated in the mind of various sectors that influenced educational policy, including Victor Clark, who also wrote a significant book on Puerto Rico, *Puerto Rico and Its Problems* in 1930 and who earlier was in charge of the island's educational system. In 1908, Clark describes the Mexican workers as "...unambitious, listless, physically weak, irregular and indolent. On the other hand he is docile, patient, usually orderly in camps..." (Gonzalez, 2000:27).

In sum, when U.S. educators began to develop a pedagogy to educate Mexicans they tapped into the materials written about Mexico. So the "Mexican Problem" was in need of a dose of "Americanization" in order to snugly fit the newly racialized subject into the racial hierarchy of the United States. Between 1912 and 1957, no less than twenty-five theses and dissertations were written citing the ideology of people like Thompson and Clark (Gonzalez, 2000:29). This racialized view of the Mexican had become a un-questioned commonsense pedagogical perspective on how to educate and "Americanize" the Mexican. Since the objective of "Americanization" was to forge a docile and obedient labor force, Mexican children were educated using "...a separate curriculum, emphasizing English and American standards of conduct, vocational education over academic work, group discipline over individuation and logically, lower expectations" (Gonzalez, 2000:36). Also, with the exception of New Mexico, in many areas of the Southwest, Spanish and some Mexican customs were prohibited as "uncivilized." In order to achieve the subordination of Mexicans the colonizer had to isolate them from a language and culture that affirmed them and that provided resources for resistance. The colonizer also had to have the Mexicans internalize Anglo-Saxon culture with all the negative content about who "Mexicans" were in the U.S. cultural imaginary.

But this process of racialization was not without challenges, particularly in those instances where the racialized subjects had access to some forms of organization. The absence of landed elites in the twentieth century intensified the social construction of Chicanos as racialized subjects yet labor organizations proved able to mediate between racialization and the subalterns. During this early period, most Mexican Americans were involved in the agricultural sector in the Southwest. California, especially, through irrigation systems that enabled the "deserts to flower" became one of the largest employers of agricultural labor in the United States.

Almaguer (1994), in his analysis of the sugar beet worker's strike in Ventura, California of 1903 provides a good example of how agricultural proletarians were able to contest their racial and class exploitation. For the first time in agricultural labor struggles, a group of Japanese and Mexican workers won a decisive victory against sugar beet growers. This was a rather unusual event in a number of ways. Union organizing among agricultural workers was not favored by the major Labor organizations in the United States. The American Federation of Labor (AFL), particularly, did not organize agricultural workers. So the sugar beet workers organized themselves under one of the first multi-ethnic unions in the United States: the Japanese-Mexican Labor Association (JMLA).

The JMLA was able to organize a strike in 1903, despite ethnic differences because they counted on a number of factors:

a. Timing of strike coincided with the need for thinning the sugar beet crops. If the weaker beets were not thinned quickly the crop could be lost. This gave the strikers some leverage with the bosses.

b. They carefully developed an ethnic sensitive, culturally appropriate democratic process where both Mexican and Japanese were informed in their respective languages, and styles of the whole organizational process. They also shared resources and developed a growing sense of camaraderie and brotherhood.

c. There was a strong influence of socialist ideology that led them to emphasize on their class position rather than on their racial status. This was reinforced by the participation of Fred C. Wheeler and John Murray from the Los Angeles Labor Council who provided moral support to the strikers throughout the negotiation process. These labor organizers were also socialist radicals from the Los Angeles labor movement.

d. They were able to maintain a very consistent policy of militantly coping with strikebreakers. Most of the time in a peaceful but militant way, they convinced most of the workers brought in to join them in their organizing effort.

Chicanos and Japanese were quite effective in contesting racialization by avoiding the kind of divisions that help the perpetuation of the process. They avoided pitting each other in merely racial terms by using their class and ethnic background as both uniting mechanisms and tools for communication and internal unity. They avoided the bosses' efforts of dividing them against each other.

This contrasts quite clearly with another important agricultural strike studied by Gilbert Gonzalez (1999), the El Monte farm worker's strike of 1933. In this case, Mexican farm workers were allied with Filipino workers. During the El Monte workers' strike, the Mexican Consul, through Vice-Consul Ricardo Hill, made sure that the strikers did not develop the strategies that led to the victory that the JMLA achieved. Hill sought to limit the militancy of the strikers; he sought to isolate particularly the most militant, some of whom were socialist or radicals. In fact, the consulate allied itself with the Los Angeles Police Department's notorious Red Squad in identifying the most active and radical Mexican labor leaders. During this period, being accused of being a socialist radical was tantamount to being accused of sedition and would ensure "repatriation" since that was a excuse commonly used to deport Mexicans during the 1930s (Balderrama and Rodríguez, 1995:48).

All of these interventions led to the demise of the Cannery Agricultural Industrial Workers Union (CAIWU) and to the defeat of the strike. In many ways, the role of the consular officers was to lessen the concern

of growers that in fact, Mexican workers were not as docile as they thought. It served to reinforce the stereotypical and racialized notion that Mexicans were innately docile and malleable. This contributed to internalizing the racial ideology by many workers who by following the lead of the consular officers led the union to its own demise and to the defeat of their strike. It also led to racial and ethnic divisions between Mexican and other workers, notably Filipinos. Here in this space, racialization progressed much further.

The JMLA, after winning the strike, collapsed in a few years. Agricultural unions are difficult to maintain because of the seasonal nature of work of their members. The only way that local agricultural unions survive is by allying themselves with larger unions, particular those in the industrial sector. The American Federation of Labor, the largest organization in that era, refused to organize agricultural workers, particularly racialized minorities. Unfortunately for the JMLA, the AFL refused to grant them a charter because Samuel Gompers did not want to have Japanese members in his union. During that specific time, the fear of Asian groups was foremost in the popular culture. African Americans had a very small presence in California and Mexican Americans were racialized as a more docile and malleable group.

In the meantime in Puerto Rico, the same Samuel Gompers who had refused to allow Japanese agricultural workers in his AFL, allied himself with Santiago Iglesias Pantin a Spanish immigrant. The leader of Puerto Rico's Federacion Libre de Trabajo (Free Labor Federation, [FLT]) which consisted mainly of sugar and tobacco workers. A significant portion of the workforce, for example was constituted by black and mulatto Puerto Ricans. For example, Prudencio Rivera Martinez, referring to the leadership of the FLT in the first decades of this century, argued that of each ten leaders "8 would be mulattoes" (Guerra, 1999:22). In Puerto Rico's case, the FLT in many ways accepted the "tutelage" of the white men in order to develop the leverage they need to deal with their local economic contenders, the sugar mill owners who were both Anglo and Puerto Rican (Rodríguez, 1988).

However, in Puerto Rico, because the labor movement had a strong presence and a strong equalitarian socialist and anarchist ideology, racialization was challenged more strongly within the labor movement than in the United States. While not often discussed by island historians, during the first decades of U.S. domination, labor activists began to engage in a public discussion of race (Suarez Findlay, 1999). In fact, while not pervasive in the Puerto Rican labor movement, socialist activists:

> "Instead of distancing themselves from blackness and racial diversity, numerous federation organizers claimed them as an integral part of Puertoricanness. Many FLT (Federation of Free Labor) members and leaders were clearly of African

descent themselves. They also affirmed this heritage for the entire working class. 'The white man was our father. The Black woman was our mother'" (1999:141).

In order to challenge the racialization process they were undergoing as workers, they constructed an identity that challenged the divide and conquer tactics of U.S. and local white elites. In fact, in satirical form they questioned the "whiteness" of the local elites, given the high degree of miscegenation in the island. In addition, the existence of significant and important political leaders who were black, like Jose Celso Barbosa, among the supporters of statehood for Puerto Rico, and Pedro Albizu Campos, among pro-independence supporters, shaped racialization dynamics. The system of bipolar racial categories that the U.S. culture had developed did not take strong hold in these initial decades as it is beginning to do in Puerto Rico today. Most of the political leadership in Puerto Rico today, from the left to the right is white.

However, the understanding that Puerto Rican activists had of racism then was one that focused on attitudes and not on the institutionalized and systemic nature of racism. The metaphors of freedom and slavery were used to unite workers in challenging racial prejudice (Suarez Findlay, 1999). However, their level of ideological sophistication was greater of gender oppression issues than of racism. In fact, most labor leaders directly addressed issues of gender oppression as important issues in the class struggle.

"In the years before World War I, leftist labor leaders recognized that women's oppression was rooted in both waged labor exploitation and the dominant norms and sexual practices of the day" (1999:143).

This understanding saw gender issues raised by institutionalized practices that went beyond attitudes and were rooted in the dominant economic system. They saw the need to transform institutions such as marriage and family in order to liberate women from oppression. Unfortunately, with the exception of labor ideologue Ramon Romero Rosa, most of the labor intelligentsia did not see the intersection of race, class, and gender. As Suarez Findlay explains: "...radical activists never acknowledged that women's racial identities might shape their experiences. Thus they implicitly recognized gender as separate and more enduring social difference than race, demanding more extended analysis and practical reforms." (1999:143).

In the educational system in Puerto Rico, racialization through "Americanization" took its course. In terms of form and content, the experience of Puerto Ricans in the island and Chicanos in the Southwest was quite different. The U.S. attempt to "Americanize" the entire

Puerto Rican population faced some obstacles. In this case, since Puerto Ricans were the numerical majority in the island, there was no need to segregate them. However, teachers were brought in from the United States to teach "American" cultural norms and folkways to domesticate Puerto Ricans and instill the kind of loyalty the United States required to maintain its colonial domination. Martin G. Brumbaugh, Commissioner of Education (1900-1901), said that "Under wise and conservative officers, the people of Puerto Rico have turned to this Republic with a patriotism, a zeal, and enthusiasm that is perhaps without parallel" (Negrón de Montilla, 1970:37).

Also, like in other areas of the United States and within Mexican economy, the process of subordinating Puerto Ricans included the dual wage system. According to Negrón de Montilla (1970), a newspaper article said in 1900:

> "The American teachers enjoy a better salary than the Puerto Rican teachers, yet instructions are given to the School Boards in the official newspaper, *La Gaceta*, that all American teachers must sign their contract for next year. No mention is made of Puerto Rican teachers, who are in more need because they earn lower salaries." (1970:55)

This dual wage system taught American teachers they were superior and taught Puerto Rican teachers that they were inferior. This institutional arrangement was part of the process to socialize the Puerto Rican population into acceptance of its new inferior status vis a vis the white "Americans."

The implementation of this educational system included the use of English as the medium of instruction and relegated Spanish to a subordinate status within the curriculum. The Puerto Rican, like the Mexican, was being domesticated into accepting its proper place within a racial hierarchy that had whites as the archetype of what Puerto Ricans should aspire to be.[23] This internalization was expected to be smooth, particularly since Puerto Ricans already were constructed in the American mind as a malleable and peaceful people. Victor S. Clark's representation of Puerto Ricans: "The great mass of Puerto Ricans are as yet passive and plastic... Their ideals are in our hands to create and mold. We shall be responsible for the work when it is done, and it is our solemn duty to consider carefully and thoughtfully today, the character we wish to give the finished product of our influence and effort" (Negron de Montilla, 1970:13).

Just like in the Mexican experience, travelers, academics, and businessmen had begun to shape in the U.S. popular mind, the notion of Puerto Ricans as children, products of miscegenation, who needed the strong paternal hand of the master in order to learn their proper role in

a racialized relationship, that between colonizer and colonized. As historian Matos Rodriguez (1999) explains in his article, U.S. writers represented Puerto Rico and Puerto Ricans as a "problem":

> "Racial stereotypes in the U.S. also reinforced the vision that Puerto Ricans were intellectually inferior people given the high incidence of 'mestizaje.' U.S. writers and government officials constructed a perfect justification for colonialism: a disorder in need of intervention, an able United States willing to serve as problem solver, and an anxious Puerto Rican people striving to improve under U.S. guidance" (1999:42).

However, this "disorder" that needs reorganization was one which had the potential for achieving a higher yet subordinate status vis a vis the United States. Thompson (1995), in his reading of *Our Islands and their People* finds that some U.S. observers believed that Puerto Ricans were somewhat redeemable:

> "[The Puerto Ricans] are a different race from the sodden populations of the Orient and the humbled and degraded masses of many European countries. When one looks into the intelligent faces of the Porto Rican girls or boys employed in the various little factories that exist in the island, he realizes that they have souls... Spanish tyranny, during the three hundred years of its iron rule, did all it could to crush the spirit of the people but the benign climate and fructifying soil counteracted the poison of official repression, and the masses of the Porto Rican are today nearer the high standard of American thought and intelligence than the common people of any other country" (1995:55-57).

These institutionalized arrangements, supported by a racist ideology spread through the economy, the educational system, criminal justice system, and religion, helping maintain the stability of the system of racialization, while integrating sectors of the subordinated groups as "gatekeepers." These institutional arrangements perpetuated white supremacy and simultaneously undermined resistance of other sectors of the racialized communities. This structural organization of racialization sets the stage for the following stage.

Placement in the Racial Hierarchy

During this third phase, the racialized group is assigned a racial status within the racial system of stratification. This process is led by how communities of color participate in what Clara Rodríguez (2000) calls "the

acceptance of and participation in discrimination against people of color" (2000:17). This stage leads into what Clara Rodríguez also describes as the "negotiations regarding the group's placement in the U.S. racial ethnic queue" (2000:18). It is within this phase that the racial "others" are constituted in the culture of the dominant and the dominated group. Since racial categories are comparative taxonomical systems, a process of categorization includes a process of comparison. The comparison and categorization not only occurs between whites and the racialized "other" but this process of comparison may include other racialized subjects. This fluid stage is shaped by historically specific correlations of power and the nature of social and economic changes taking place within the United States, or the colonial spaces of racialization.

Precisely because the system is based on comparative taxonomies, new groups entering the racialized system begin to internalize the norms that guide and maintain the racial hierarchy. As these groups are being socialized and assimilated, they attempt to gain leverage by discriminating against the group immediately below or close to their own standing in the racial ladder. The Irish discriminated against blacks to establish their "whiteness" or more accurately, their "non-blackness," and assure a better placement in the racial ranking. Blacks became the "other" that whitened them. Boricuas and Chicanos in various degrees attempt to distance themselves from African Americans or other Latinos. This distancing also takes place within racialized groups, particularly in terms of the native versus the foreign-born.

During the early representations of Puerto Ricans in the United States the Filipinos became the racial "other" that mediated the racial status of Puerto Ricans in the public imagination. In 1917, all Puerto Ricans were granted U.S. citizenship, an anomalous act given that a significant proportion of the population was, in the U.S. racial system, "non-white." There were a number of factors involved, one is geopolitical, the United States wanted to assure control over Puerto Rico for strategic reasons. Or, like Pedro Albizu Campos, the nationalist leader, said, "The U.S. wants the cage, not the birds." Secondly, many members of Congress perceived the island as the "whitest" of the Antilles.[24] But this process that enabled Puerto Ricans to be granted U.S. citizenship in 1917 included the comparative perception that they were less socially distant than Filipinos in U. S. popular culture (Cabranes, 1979:17-18). Sectors of the U.S. Congress were concerned about opening the doors to a nation of "orientals" if Puerto Rico became a precedent for the Philippines. Until it was clear that the Philippines would not be annexed Congress would not grant statutory U.S. citizenship to all Puerto Ricans. This process of racialized comparison vis a vis Filipinos is also present in museum representations of Puerto Ricans and Filipinos during the early twentieth century (Duany, 2002).

Puerto Ricans living in the United States had a different experience from those in the island. Jesus Colon (1961), in his collection of stories from his experience in New York in the early decades of the twentieth century, provides some glimpses of how some Puerto Ricans faced the racially bifurcated system in the United States. Puerto Ricans in the United States experienced racialization by being perceived as non-white. In the early days many lived within African American communities and experienced racial discrimination in employment (1961:44). Colon, a socialist and as a self-educated man who had significant writing skills, had been hired to do some part-time transla-

tions for a film agency that distributed a film series popular in the Spanish-speaking community. They liked his work so much they offered him a job. When Colon shows up at the agency's door, the office manager says: "Yes I wrote that letter.... That was to be your desk and typewriter. But I thought you were white" (Colon, 1961:51).

This experience also was reproduced with Puerto Rican musicians who performed in the United States. Juan Flores (2002) tells the story of Davilita, the Puerto Rican musician, who recalled how Puerto Ricans and Cubans, who were the darkest among Latinos in the United States, were paid less than other Latin Americans (Flores, 2002:69). In addition, Puerto Ricans experienced discrimination in cultural centers begun by Spanish immigrants. In her book on Puerto Rican musicians, Ruth Glasser (1995) explains how Asturian, Galician, Valencian, and other Spanish cultural clubs and centers had exclusionary policies that excluded non-whites. In their effort to maintain their status as aspiring whites, Spanish immigrants coped by racially discriminating against Puerto Ricans. A similar experience occurred within the Cuban community, between black and "white" Cubans in Tampa, Florida at the turn of the century. The racial codes of the south divided "white" from black Cubans and in many ways this went unchallenged by Cubans aspiring to a "white" status (Santiago-Valles 2000:15-16).

In the Mexican experience, differences between native and foreign-born in the United States signify different status positions within the Mexican American community. While the Mexican American is racialized and subordinated to whites, a foreign-born, non-citizen Mexican occupies a lower position in the racial hierarchy. The conflicts that existed in

the Mexican community in the 1930s when close to 1 million Mexicans were "repatriated" raised the issue of who occupied a lower racial status within the Mexican American community (Balderrama & Rodríguez, 1995). Those who were not repatriated were able to avoid, and negotiate, temporarily, being placed in the lowest racial status possible in the Southwest during this period, because at least they, were "Americans."

Also, the conflicts between the "Spanish" Mexicans and the "Indian" Mexicans, which arose as groups negotiated their standing within the racial hierarchy were rooted in this acceptance of the racial hierarchy and an attempt to leverage a higher status by distancing themselves from the lower racial status (Almaguer, 1994). The creation of a "hispano" category in New Mexico was also a way of establishing distance between the newly arrived Mexican immigrants and the native New Mexicans of Mexican ancestry. "Mexican" had become so racialized that Mexican Americans would rather be "Spanish" or "Hispano" than "Mexican." By assuming this tactical posture they reinforced a system that in everyday practice, would not make any meaningful distinction between "Mexican" and "Hispano." In some states like Texas, the distancing was so great that the Mexican elites at times even allied themselves with the Ku Klux Klan, hoping to achieve in this alliance a measure of whiteness (Acuña, 1988).

Among Puerto Ricans, the internal distinctions between darker and lighter skinned Puerto Ricans (colorism or pigmentocracy) became more pronounced. The United States, in its "Americanization" process, also tended to narrow the range of racial categories in the racial continuum so prevalent in the Caribbean and Brazil (Rodríguez, 1997). The ideal "Puerto Rican" was not a real, concrete mulatto or mestizo Puerto Rican but a "Spanish" Puerto Rican. For some, the real "Puerto Rican" was white, and, could trace her/his lineage to Spain (never to Africa). Lillian Guerra (1998) explains how Puerto Rican historian, Cayetano Coll y Cuchi, who was educated in the United States begins to question U.S. imperial policies in Puerto Rico by assuming a "hispanic" Puerto Rican identity. This resistance identity, however, was still problematic:

> "Yet, importantly, the reference point for the resistant identity that Coll y Cuchi discovered within himself he did not articulate as essentially "Puerto Rican," but as Spanish. Coll y Cuchi's defensive prescription against Americanization's critique of all things Puerto Rican as well as his own avowal of that critique were both equally colonial" (Guerra, 1998:46).

These efforts to "whiten" the image of being a Puerto Rican as a way of resisting racialization through "Americanization" led to a process of whitening one of the most important symbols of "Puertoricanness," the *jibaro* or the icon of the Puerto Rican peasant.

This symbol of a "true Puerto Rican" began to spread through Puerto Rican popular culture during the nineteen century. The opposite racial "other" were the Spanish then, but in the twentieth century, the "other" were U.S. whites and their process of "Americanization."

Lillian Guerra (1998) further develops Jose Luis Gonzalez' (1993) analysis of how the *jibaro* became an instrument that was used as a pivot to leverage into a whiter status within the racialized hierarchy in Puerto Rico. The myth of the *jibaro* as representation of true "Puertoricanness" was pivoted on a "denial of an Afro-Mestizo historical reality from which many Puerto Rican customs and world views were derived—even by creole peasants, the *jibaros* themselves" (1998:55).

However, U.S. white colonizers were not entirely convinced:

> "Brigadier General George W. Davis, one of the colonial governors of Puerto Rico, states that 'between the Negro and the peon there is no visible difference.' Davis found it difficult to 'believe that the pale, sallow and often emaciated beings' were indeed 'the descendants of the conquistadors...'" (Santiago-Valles, 1994:45)

"How americans see the "natives" their plan.

The "civilizing" mission of the United States, utilized the Americanization efforts as a way of bringing the "native" into a close, yet not equal status with U.S. whites. The natives were constructed as amoral, primitive, violent, childish, overly sexual beings that required domestication (Briggs, 2002). The multi-valenced image of Puerto Ricans provided a contradictory image of the new colonial subjects; they were seen as both docile yet violent, innocent yet amoral, it was a version of the "noble savage." Thompson (1995) describes how Puerto Ricans were read in their pictorial representations as living in Eden yet engaging in "uncivilized" behaviors that were not conducive to equal status with the colonizer.

> "They [the Puerto Ricans] live so close to nature that the things which would seem improper to us are with them the innocent affairs of their daily life. In many respects they are still in that Edenic state which thinks no evil and consequently knows none" (Thompson, 1995:30).

This characterization also leads to dehumanizing Puerto Ricans, because rational people weigh the consequences of their actions; however, "animals" are judged by "instincts" not "reason."

> "Morals, in the technical sense, they have none, but they cannot be said to sin, because they have no knowledge of the law, and therefore, they cannot commit no breach of law. They

are naked and are not ashamed... There is evil, but there is not the demoralizing effect of evil. They sin, but they sin only as animals, without shame, because there is not sense of being wrong" (Thompson, 1995: 31).

Also, the natives, in order to fit within the new system had to be reshaped in their sexuality and family life. "Americanizing" became a way of transferring the Yankee moral standards into the everyday practice of the subaltern. Suarez Findlay (1999), clearly demonstrates the almost evangelical way colonial administrators sought to alter the Puerto Rican:

> They endeavored to homogenize their new colonial subjects sexually, to reduce diverse popular sexual practices and morals to a unified standard of heterosexual marriage and two-parent families, thus instilling their Anglo-Saxon, bourgeois social and cultural ideas in the island's populace" (Suarez Findlay, 1999:111).

Both Mexicans and Puerto Ricans find placement in the new racial order and contradictorily, contribute to their own subordination. The new racial identity and status creates competition within and between groups, all seeking to leverage the most advantageous and less stigmatizing position within a hierarchy where whites are at the top while the subalterns are divided against each other.

Crystallization of a Racial Identity

The fourth and final stage is the "crystallization of a racialized identity." This process of individuation takes place through the systemic processes of assimilation, "Americanization," and homogenization. During this phase, the internalization of racist oppression becomes a signifying characteristic of being that jointly, with institutional arrangements, serves to reinforce the systems at the individual level and limit the process of contestation at the systemic level (Rodríguez, 2002a). Internalization is a major factor limiting resistance, and as described by Franz Fannon (1986) and later described by Pan-Africanist Steve Biko, as "the most powerful weapon of the oppressor is the mind of the oppressed." It is within this stage where the racial system finds its strategic self-perpetuating mechanisms.

The internalization of racist oppression becomes the *carimbo* or branding that marks the racialized subject. A mark that is not physical but socio-psychological.[25] The power of the changes in culture and identity that take place in this stage, is that these new forms of being and behaving do not appear as the products of coercion, they are perceived as innate to the individual and the culture. A racialized culture and iden-

tity, either "Mexican American" or "Boricua," is created in response to and in contestation of the process of racialization. Therefore, the individual and groups that arise as racial groups, Mexican Americans and "Boricuas," not only are racialized by the institutions and systems of white supremacy, they are also racialized by colonized and racialized cultural practices. They are colonized from within the cultural spaces of these communities. These new racialized cultures are constructed by oppressed communities using, in these cases, Mexican and Puerto Rican cultural elements together with these new cultural traits that arise out of an experience of oppression.

However, at times these new learned behaviors are divisive and self-destructive. The sense of self that is constructed in this stage of racialization is one imbued with a sense of powerlessness. It is the mode by which "race," in its political sense, becomes a lived reality. Subordination becomes embedded in the culture in subtle and powerful ways. *Parejeria* and *pochismo* in the Puerto Rican and Mexican American contexts don't lead to liberation, yet provide the means to survive in hostile environments.[26]

Through this socio-cultural process, identities are socially constructed to "fit" into the racial hierarchy; this enables white supremacy to extend the power of racism into the deepest recesses of the personhood of the subaltern.[27] Internalized Racist Oppression (IRO) leads racialized subjects into behaviors that are, at times, the outcome of coping mechanisms. Other ways of coping in a racialized society include denying one's true self and mimicking the dominant archetype. In a society where the racial categories are fluid, and where gradations of color are what determines a person's racial status it is possible to "pass" and become "white."

In Puerto Rico, during this period an interesting phenomenon, the "statistical disappearance" of blacks and the "whitening" of the Puerto Rican population took place. The process of seeking whiteness in order to avoid the stigmatization inherent in the process of Americanization had a deep impact on the sense of racial identity developing among Puerto Ricans. In 1910, 29.98% (335,192) of the population identified itself as mulatto and 4.49% (50,245) as black. By the next decennial census in 1920, there were 7.5% less blacks and mulattos in the census (Guerra, 1998:221). Concurrently, this decline in persons of color was accompanied by an increase of 7.5% in the number of whites. Nearly 34,000 mulattos and blacks disappeared statistically from the census data.

As Guerra (1998) and Gonzalez (1993) have pointed out, Puerto Rico during the eighteenth and early nineteenth century had a population with a high percentage of blacks and mulattos. Contrary to the experience of countries like Argentina, Chile, Uruguay and Costa Rica, whose immigrations policies whitened these countries, Puerto Rico's attempts failed (Bonilla-Silva & Glover, 2005). Although there were thousands of

whites who migrated from Haiti, Spain, and other parts of Europe prompted by the liberal immigration incentives of the 1815 *Cedula de Gracias*, this whitening process was balanced by another illegal immigration of thousands of blacks from the English-speaking West Indies. In fact, the first census of Puerto Rico carried out by the U.S. government in 1899 showed that 38.2% of the Puerto Rican population was non-white (Duany, 2002:248). By 1920, the non-white population, statistically speaking, fell to 27.0% without any major emigration of black Puerto Ricans taking place.

Additionally, according to Guerra (1998), there was no significant migration of whites into Puerto Rico from 1910-1920 to justify a 7.55% increase in the white population. The only thing that had changed is that Puerto Ricans did not want to be Black. To be black in an "Americanizing" colony meant being left in the lowest rung of the racialized colonial order. This was not a process of genocide in the traditional sense but it was a process where certain forms of representation and identity were vanquished in the culture. The African in Puerto Rico could not be physically exterminated but it could be eliminated as a form of identity and an expression of self.

But contrary to the racialization of Mexicans before the 1890s in the United States, this tendency toward racializing the new subjects during the early part of the twentieth century is rooted in the influence of pseudoscientific racism (Shipman, 1994). As mentioned early, Mexicans before the 1890s are seen as a culturally distinct people. They are an "ethnic" group, which although racialized and subordinated are still considered to be in a higher status than American Indians or African Americans. Mexicans, in the newly conquered states were Christian (albeit Catholic), spoke a European tongue (albeit Spanish) and were not as dark (albeit brown) as the other two "others." As long as the Mexican population was not completely subordinated, they were perceived as culturally different.

During the twentieth century they become racially distinct in the new racialized order shaped by a new popular culture that biologized difference. In the documentary "Los Mineros," directed by Paul Espinosa and produced by Hector Galan in 1991, we are told the history of the racialization of a mining community in Clifton Morenci Arizona during the first four decades of the twentieth century. Sylvester Morris, a mine owner, is quoted: "My own experience has taught me that the lower class of Mexicans are docile, faithful, good servants, capable of strong attachments when firmly and kindly treated. They have been "peons" for generations. They will always remain so, as it is their natural condition." One could easily substitute Mexicans for any animal and the description would still be consistent. The distinction had transformed Mexicans into less than whites, not only culturally, but also as a biologically distinct race of people. Unfortunately, this process leads to internaliza-

tion of the norms of white supremacy. The racial construct then, becomes "normalized."

In terms of gender, there is a cultural dynamic that reflects how a racialized subject develops through gender role socialization. This can be seen among Mexican American working class women during the 1930s in the United States. In Vicky Ruiz' (1996) study on acculturation and child rearing practices we notice the internalization of racist oppression in quite a distinct way. For example, families engaged in the practice of steering women away from members of their own group and promoting marriage with whites. So that child-rearing practices are not only "gendered" they are simultaneously "racializing." This is also practiced in Puerto Rican and other Latin American cultures. This child-rearing practice is labeled as *mejorar la raza* or improving the race. This is a way of "whitening" one's offspring so that they will be able to "pass" as whites and leave the racialized community behind. It becomes an individualistic way out of subordination, but one that reinforces the same system it pretends to challenge. This is a reflection of how we internalize the racialized images the racializer directs at us.

Vicky Ruiz also talks about how the culture viewed Mexican woman as "morally loose, Latina actresses in Hollywood found themselves typecast as hot blooded women of lower repute." It is assuming that almost animalistic urges and instincts exists in groups that are now racialized as sub-persons. This experience of racializing the sexuality of Chicana also took place among Puerto Rican women in Puerto Rico. However, the active labor socialist-feminists at least contested some of the sexist discourse. The FLT in Puerto Rico actively organized women workers and provided a culture that developed the leadership skills of women.

This racialized view of Puerto Ricans is contrasted with that of Mexicans. In the relationship between Anglos and Mexican, the racialization of Mexicans is rooted in assumption of how miscegenation processes "tainted" Spanish blood (already a questionably "racially pure" European group given the role of Romans, Muslims, Jews, and Africans in Iberia). The focus is on the specific role of indigenous ancestry. In Puerto Rico's racialization, the process pivots around the assumed African ancestry present in all Puerto Ricans. But it is in the United States, rather than in the island where the African ancestry of Puerto Rico becomes a clearly stigmatizing biological characteristic.

Mark Reisler gives us a glimpse of how Anglo perceptions of this racialized subject during the 1920s were deeply biologized, and how they shaped public policy. He points out how the debate about restrictions in immigration took place within the same set of discursive racialized themes: Mexicans in the United States are an inferior group, that is "docile, indolent and backward."

The weakness of organizations like labor unions among Mexican Americans and their exclusion from political parties led to a different

level of racialization in the mainland. For example, on one side of the debate about restricting immigration were those who argued that bringing into the nation persons who had those kinds of qualities would alter, stain, and dilute the allegedly higher set of qualities, which were part of the contributions of people of European stock. In other words, since they assumed that cultural characteristics were rooted in race, and Mexicans represented a racial group with Indian blood, these characteristics might enter the "American" gene pool through the feared process of miscegenation. But in this hierarchy of racialized groups, Puerto Ricans fared worst.

The growers of California in the 1920s wanted to have access to cheap labor to reduce the costs of agricultural production. White labor was not willing to do the hard backbreaking work in the fields so growers depended on Filipino, Japanese but mostly Mexican labor. Growers, in order to protect their source of labor power they argued that if the government curtailed Mexican migration they would have to look for another source. They express a clear fear of bringing blacks and facing in California what they described as the "racial problems" of the South. But particularly they feared being forced to bring Puerto Ricans because, in the words of George Clements, the director of the Los Angeles Chamber of Commerce agricultural department:

> "While they all have Negro blood in their veins, the greater part of them are without those physical markings which can only protect society. They are red-headed, freckle-faced, thin lipped Negro hybrids with the vicious qualities of their progenitors" (Reisler, 1996:36).

Puerto Ricans are tolerated within the confines of the island, there they are perceived as reformable racialized subjects. However, in the mainland they are perceived as a threat. A threat in the sense that since miscegenation is so pervasive among this population it is not always possible to distinguish who is really a "white" Puerto Rican and who is not. This obviously could lead to further miscegenation with the white population tainting and degrading the white race. This is particularly troubling for a system based on white supremacy since the subordinates are already perceived as overtly sexual beings. Leo Stanton Rowe (1908) warns the United States that:

> "A country in which the mass of the population has been kept in either slavery or in a condition of social inferiority is certain to retain the sexual relations of a primitive period for a long time after the causes giving rise to these relations have disappeared" (Rowe, 1908:98).

The fear of "mongrelization" leads the supporters of imperialism and expansion to call for a settler policy in Puerto Rico. It is suggested that white Americans should begin to settle Puerto Rico to insure control and avoid the invasion of inferior races into the United States (Healey, 1970).

Conclusions

Unfortunately, race was and continues to be an enduring social difference, and its analysis and systemic challenge then and today still poses a contemporary challenge to an anti-racist social movement and perspective. Racialization is a crucial concept that provides insights into the way racism works in the United States and the Caribbean.

Racialization is a process that reclassifies groups into a lower racial status. Racialization is a process of subordination and domination. It is rooted in an intellectual scientific tradition that has permeated the popular culture of this era in the United States and that utilizes the structure for creating meaning during this period to biologize differences. Racism and racialization, rather than being the cumulative effect of individual actions, are better understood as part of a pattern that is constructed in a systemic way. In other words, all societal institutions practice racialization in particular ways using the pre-existing conceptual materials proper to the tradition (educational systems, previous racial hierarchies, religious systems, media, etc.). Racialization has a structure that can be discerned, with different consequences and methods identified with each stage.

Racialized individuals both challenge and contribute to the process of racialization. The role of internalized racist oppression is crucial to understand how racialization impacts the sense of self. We need to look at how racialized groups challenge racialization when they unite with other racial groups in actions that challenge the stereotypes, or reinforce it when they contribute to reinforce the stereotypes used to construct racialized images.

This process of racialization leads to the homogenization of ethnic groups and their transformation into a racial group that obliterates the heterogeneity of Puerto Ricans and Mexicans as an ethnic group. The colored lens used by the racializer blinds him to the diversity of racial groups existing within the racialized group. The impact of this perception is so powerful that the subordinated racialized groups assumed the label of the racializer. Among Puerto Ricans in New York, Clara Rodriguez in her book *Puerto Ricans Born in the USA* finds that Puerto Ricans describe themselves "darker" than what they appear. This is particularly more evident among those who have lived in the U.S. the longest.[28]

The intersection of race, ethnicity, class, and gender during this period needs to be looked at more closely within a theoretical framework. There is a need to look at racialization within the Spanish period in Puerto Rico to contrast and more clearly demarcate its differences from racialization under the United States. The economic process, the institution of slavery, and other important structural components of the racial system under Spain have been researched, but there is a need to connect all of these within a theoretical framework that focuses on racialization, particularly after the abolition of slavery in 1873.

There is also a need to look and contrast the experiences of Puerto Ricans in the United States and the island. The racialization of Puerto Ricans in New York during this period is quite distinct from what was taking place in Puerto Rico. How can we otherwise explain why one of Puerto Rico's leading intellectuals in the United States, Arturo Alfonso Schomburg, a progressive black Puerto Rican, contrary to Pedro Albizu Campos in Puerto Rico, chose to lead an African consciousness movement in the mainland. Albizu Campos, on the other hand, chose the nationalist road to unite Puerto Ricans irrespective of race. Two powerful Puerto Rican intellectuals of African ancestry chose two different roads to address and challenge oppression.

Racialization is a process that has its greater impact on groups. In others words, although certain Mexican or Puerto Rican individuals may be able to "pass" and eventually become "whitened" that has not been the experience for the entire social group of Puerto Ricans and Mexicans during the last 150 years. There were points in time where this might have happened, particularly after World War II, but the racially stratified system was reinforced after the 1960s, another area that needs to be explored. After WWII, Chicanos were in the process of becoming "whitened." Their political tactics were not rooted in a "non-white" grounding but in the hope of achieving whiteness. World War II veterans were able to achieve a modicum of status and economic position through the GI Bill, FHA, etc. They had been able to move, particularly in California, to the aging suburbs, but suburbs still. They were able to enter many unions and slowly it seemed that the process of integration was going to happen. One index of this was the increasing Mexican support for the Republican party (Reagan, later Nixon, etc.) and the early integration into the Democratic Party (Viva Kennedy! Clubs) but the economic restructuring that began to be salient in the 1960s, the re-racialization that took place ironically as a result of the Civil Rights movement, and the increased immigration brought about by the 1965 migration law shifted the course of racialization again.

For Boricuas as well as Chicanos the challenge will be how to resist racialization in light of the increasing economic polarization within both communities. There are large growing middle class and upper middle class among both communities, which have less and less contact with

the working class majorities of the communities. It is the working class segment of both communities, that are being racialized more intensely, and they still constitute the majority among the Latino population of the United States. Any anti-racist agenda in the United States and Puerto Rico will most likely include a clear linking of class, race, ethnicity and gender if it is to be successful in the dismantling of white supremacy and racism in the United States.

References ● ● ● ● ●

Acuña, R. 1988. *Occupied America*. New York: Harper Collins.

Allen, T. W. 1994. *The Invention of the White Race Vol One: Racial Oppression and Social Control*. London: Verso.

Almaguer, T. 1994. *Racial Faultlines: The Historical Origins of White Supremacy in California*. Berkeley: University of California Press.

Anderson, B. 1991. *Imagined Communities: Reflections on the Origin and Spread of Nationalism*. New York: Verso.

Ayala, C. J. and L. W. Bergad. 2001. "Rural Puerto Rico in the Early Twentieth Century Reconsidered: Land and Society, 1899-1915" *Latin American Research Review* 37 (2):65-97.

Balderrama, F. E., and R. Rodriguez. 1995. *Decade of Betrayal: Mexican Repatriation in the 1930s*. Albuquerque, NM: New Mexico University Press.

Bonilla-Silva, E. and K. S. Glover. 2005. "'We Are All Americans': The Latin Americanization of Race Relations in the U.S." Manuscript.

Briggs, Laura. 2002. *Reproducing Empire: Race, Sex, Science and U.S. Imperialism in Puerto Rico*. Berkeley: University of California Press.

Brodkin, K. 1998. *How Jews Became White Folks and What That Says About Race in America*. New Brunswick, New Jersey, Rutgers University Press.

Cabranes, J. A. 1979. *Citizenship and the American Empire*. New Haven, CN: Yale University Press.

Carrion, J. M. Ed. 1997. *Ethnicity, Race and Nationality in the Caribbean*. Rio Piedras: University of Puerto Rico, Caribbean Studies Institute.

Collins, R. and M. Makowski. 1998. *The Discovery of Society*. Boston: McGraw Hill.

Colon, J. 1961. *A Puerto Rican in New York and Other Sketches*. New York: Mainstream Publishers.

Davila, A. 2001. *Latinos Inc.: The Marketing and Making of a People*. Berkeley: University of California Press.

Duany, J. 2000. "Neither White nor Black: The Politics of Race and Ethnicity among Puerto Ricans on the Island and in the U.S.

Mainland," revised version of paper presented at the conference "The Meaning of Race and Blackness in the Americas: Contemporary Perspectives," Brown University, Providence Long Island, February 10-12, 2000.

Duany, J. 2002. *The Puerto Rican Nation on the Move: Identities on the Island and in the United States*. Chapel Hill, NC: University of North Carolina Press.

DuBois, W. E. B. 1906. *The Souls of Black Folks*. Greenwich, CT: Fawcett.

Falcon, A. 2005. *Atlas of Stateside Puerto Ricans*. Washington, D.C. Puerto Rican Federal Affairs Administration.

Fannon, F. 1986. *The Wretched of the Earth*. New York: Grove Press.

Flores, J. 2000. *From Bomba to Hip Hop: Puerto Rican Culture and Latino Identity*. New York: Columbia University Press.

Flores, J. 2002. "Islands and Enclaves: Caribbean Latinos in Historical Perspective" in *Latino: Remaking America*. M. Suarez-Orozco and M. M. Paez, Eds. University of California Press, pp. 59-74.

Glasser, R. 1995. *My Music Is My Flag: Puerto Rican Musicians and their New York Communities*. Berkeley, CA: University of California Press.

Godinez, V. 2001. "'Los otros Hispanos' often assimilate twice." Orange County Register, August 15.
http://www.ocregister.com/features/census/other00815cci3.shtml

Gonzalez, G. and R. Fernandez. 1998. "Chicano History: Transcending Cultural Models" in *The Latino Studies Reader: Culture, Economy and Society*. Antonia Darden & Rodolfo Torres, Eds. London: Blackwell Publishers, pp. 83-100.

Gonzalez, G. and R. Fernandez. 2002. "Empire and the Origins of Twentieth Century Migration from Mexico to the United States" *Pacific Historical Review* 71 (1):19-57.

Gonzalez, G. and R. Fernandez. 2003. *A Century of Chicano History: Empire, Nations and Migration*. New York: Routledge.

Gonzalez, G. 1990. *Chicano Education in the Era of Segregation*. Philadelphia: The Balch Institute Press.

Gonzalez G. 1999. "The 1933 Los Angeles County Farm Workers Strike" in *Latino Social Movements: Historical and Theoretical Perspectives*. Rodolfo Torres and George Katsiaficas, Eds. New York: Routledge, pp. 111-140.

Gonzalez G. 2000. "The Ideology and Practice of Empire: The U.S., Mexico, and the Education of Mexican Immigrants," (Manuscript), University of California, Irvine.

Gonzalez, J. L. 1993. *Puerto Rico: The Four- Storeyed Country*. Princeton, NJ: Marcus Wiener Publishing.

Gonzalez, M. G. 1999. *Mexicanos: A History of Mexicans in the United States*. Bloomington, IN: University of Indiana Press.

Griswold del Castillo, R. 1990. *The Treaty of Guadalupe Hidalgo: A Legacy of Conflict.* Norman, PK: University of Oklahoma Press.
Griswold del Castillo, R. et al. 1991. *Chicano Art: Resistance and Affirmation, 1965-1985.* Phoenix, AZ: University of Arizona Press.
Guerra, L. 1998. *Popular Expression and National Identity in Puerto Rico: The Struggle for Self, Community and Nation.* Gainesville, FL: Florida State University Press.
Guerra, L. 1999. "The Promise and Disillusion of Americanization: Surveying the Socio-Economic Terrain of Early Twentieth Century Puerto Rico" in *CENTRO* XI, (1): 9-31.
Haney Lopez, I. F. 1996. *White By Law: The Legal Construction of Race.* New York: New York University Press.
Harris, M. 1997. *Culture, People and Nature: An Introduction to Cultural Anthopology.* New York: Longman.
Healey, D. 1970. *U.S. Expansionism.* Madison: University of Madison Press.
Ignatiev, N. 1995. *How the Irish Became White.* New York, Routledge.
Inter-University Program for Latino Research. 2002. "Race for Hispanic Country of Origin by regional Division and State in Census 2000."
http://www.nd.edu/~iuplr/cic/his_org_9-02/ethenic_id.html.
Keen, B. and K. Haynes. 2000. *A History of Latin America.* Boston: Houghton Mifflin Co.
Kugel, S. 2002. "Latino Culture Wars" New York Times, February 24.
Karenga, M 2002. *Introduction to Black Studies.* Los Angeles, CA: University of Sankore Press.
Klor de Alva, J. J. 1997. "The Invention of Ethnic Origins and the Negotiation of Latino Identity, 1969-1981," in M. Romero, P. Hondagneu-Sotelo, and V. Ortiz Eds. *Challenging Fronteras: Structuring Latina and Latino Lives in the U.S.* New York: Routledge.
Maldonado, E. 1979. "Contract Labor and the Origins of Puerto Rican Communities in the United States. *International Migration Review* 13(!): 103-21.
Matos Rodriguez, F. V. 1999. "Their Islands and Our People: U.S. Writing About Puerto Rico, 1898-1920." in *CENTRO* XI, (1):33-49.
Menchaca, M. 1995. *The Mexican Outsiders: A Community History of Marginalization and Discrimination in California.* Austin: University of Texas Press.
Mirande, A. 1987. *Gringo Justice.* Notre Dame, IN: Notre Dame University Press.
Montejano, D. 1987. *Anglos and Mexicans in the Making of Texas, 1836-1986.* Austin, TX: University of Texas Press.
De Montilla, A. N. 1971. *Americanization in Puerto Rico and the Public School System: 1900-1930.* Rio Piedras: Editorial Edil.

Nieto Phillips, J. 1999. "Citizenship and Empire: Race, Language, and Self-Government in New Mexico and Puerto Rico, 1898-1917." in *CENTRO* XI, (1):51-74.

Oboler, S. 1995. *Ethnic Labels, Latino Lives: Identity and the politics of (re) presentation in the United States.* Minneapolis: University of Minneapolis Press.

Oboler, S. 1997. "So Far From God, So Close to the United States: The Roots Of Hispanic Homogenization" in *Challenging Fronteras: Structuring Latina and Latino Lives in the U.S.* M. Romero, P. Hondagneu-Sotelo and V. Ortiz, Eds. New York: Routledge, pp. 31-54.

Omi, M. and H. Winant. 1986. *Racial Formation in the United States.* New York: Routledge.

Perez, G. "Puertorriqueñas rencorosas y Mejicanas sufridas: Constructing Self and Others in Chicago´s Latino Communities." CENTRO Talks http://www.prdream.com/patria/centro/02_26/perez.html.

Phelan, J. 1968. "Pan Latinism, French Interventionism in Mexico and the Genesis of the Idea of Latin America," in *Conciencia y autenticidad historicas.* Juan A. Ortega y Medina Ed. Mexico: UNAM, pp. 132-141.

Reisler, M. 1996. "Always the Laborer, Never the Citizen: Anglo Perceptions of the Mexican Immigrant during the 1920s." in *Between Two Worlds: Mexican Immigrants in the United States.* D. Gutierrez, Ed. Wilmington, DE: SR Books, pp. 23-43.

Rodriguez, C. 1989. *Puerto Ricans: Born in the USA.* New York: Unwin Hyman.

Rodriguez, C. 2000. *Changing Race: Latinos, the Census and the History of Ethnicity in the United States.* New York: New York University Press, p.8.

U.S. Bureau of the Census. *Census 2000 Summary File 1 (SF1) 100-Per cent Data, Detailed Tables for States.* April 2000. www.census.gov.

Rodríguez, V. M. 1988. *External and Internal Factors in the Organization of Production and Labor in the Sugar Industry of Puerto Rico, 1860-1934.* Unpublished Dissertation. Ann Arbor, MI: University Microfilm International.

Rodríguez, V. M.1997. "The Racialization of Puerto Rican Ethnicity in the United States" in *Ethnicity, Race and Nationality in the Caribbean.* J. M. Carrion Ed. San Juan, Puerto Rico: Institute of Caribbean Studies, University of Puerto Rico, pp. 233-273.

Rodríguez, V. M. 2000. "Censo 2000: Nacion, raza y el discurso independentista" in two parts in *Claridad.* January 7-13, 2000, pp. 14, 31, and January 14-20, 2000, p. 14, 31.

Rodríguez, V. M. 2002a. "Internalized Racist Oppression and Racialization in Latino Politics in the United States." Manuscript. California State University, Long Beach.

Rodríguez, V. M. 2002b. "Racism and Identity in Puerto Rico" paper presented at the Fourth meeting of the Puerto Rican Studies Association, Congress Plaza Hotel, Chicago, IL.

Roediger, D. R. 1991. *The Wages of Whiteness: Race and the Making of the American Working Class.* London, Verso.

Romero, M., P. Hondagneu-Sotelo and V. Ortiz Eds.1997. *Challenging Fronteras: Structuring Latina and Latino Lives in the U.S.* New York: Routledge.

Rosaldo, R. 1989. *Culture & Truth: The Remaking of Social Analysis.* Boston: Beacon Press.

Rossides, D. 1978. *The History and Nature of Sociological Theory.* Boston: Houghton Mifflin.

Rowe, L. S. 1904. *The United States and Puerto Rico.* New York: Longman & Green.

Ruiz, V. 1996. "Star Struck: Acculturation, adolescence, and the Mexican American Woman, 1920-1950." *Between Two Worlds: Mexican Immigrants in the United States.* in D. Gutierrez, Ed. Wilmington, DE: SR Books, pp.125-147.

Sanchez Korrol, V. 1983. *From Colonia to Community: The History of Puerto Ricans in New York City, 1917-1948.* Westport, CN: Greenwood Press.

Santiago-Valles, K. A. 1982. "La concentracion y la centralizacion de la propiedad en Puerto Rico (1898-1929)," in *Homines* VI (2):15-42.

Santiago-Valles, K. A. 1994. *"Subject People" and Colonial Discourses: Economic Transformation and Social Disorder in Puerto Rico: 1898-1947.* Albany: SUNY Press.

Santiago-Valles, W. F. 2000. "Difference in Codes Racialization of Color and Class Among Cubans & Puerto Ricans at the Beginning of the Twentieth Century. Lessons for 21st Century Coalitions," paper read at the IV International Puerto Rican Studies Association Conference, University of Massachusetts, Amherst, October.

Selden, S. 1999. *Inheriting Shame: The Story of Eugenics and Racism in America.* New York: Teachers College Press.

Shipman, P. 1994. *The Evolution of Racism: Human Differences and the Use and Abuse of Science.* New York: Simon and Schuster.

Souza, B.C. 1984. "Trabajo y Tristeza—'Work and Sorrow': The Puerto Ricans of Hawaii, 1900-1902" *Hawaiian Journal of History* 18:156-73.

Spring, J. 1997. *Deculturization and the Struggle for Equality: A Brief History of the Education of Dominated Cultures in the United States.* New York: McGraw-Hill.

Suarez Findlay, E. J. 1999. *Imposing Decency: The Politics of Sexuality and Race in Puerto Rico, 1870-1920.* Durham, NC: Duke University Press.

Stewart, A. 2000. "Internalized racist Oppression, IRO." Manuscript. Crossroads Institute Core Training Manual, Chicago, IL.

Takaki, R. 1983. *Pau Hana: Plantation Life and Labor in Hawaii, 1835-1920.* Honolulu: University of Hawaii Press.

Taylor Haizlip, S. 1995. *The sweeter the juice : a family memoir in black and white.* New York : Touchstone.

Thompson, L. 1995. *Nuestra isla y su gente: La construccion del "otro" puertorriqueño en* Our Islands and their People. Rio Piedras, PR: Centro de Investigaciones Sociales y Departamento de Historia, U.P.R.

Turner, J. K. 1911. *Barbarous Mexico.* Chicago: N.P.

Vega, B. 1984. *Memoirs of Bernardo Vega.* C. Andreu, Ed. New York: Monthly Review Press.

Endnotes ● ● ● ● ●

1. I want to thank William Fred Santiago, Marie Ramos Rosa, Juan Manuel Carrion, Ann Stewart, Robette An Dias, Joseph Barndt, partners of Crossroads, Rudy Acuña, and many others for insightful conversations and guidance on this topic. I also want to thank my wife and partner Laura, for teaching me about being a Boricua in the United States. I also want to thank the anonymous reviewers for their precise and helpful suggestions. Throughout this essay my definition of racialization is rooted in the process to "signify the extension of racial meaning to a previously unclassified relationship, social practice or group." (Omi & Winant, 64). This racial meaning is constructed on the basis on some assumed biological characteristics that are assumed to represent some essential difference. The final outcome of racialization is the construction of a racial group that is then seen and experienced as a subordinate, homogeneous category of people in a hierarchy of racial groups.

2. There is a vast literature that has contributed to the ideological deconstruction of the racialization process in the United States. Racialization's genealogy has its origins in the efforts of the plantation elite to divide and conquer poor whites and black indentured servants in the plantation economies of the early U.S. colonies (Allen, 1994, 1997). We have come to understand the legal process of delineating the boundaries of the politically constructed racial categories (Haney Lopez, 1996) and there is significant amount of work on construction of "whiteness" and the racialization of European immigrants (Roediger, 1991; Ignatiev, 1995; Brodkin, 1998) . These ef-

forts have deepened our understanding of how the categories are constructed and how new ethnic groups are incorporated into the racial system.

3. I will use the concept of "people of Latin American origin," (Mexican or Puerto Rican) to differentiate from "Latinos/Hispanics," which is what I will use for these groups after racialization. I recognize that the category "Latino" is often used among academics who challenge the Eurocentricity of "Hispanic" (Oboler, 1995; Acuña, 1996, 2000) and the process of "whitening" people of Latin American origin, but that term is also as problematic as "Hispanic." The concept of "Latin America," was coined by Francophiles during the nineteenth century to present a counter hegemonic myth to Anglo-Saxon expansion. This makes both "Hispanic" and "Latino" problematic since they are both the outcome of European efforts to triangulate the process of controlling the new nations and groups from the Americas (Phelan, 1968).

4. Suzanne Oboler (1997) argues that this process of homogenization is a product of the experience of people of Latin American origin within the United States. Despite the linguistic similarities, the historical experience, the population racial make-up and their relationship to the United States, created significant cultural differences among Latin American nations.

5. In New York, for example, Latin Americans become racialized within the Puerto Rican "melting pot." While Puerto Ricans are losing the numerically predominant position in an increasingly diverse Latino New York, the Puerto Rican culture is still a significant avenue for Latin Americans to participate in the Latinization of New York (Kugel, 2002). A similar process exists in Southern California, for example where other people of Latin American origin become acculturated in a Mexican cultural milieu (Godinez, 2001).

6. DuBois by "double-consciousness" meant that process of racialization where people of African descent are provided with a racialized encasement that feels uncomfortable because it is an identity created to dominate and control. "It is a peculiar sensation, this double-consciousness, this sense of always looking at one's self through the eyes of others, of measuring one's soul by the tape of a world that looks on in amused contempt and pity. One ever feels his two-ness,—an American, a Negro; two souls, two thoughts, two unreconciled strivings; two warring ideals in one dark body, whose dogged strength alone keeps it from being torn asunder" (1906:12).

7. For a description of the racialization of Puerto Rican ethnicity see Rodríguez' (1997) description of the racialization of Puerto Rican ethnicity.

8. As Nieto-Phillips has argued in his helpful historical comparison of the New Mexican and Puerto Rican experience under imperialism,

although the histories of Mexican Americans and Puerto Ricans are quite distinct, at times "at various points in time and in the context of U.S. imperialism, (are) inextricably connected..." (1999:51).

9. Vicente Ramon Guerrero Saldaña (1782-1831) was the second president of Mexico. He had been a Lieutenant Colonel in the Mexican War of Independence. Of African and Indian heritage he was a brilliant military strategist. He was executed in 1831 after leading a rebellion against General Anastacio Bustamente. However, leftist Leonardo Zavala and conservative Nicolas Bravo, who also rebelled against the central government were sent into exile, only the black Guerrero was executed.

10. The "one drop rule"or the rule of hypodescent assigns the offspring of a mixed race couple the less prestigious status of the two parents. Therefore, a black and white couple's child will be "non-white." Within this system black women can never have a "white" child but a white woman can have a "non-white" child. See Harris (1997).

11. See Taylor Haizlip (1995) for a historical account of "passing" within the African American community.

12. U.S. Census Bureau, Census 2000 Redistricting. Summary Files, Tables PL and PL 2.

13. Bonilla-Silva (2005) has argued that the ideology of "color-blind" racism that pervades Latin America leads people to not see race as a social reality. See Rodríguez (2002b) and Rodríguez (2000), an article on the background politics behind the use of race questions in the census in Puerto Rico.

14. Race has two definitions that are used in this work in different contexts, one, "race" as a demographic characteristic, as it is used by the census and "race" as a political concept. In the demographic sense race "reflects a social definition of race recognized in this country" (U.S. Bureau of the Census). Politically, however, "race" is "a social category used to assign human worth and social status using Europeans as a paradigm..." (Karenga, 2002).

15. The influence of "Taylorism" in pedagogical thought during the first decades of the 20th century was rooted in the need to "train" and domesticate (not educate) workers for the brutish work in assembly lines of industrial production. Most of the workers were immigrants from Mexico, Puerto Rico and Southern and Central Europe, these were some of the most racialized European immigrant groups. For Mexico see Gilbert Gonzalez (2000).

16. The Carnegie Institution in 1903 awarded Charles Benedict Davenport $34,250 for "the formation and continuance of the Station for the Experimental Study of Evolution in Cold Spring Harbor, New York." He also became a leader of the American Breeders Association and its Eugenics section where he researched "heredity in the

human race and emphasize the value of superior blood and the menace to society of inferior blood" (Selden, 1999:4).

17. Renato Rosaldo (1989) argues that culture is a marker of difference, in a society with social stratification. "As one approaches the top rungs on the ladder of social mobility, however, the process reverses itself. At this point one begins a process of cultural stripping away" (201). Also, this ideological process tends to obscure power in the relationship between social groups "Yet analysts rarely allow the ratio of class and culture to include power. Thus they conceal the ratio's darker side: the more power one has, less culture one enjoys, and the more culture one has, the less power one wields" (202).

18. Most of the early Anglo immigrants into the Southwest were men who sought new avenues of upward mobility. Many Anglos married into the Mexican elite by marrying their daughters. In Arizona, for example "Between 1872 and 1899, intermarriage remained high, with 148 of 784, or 14% of all marriages, being between Anglo men and Mexican females; during the same period only 6 involved Mexican men and Anglo women." (Acuña 1988: 89). In California, a similar process occurred; in some ways it was a way, for the Anglo elite to assure an incontestable "white" status for their progeny (Acuña, 1988:116-118).

19. Another reason for the form of resistance was the level of violence and criminalization used against Mexicans after the Mexican American War that ended in 1848. See Alfredo Mirande (1987) for a historical description of the demonization and violent subordination of Mexicanos.

20. The Platt Amendment, imposed by the United States, allowed the United States to maintain a naval base in Cuba (Guantanamo) and to intervene any time it thought necessary to "preserve Cuban independence" (Keen & Haynes 2000:431).

21. A recent inquiry into the land tenure of Puerto Rico from 1899-1915 by Cesar J. Ayala and Laird W. Bergad, (2001) argues that land tenure in fact became less concentrated in the early years of U.S. imperial hegemony. However, the power of U.S. sugar and tobacco interests, while mediated in more nuanced ways than thought before, still exercised hegemony over the island's agricultural economy.

22. The role of labor brokers in attracting Puerto Rican labor to the United States was made easier after Puerto Rico's economic debacle caused by U.S. policies following the Spanish-American War of 1898 see E. Maldonado (1979); B.C. Souza (1984).

23. A process of subordination that was utilized in various shapes and forms in the racialization of Native Americans/Indians, African Americans see J. Spring (1997) who provides a good synopsis of the impact of imperial education on the subaltern.

24. The perception that most Puerto Ricans were "white" in the eyes of congress was crucial to conferring citizenship to Puerto Ricans. Since the 1790 Naturalization Act, only whites could become U.S. citizens. This did not change until the 1951 Walter-McCarren Act, which opened the door to "non-whites" being able to become U.S. citizens.

25. Internalized Racist Oppression (IRO) is defined by anti-racist trainer Anne Stewart (2000) as a "complex, multi-generational process of socialization that teaches people of color to believe, accept and live out a negative societal definition. These behaviors contribute to the perpetuation of the race construct."

26. "Parejeria" is one way of individually challenging dominant groups or individuals without outright confrontation. "Pochismo" is a culture that arises out of being rejected in the mainstream for not being fully "American" and from rejection in the Mexican culture for not being "Mexican" enough. "Rasquachismo" or the particular worldview of the Chicano underclass, can also be a coping mechanism for a life of powerlessness, however, in Chicano art, especially the work of Tomas Ybarra Fausto transforms this stance into a form of cultural resistance (Griswold Del Castillo, 1991)

    Other racialized coping mechanisms are gendered; Gina Perez in her lecture "Puertorriqueñas rencorosas y Mejicanas sufridas: Constructing Self and Others in Chicago's Latino Communities" at the CENTRO of Puerto Rican Studies explains how these gender based coping mechanisms where stereotypes are then presented as positive traits that while they do not challenge racialization, but they help survival. CENTRO Talks, http://www.prdream.com/patria/centro/02_26/perez.html.

27. The impact of racism on the sense of self of subordinated, racialized groups was first discussed sociologically by African American sociologist W. E. B. Dubois (1961). The classics by Albert Memmi, Franz Fannon broadened this understanding into the colonial experience. Contemporary anti-racist theory and perspective identifies this racialized identity as "internalized racist oppression" (Rodriguez, 2002a).

28. In some exploratory focus groups that I carried out among students in a course at the University of Puerto Rico (1998) I found that those who had lived in the United States (there is significant "circular migration" in Puerto Rico) were more likely to describe themselves using color categories that were darker than those used by the other respondents who rated them. This phenomena is called by Rodriguez as the "browning tendency," an index of racialization.

● ● ● ● ● ● ● ● ● ● ● ● ● ● ● ● ●

The 1992 "Angelazo,"
Los Angeles, U.S.A.:
"A House Divided Against Itself..."[1]

Abstract

The events that rocked the city of Los Angeles on May of 1992 opened a new chapter in race relations in the United States. These events became a metaphor about what is ailing U.S. society. The United States is not a society neatly divided into black and white Anglo-Saxon worlds, it is a shattered glass whose pieces represent the various racial and ethnic groups that strive to become a part of the "mainstream." The mainstream is the concrete fulfillment of the materialistic "American dream." Its realization, in the concrete lives of the myriad of the majority of the communities of color communities that make up the United States, is becoming increasingly elusive.

Despite expectations to the contrary, the Los Angeles rebellion did not create a significant change in attitudes toward one of the root causes of racial/ethnic antagonism in Los Angeles. A survey carried out by UCLA professor, Lawrence Bobo, (1992) following the events, indicated that social barriers to mobility were still not seen as the main culprits for high poverty levels among minorities. The worldviews of Latinos and blacks were relatively similar in that 76% of blacks and 68% of Latinos felt that "social barriers" in some sense "caused" higher poverty amongst these groups. On the other hand, only 50% of Anglos and 57% of Asians feel that social barriers were to blame for poverty levels. In fact, only 61% of Anglos and Asians feel that more spending to assist Latinos and blacks is necessary to resolve poverty levels. These attitudinal levels were not changed significantly by the events in Los Angeles (Mandel, 1993). The "two nations" the Kerner Commission talked about in the 1960s is still present in the southern California social landscape. Two worlds and two perspectives: one an individualistic understanding of social ills held by whites, and one a more systemic, institutional perspective that shapes the understanding of communities of color.

Introduction

On April 29, 1992, when the Simi Valley, California white jury delivered a not guilty verdict for four Los Angeles policemen that were being tried in the beating of African American Rodney G. King, the city was stunned in disbelief. As the news spread like a wildfire throughout the city, Los Angeles became engulfed in rioting, looting, shooting, and protests.

While the initial incidents of violence took place within a sector of the African American community of South Central Los Angeles, in a few hours they had spread to the Latino, and other racial/ethnic, communities within the city. Forty-one (out of fifty-three who died) that were killed by gunshot wounds, ostensibly by the "forces of order," nineteen were Latinos. One policeman who killed a Salvadorean national the second night had fatally shot an African American person in 1987, an incident that had been protested by the black community forcing Chief Gates of the Los Angeles Police Department (LAPD) to criticize the police officer. Eventually, more than twenty cities in southern California experienced incidents of violence and protest.

Thousands of California local and state police forces, supported by units of the U.S. armed forces patrolled the city of Los Angeles in the days following the worst urban social conflagration the United States has ever experienced. Further, hundreds of Immigration and Naturalization Service, Federal Bureau of Investigation, and Alcohol, Tobacco and Firearms agents, swept the city's communities like a swarm. Undocumented immigrants particularly were singled out and became, all of a sudden, blamed for what ails southern California.

Units of the Marine Corps that were deployed in the city following the disturbances had been part of the troops that had participated in the military action against President Manuel Noriega in the republic of Panama. Also, some of the army units deployed throughout the city from Fort Ord, California, had been involved in combat against Iraq in the Persian Gulf.

During the uproar, fifty-three persons lost their lives while 2,400 more were injured and thousands arrested. More than a thousand structures were set on fire and damages reached hundreds of millions of dollars in direct losses in this city, better known for its film industry and palm trees than for its social conflicts. Los Angeles, the second largest city of the United States was rocked by such an outburst of rage that analysts are still trying to discern its causes. But, "public opinion" had already made up its mind about the culprits.

In the aftermath of the disturbances, a *Los Angeles Times* poll in May 1992 found that 50% of those polled called for moral leadership from within inner-city communities (read blacks and Latinos) and a CBS poll found that 43% of those polled attributed the causes of the incidents to "breakdown in family values" while only 35% blamed "govern-

ment neglect." This predominantly white majority public opinion was the target of former Vice President Dan Quayle's comments that year about family values. The subtle message was that "these people" lived immoral lives and therefore engaged in immoral acts of violence. This criminalization of what was a violent social action led officials to ignore almost completely the underlying causes of the rebellion. The "Law and Order" theme used so effectively to quash the social movements of the 1960s, was reinvigorated in liberal California.[2]

The events, plastered on prime-time television, broadcasted live for hours, seemed to be beamed from a far away third-world nation. Yet, through the great technological advances of satellite, microwave communications, video, and computer graphics we could experience the rage and feel the heat of the fires right in our own living rooms.

Despite the intensive media coverage and the thousands of words that have attempted to capture the context for this "Angelazo," many were grappling for an explanation. Despite visits to the ravaged local neighborhoods by politicians of all stripes, including then President George Bush Sr., despite its impact on the 1992 elections discourse, local, and state commissions report, it still seems that the national elites have not discerned the content of the message sent by this rebellion.

While some analysts have focused on the broad participation of all ethnic sectors as evidence of the class basis of this rebellion, the overwhelming majority of those involved were African American, Latino, and Asian. Race and ethnicity were the most important factors in any contextualization of this rebellion. What happens in American society is that being Latino or black means a greater likelihood of being in a subordinate social and economic class. Communities of color clearly understand this reality, but the white elites still do not.[3]

Additionally, although the media has tended to characterize this conflict as a black/white issue, in fact, this is probably the first "multicultural" uprising in the United States. While the media and the Hollywood industry still represented Los Angeles as a black and white city, the reality is that in 1992, 39% of the population was Latino, by the year 2000, the Latino population rose to 45% of all Angelinos, and whites, who represented 39% of the population in 1992, declined to only 32% of the population in 2000. Despite the portrayal of Los Angeles in 1992 as an Anglo and African American cauldron of conflict, only 10% of the city's population was black. Within the Los Angeles Unified School District, more than thirty languages were spoken in the classrooms. This city is probably the most multilingual city in the United States, it is also a place where various forms of bilingual education became the law of the land.[4]

Ironically, the center of the rebellion was South Central Los Angeles, for example, this district, which encompasses the area most devas-

tated by the 1992 rebellion and the 1965 Watts uprising, is today 50.1% Latino and 44.8% black. Within the city of Los Angeles proper, more than 40% of the population is foreign-born. This is an area that increasingly has become more polarized and stratified.[5]

Collective Behavior in the United States

What took place in Southern California cannot be reduced to individual psychology. Focusing on individual psychology will confuse and lead away from developing a frame of reference that will make sense of these events. The focus needs to be on the social and collective nature of human social life. Collective behavior is an inherent part of our humanity and must be placed within the context of ordinary people responding to extraordinary situations.

During the last decade of the nineteenth century, a French sociologist, Gustave Le Bon, was asking himself the same questions we pose today. Why do people participate in such seemingly irrational political or social upheavals? Le Bon was partially responding to some of the social conflicts that accompanied the modernization and industrialization of France.[6] Today, those who speak about "animalistic behavior" are for the most part coinciding with Le Bon's analysis. He thought that people's behavior in crowds is reduced to the "lowest common denominator." The main difference with what happens today in the United States and what happened in France during the eighteenth century is the intense process of racialization that accompanies these characterizations of those who engage in social protest (Rodriguez, 2005). This process of racialization becomes intensified if the protestors are persons of color.

Le Bon notwithstanding, the issue is not so simple. While it may give us a false sense of understanding and social distance from the behavior pervading the social conflagration in Los Angeles, to label such behavior as sub-human truly misses the point. These were not only violent irrational outbursts growing out of frustration, in reality there was a rational structure to these events. There was leadership, division of labor, and clearly discernible behavioral patterns and a process in these events.[7] These were not the first or the last of these scenes in the United States' race/ethnic relations drama.

One characteristic of these events is that just like in the 1965 Watts insurrection, during the Los Angeles 1992 insurrection one could see looters stopping at red lights and crosswalks with their trunks full of stolen goods. We also could see looters helping other female looters when they tripped over and fell to the floor because of the heavy load they were carrying. How can we make sense of such seemingly contradictory images?

First, as much sociological research has clearly demonstrated, not all members of a crowd share the same emotions and feelings. During the 1970 Kent State riot, which resulted in the killing of four students and the wounding of nine others, participants were shown to have different feelings and proclivities. The crowd that seemed to confront the National Guard was not a homogeneous mass. There was no "herd instinct."

The violence that has pervaded this city was indicative of a social insurrection. As in other similar events through history we will eventually find that many ordinary people were part of the set of events that rocked the city.[8] We can be made to feel more guarded and protected by labeling the participants as anarchic "hoodlums" or "riff raff" but we must not allow ourselves to be coddled into a false sense of security.

For example, recent 1990 census data provides proof of this fact. The first outbursts of this rebellion originated not from the poorest districts of Los Angeles but from its most stable neighborhoods. This tends to support the notion of the "continuing significance of race" within American society. The basic sense of frustration arising from African Americans was their treatment as second-class citizens, even when gainfully employed and living stable lives (Dunn & Hubler, 1992). Latinos, who are historically represented as passive, docile, and malleable, engaged in collective behavior in areas like Pico-Union, a center of newly arrived Central American immigrants. A significant number of these Central American immigrants—Salvadoreans, Guatemalans—are also political refugees. While most of them are poor, they are part of the working poor and not part of a "welfare dependent," stigmatized and "inner city" lumpen population so prevalent in the popular culture's imaginary.

Genesis of the Social Despair

This social insurrection evidenced the fine and tenuous basis of community in Los Angeles in a way that no natural disaster had ever accomplished. The bond that holds society together is the shared agreement that legitimizes social norms. These rules have power over us because we have some sense that they have some measure of reasonability and fairness and that they somehow apply to all persons.

This tenuous consensus was shattered by the jury's verdict on April 29, 1992. The majority of the residents of Los Angeles, as surveys clearly evidenced, felt that the verdict was a miscarriage of justice. Simi Valley, where the trial took place, while not the bigoted community the media had projected is still, sociologically, very distant from Los Angeles's rich ethnic diversity. This city had become a site where law enforcement of-

ficers found refuge while working for the city of Los Angeles, but it was also a "refuge" for other whites and upwardly mobile minorities to escape from Los Angeles' problems. In some ways, it was a site for "white flight" just like Orange County was during the 1960s and 1970s.

But this verdict was merely a catalyst that unleashed many forces that were festering in U.S. society. Forces that had accumulated with an intensity and a force that had weakened and undermined the hold of social norms over people's behavior. Los Angeles had become a matrix where various ethnic communities, while sharing common geographic spaces at some points of their everyday life, lived in separate cultural spaces. One cultural space was marked with material abundance, in which law enforcement was really there to "protect and serve," although the other cultural spaces were marked by poverty, declining social services in deteriorating neighborhoods, and a law enforcement system that harassed and stigmatized them. The bonds that created community were facing a challenge, and they had lost their legitimacy. For communities of color, the daily experience of racialization perpetuated their growing sense of them as "nonwhite" which in our society means not dominant, not entirely "American" not fully human (Chavez, 2002). Particularly for Latinos, this sense of "otherness" was clearly expressed in popular culture expressions like the late 1990s Chicano rap of Kid Frost where a sense of being the "racialized other" was clearly expressed in the lyrics (Chavez, 2002).

These bonds that keep Los Angeles society and most United States communities together, especially in large urban areas, were weakened during the previous two decades before the rebellion. The process of healing that supposedly took place after the 1965 Watts rebellion never reached fruition. The roots of that incident and this recent one have hardly been addressed. The origins of this crisis lie not in the Rodney G. King trial and its aftermath, but deep in the core of contemporary U.S. society. The rendering of the verdicts were just a spark that hit the powder keg of the nation.

Joining the Ranks of the Third World?

Some regions of the United States are increasingly becoming mirror images of the countries that we have disdainfully labeled the "third world." Third world nations that confront declining incomes and rising external debts have historically been fertile ground for social unrest. Globalization has meant the reproduction of third-world conditions inside of the metropolis. Because parallel to these super exploited nations in the global economy, large segments of U.S. society have become places where rising poverty, despair, hopelessness, and rage, are only contained

by the state's coercive apparatus. Law enforcement has clearly assumed the role of an occupying army in these barrios and inner city cores.

The Los Angeles Police Department had become in the last decade before the rebellion probably one of the most "militarized" and proactive police departments in the United States. Its policy of active enforcement (with very high arrest rates of minorities) is almost the civilian counterpart of "low intensity conflict" strategies carried out by U.S. military in the Third World in the 1980s. The cuts in the state's budgets as a result of Proposition 13 led to a reduction in the budgetary resources invested in policing in Los Angeles, then LAPD Chief of Police Daryl Gates, militarized the department in order to face a large community with fewer resources. In fact, despite the talk about how armed the populace of Las Angeles was, not one policeman died during the rebellion. Of the 239 shooting victims, only three of them were policemen. Law enforcement agencies had overwhelming firepower while the rebellious masses did not.

One of the reasons for the militarization of the Los Angeles Police Department is the very small ratio of policemen to the large population of Los Angeles. Other cities like New York had twice the number of police officers that Los Angeles had. In some sense the LAPD had to adapt to the challenge of a relatively small police force. Obviously, they chose to implement a racist policy on what was in fact a society bursting with social problems. These communities became the new "internal third worlds."

In some sense, these places have been created by processes of segregation that, although more subtle, hidden, and covert than thirty years before, still have the same overall effect. Institutional racism is still alive and well and operates in more covert ways than in earlier decades. Real estate, insurance, and banking have for years used and still use illegal redlining practices to avoid investing social and economic resources in these internal "third worlds."

Recent studies of the banking system have evidenced clear patterns of discrimination in lending practices. The Atlanta Journal/Constitution newspaper published a series in 1988 that evidences this clear pattern of discrimination.[9] These inner-city districts have become places where despair and hopelessness abounds and from these emotions, righteous indignation and rage are just a short step away. A decade after the rebellion, studies document that these segregating and discriminating practices continue today (Stein & Laila, 2003; Turner et al., 2002).

The rage was also fueled by heavy-handed police tactics within these minority communities. The LAPD was criticized by the Christopher Commission, a commission whose role was to audit the police department's activities in light of heavy public criticism. Similarly, dur-

ing the summer of 1992, a study completed for the Los Angeles County Supervisors sharply criticized the Sheriff's Department record of police brutality, particularly against members of minority groups. These law enforcement agencies have compounded the inner-city problems by trying to deal with issues for which they have no cultural competency.[10]

During the rebellion, the rage overflowed the upper edges of the forces of order's ability to contain it. During those days, for a brief period of time, the streets of Los Angeles were in the power of the masses, anarchic masses notwithstanding.

What underlies the forces that were unleashed by the opening of the floodgates? What raw nerve was snapped when the Simi Valley jury delivered its verdict of not guilty for four white policemen?

Growing Social Inequality

It seems obvious that in the last two decades before the rebellion social inequality had become more visible and intense in the United States. Numerous politicians of all political stripes blamed both the Ronald Reagan and George Bush Sr. administrations for creating the conditions for the social unrest. The truth of the matter is that the roots of the growing chasm between the rich and the poor could not be placed entirely on the lap of the Reagan and/or Bush administration. In reality, while the social and economic policies of both the Reagan and the Bush administration compounded the increasing polarization, they did not create this social trend.

The growing gap that divided the United States then and today has its origins some decades ago when the nation was healing the wounds caused by segregation, separation, and racial hatred. While these attempts to heal were being made a social chasm was being built right underneath society's efforts. The progress that was being achieved gradually in certain programmatic efforts were being set asunder by larger, structural changes in the character of the nation's economic system. In fact, the police forces were handed a situation that they are not able to cope with. During those days debates in the United States about "community policing" created much discourse but never became the panacea that many of its proponents hoped it to be.[11]

While the "great society" efforts were being implemented, the process of restructuring and de-industrialization was rapidly gaining momentum throughout the United States. In addition to the dismantling and de-funding of federal programs like Aid for Dependent Children and Families (AFDC), other major structural changes were impacting the destiny of the poor.[12] These poor also include the high percentage of communities of color like Latinos and blacks who are poor. This social

and economic trend has had a dramatic impact on this nation's social structure and specifically on the relationship between the socio-economic classes of the United States. This secular social trend has challenged the U.S. middle class, has created a seemingly permanent group of persons mired in poverty (which in the popular culture are constructed as people of color), and has made even more difficult the forging of a national political consensus.

A Post-Industrial Society for a Global Economy

One result of the rationalization of the United States industrial production has been the relative de-industrialization of its economic base. As industries have vied to compete in the global market they have abandoned local U.S. communities and located their manufacturing processes in places where the costs of production are lower.[13] From the northern border of Mexico to the Asian nations of the Pacific Rim, U.S. capitalism has globalized even farther its manufacturing activities.

This process of rationalization has had two faces, one, the process of corporate restructuring undertaken by major industrial and financial enterprises, and two, de-industrialization. The corporate restructuring is one way that corporate America has utilized to create leaner and supposedly more efficient units that can compete more effectively in today's markets. One result of corporate restructuring has been the merger mania that has engulfed many corporate sectors in the last few years. Another contemporary outcome has been the "outsourcing" of productive activities to other parts of the world, including highly skilled work.

The merger process has obviously not created new productive capacity but has allowed many corporate firms to reduce costs in order to pay for the high costs of buyouts and mergers. Additionally, they have, in some cases, been able to streamline their bureaucracies and focused their services on the most profitable areas while outsourcing others. At the same time, many workers and middle-level management had found themselves without a job in an increasingly weakened economy.

Parallel to this process, the de-industrialization trend that has changed the character of the U.S. economy in the last two decades has eliminated hundreds of thousands of good paying, union-protected manufacturing jobs throughout the nation. Jobs that provided the economic basis for the rise of many United States workers to a middle-class status in the U.S. stratification system. Jobs that because of the apprentice programs had provided an entry-level door into the economy and specifically entry into the industrial sector for many young U.S. citizens. These entry-level jobs, which are paths to further advancement into a secure middle-class status, have experienced a dramatic decline.[14]

This process has also changed the character of the United States' large urban areas which have experienced dramatic transformations. Urban areas used to be centers of manufacturing, today they are centers of a myriad of services. From financial to information transfer services to trade and commerce, cities today have become emblematic of the post-industrial economy.

In substitution for manufacturing jobs, this service sector has created a significantly large number of jobs. But, these jobs seem to be polarized between jobs that require high levels of education at one end and low-skill, low-paying jobs at the other end. Many people of color and poor whites have found themselves locked out of the economy by this new "post-industrial" economy. The present state of extreme poverty experienced by some groups like Puerto Ricans and African Americans in New York and Chicago are partly the result of these urban transformations.

Race, Poverty, and Social Inequality

The very latest poverty statistics released by the Census Bureau in August of 1991 were startling to say the least. In general, there were 2.1 million more poor persons in the United States since 1989. The poverty rate had increased from 12.8% in 1989 to 13.5% in 1990.

In fact, one in five U.S. children lived in poverty and not only did they continue to be overrepresented among the poor, this proportion of children who are poor continued to increase. Among all the industrial nations of the world the United States had the highest proportion of children who are poor. This nation, among industrialized nations of the world, was the nation with the highest infant mortality rate.

Michael B. Katz, a historian whose work has focused on U.S. history, and especially on the history of our welfare system, published a book in 1989 entitled, "Undeserving Poor." The subtitle: "From the War on Poverty to the War on Welfare." This is a very clever description of what we have been seeing in the United States during the last fifteen years.

Katz explains that definitions of who are the deserving poor have shifted and that social policy and the popular culture's understanding of the poor hardly ever has had much to do with the reality of poverty. Today is not much different than yesterday. The possible exception is that in California, being poor means being Latino or black, not white.

When people think about a family on welfare, a distinct image appears in people's minds: an African American or a Latino woman with a large number of kids. This image rises despite the overwhelming social scientific evidence that this is far from the truth. In fact, the average family on welfare during the early 1990s was made up of 2.2 persons.

The 1992 electoral campaign of white supremacist David Duke was barely defeated. Yet it was effective in gathering a large proportion of Louisiana's highly educated young voters. The subtle, encoded messages were clearly understood by the electorate. When Duke mentioned in his speeches the "underclass" people knew exactly who he was talking about.[15] When he talked about "blood sucking welfare cheats," everyone, without using any epithet, knew who he was referring to. Popular culture in the United States has reached a very coherent consensus. Blacks and Latinos are sucking our resources by their indiscriminate use of the welfare system.

The reality is so different.

First, at least half of the poor are not black or Latino, they are white. An essay in the December 16, 1991 edition of *Time* by Barbara Ehrenreich provides some interesting statistics about this issue. Unfortunately, some of her statistics are misleading because in her essay she says that whites constitute 61% of those receiving welfare when in fact, those figures include a good percentage of Latinos who classify themselves as whites.

Nevertheless, whites still constitute a major portion of those on welfare. The major difference is that Latinos and blacks constitute 66% of the poor in our central cities.[16] Obviously, when the media and people in our communities see the images of the central city poor they assume that the overwhelming majority of the poor are black or Latino across the nation.

Conversely, in non-metropolitan areas, those areas outside of our cities, including rural areas, are very different with respect to who are the poor. Only 29% of the poor who live outside of our large metropolitan areas are Latino or black. While being poor may not seem qualitatively different whether it is in a non-metropolitan area or a rural area, the reality is that it does make a difference.

Racial and economic segregation is sharper within the core of U.S. cities. In other words, most of one's neighbors in the city core will also tend to be poor and persons of color. This is not always the case outside of metropolitan areas. Neighborhoods in general are less segregated and the poor can very often be found among the middle and working classes. Hidden and unobtrusive, but they are there. The stigma is less powerful in the suburbs, particularly for poor whites, than it is for people of color within the city core.

Inner Cities: Economic Deserts

Metaphorically, the inner core of our cities are like deserts; they are economically arid, dry and barren, truly devoid of anything, including hope. In fact, the etymology of the word *desert* goes back to the Latin word

desertum or abandoned. That is the best description of the effects of the process that has transformed the heart of our large urban areas.

The corporate restructuring and de-industrialization of the United States that received its momentum a few decades ago is the underlying context for the changes experienced by our cities. They are also the stage within which communities like South Central Los Angeles, South Bronx, West and South Chicago have been transformed in areas of anger and despair.[17]

For example, Puerto Ricans and other Latinos are facing tremendous economic and social challenges. While the poverty rate in 1990 for Latinos in general was 28.1%, 40.6% of Puerto Ricans lived in poverty. In 1990, 51.2% of Puerto Rican children lived in poverty (U.S. Census 1991). Thirty-nine percent of households are female headed households. The rate for African American female headed households was 48.1 %.

The accumulation of disadvantages brought by a legacy of racism, the present dynamics of institutionalized racism, coupled with the basic economic transformations the nation is undergoing, have created a wasteland inhabited by people of color in the heart of what used to be the industrial hubs of the United States.

Epilogue?: Forging a Political Consensus

The trial that the United States faces is seemingly overwhelming. There are no recipes, no herbal teas and no home remedies that can magically heal the wounds. How can the United States reach a political consensus that will facilitate a national concerted effort to address these economic, social, and political challenges? A consensus in the past was established by heralding all the moral outrage that was present within the majority Anglo/white community about the moral injustice of segregation. That reservoir of moral outrage is empty today. In fact, we are running on empty.[18] The 1992 U.S. presidential elections probably raised some hopes but the problems are structural in character. Today, with terrorism and homeland security being the major focus, the theme of racial justice is not part of the national political discourse.

During the cold war a consensus for raising military budgets was built around the notion of a "common enemy." The evil empire was the analgesic that allowed us to endure the pain of social cutbacks, reduced services, and decreasing maintenance of the nation's social and economic infrastructure. Then as today, the United States is experiencing social problems that are blooming.

Yesterday, policy planners were concerned with building a defensive/offensive capability that would protect the national integrity and security of the United States. Today, every child that has to grow and be socialized within the economic deserts that plague the nation's urban

areas is a bomb waiting to explode. The concern for terrorism that pervades our contemporary culture focuses on the external, global issues at the expense of the internal and domestic social and economic challenges. Instead of social programs, urban issues receive legal repression. The recent passage (1998) by 62% of Californians of Proposition 21, to increase penalties and make it easier to send juveniles into the criminal justice system will potentially continue the stigmatization and criminalization of communities of color.

Unfortunately, today there is no "evil empire" to force the majority into a consensus, since the moral outrage reservoirs are empty, what remains is narrow self-interest.[19] This can also be a productive path if developed creatively. What is at stake today is the issue of national unity, a major historical concern for the founders of this nation as well as contemporary analysts.[20]

The real issues of national security that have obsessed the United States for so long are today of a domestic nature. While we focus on other lands the acid that corrodes the United States' social and economic structure is not external but spawned by national policies and economic rationality. More dangerously, as we move deeper into the twenty-first century the basis for this nation's democratic processes in an increasingly culturally diverse society are being undermined by economic processes.

Hanna Arendt said during the 1970s, and Arendt is far from being a liberal, that the main contradiction of the capitalist system is that it presupposes that people can be politically equal even though they are economically unequal.

The United States is slowly pulling the economic rug out of the foundations of its democratic system. A nation that demographically is rapidly changing and becoming more racially and ethnically diverse, a nation that is becoming more economically polarized, is a "house divided against itself." A house divided against itself can only collapse.

Epilogue to an Epilogue:
or "How Los Angeles' Wounds Fester"

> "It cannot be denied that the masses revolt from time to time, but their revolts are always suppressed. It is only when the dominant classes, struck by sudden blindness, pursue a policy which strains social relationships to the breaking-point, that the party masses appear actively on the stage of history and overthrow the power of oligarchies."
>
> Robert Michels (*Political Parties*, 1911)

Robert Michels, a German political sociologist, in his thesis about the "Iron Law of Oligarchy" states that large organizations can not but be undemocratic. In the same way, a society dominated by large organizations will also tend to be undemocratic. If we examine the events of 1992 Los Angeles, what would be Michel's diagnosis? Have we expanded democracy to include the "others"? Are we left with nothing but cynicism to build on?

Unmet Expectations

LAPD Officers Stacey Koon and Laurence Powell were indicted for violating the civil rights of Rodney King on April 30, 1992. On April 16, 1993, both officers were found guilty of one count for violating Mr. King's civil rights and later sentenced to thirty months in a federal correctional camp. While the tension over the impending verdicts was lifted, the core issues that gave rise to the uprising remain even today (2005). Most knowledgeable observers of the communities that make up Los Angeles never expected anything serious to occur, even in the event of another acquittal of all the defendants. There were not high expectations for a just verdict that year. This explains the kind of euphoria that swept many communities of Los Angeles in response to the guilty verdicts on these two officers that became symbolic of the abuse against an entire community.

In some sense the expectations about how the Los Angeles insurrection would change national discourse on the challenges that face our nation's cities were unfounded. A 1994 poll by the *New York Times* and CBS evidences that the racial/ethnic divide is alive and well in America. Only 37% of Americans believe race relations were good. Blacks and whites still have widely different perspectives on solutions to race relations issues and problems. While 66% of blacks still support preferential hiring when there has been job discrimination in the past, this policy only received the support of 28% of whites. In 1996, the voters of California voted in favor of Proposition 209 to dismantle the use of affirmative action in the public sphere. Again, this measure indicated the continuing racial polarization that pervades California as the majority of whites voted in favor of the proposition and the majority of people of color voted against it.

Many white Los Angelenos, given the worsening economic conditions in California would probably agree with Sheila Watson, a forty-four-year-old homemaker from Moyer, Alabama who told the *New York Times* in 1994 that "Things have changed for the worse for white people." It is then not surprising to find that although change has occurred in Los Angeles following the riots, the fundamental causes of the uprising have remained untouched. We have changed without changing.

Los Angelenos also wanted "change." The effect of the insurrection was devastating to the city. Its sense of identity had been shattered. Los Angeles had always projected itself as the most diverse city in the nation and saw its strength precisely in that diversity. Many now feel that its diversity rather than its strength might be its Achilles heel and its weakness.

A Cacophony of Ironies

The first effort at healing the wounds of the city involved naming a white male to head the efforts to re-build Los Angeles after the insurrection. Peter Ueberroth, a businessman from Newport Beach and whose claim to fame had been organizing the successful 1984 Los Angeles Olympics. Unfortunately, the title of his efforts, "Re-build L.A. Foundation" did not bode good things for Los Angeles. Some have argued that Los Angeles should not be rebuilt, rather recreated on a more just foundation.

But Ueberroth is a good organizer and a well connected businessman, but as many of the efforts in the aftermath of the insurrection, his efforts are tinged with irony. The fact that he is from Orange County, the county adjoining Los Angeles, is in itself ironic. For years after the 1965 Watts rebellion this county became the haven for the white flight that ensued in the 1960s and 1970s. Now, the knights in white shining armor that were to save the city would have to come from those communities that had abandoned the city earlier. He proposed to re-build Los Angeles without the use of public funds (in May 1994, Mr. Ueberroth resigned his position with Rebuild LA).[21]

Another irony was the naming of Willie L. Williams as the first African American to ever manage the LAPD with 9,000 officers and 3,000 civilian staff, covering an area of 467 square miles (1209 km^2). The new chief of the LAPD replaced Daryl Gates whose term was marked by controversy and was sharply criticized by the Christopher Commission. Chief Williams comes from the police department that was involved in the bombing of a whole inner-city block to end a standoff between the Philadelphia Police Department and the Black nationalist group, MOVE. One wonders what is kept in store for this city in terms of "riot control" in future civil disturbances? Members of the LAPD have disclosed, as they were preparing for the rendering of the verdicts on the Rodney King 1993 civil rights case, that they will have greater flexibility this time around in dealing with "crowd control." But Chief Williams only lasted until 1997 when Bernard Parks, also African American, was named chief until 2002, when again a white police chief was named, William Bratton.[22]

The final irony lies in that one of the last acts of the Bush administration was to order the justice department to prosecute the four police

officers for violating the civil rights of Rodney King . The prosecuting team did a very effective job in presenting a strong case against officers Koon and Powell. They also were able to have a multiracial jury despite the defense' efforts to eliminate African Americans from the process. On April 16, 1993, only Koon and Powell were found guilty of violating Rodney King's civil rights, and they spent thirty months in federal correctional camp. Rodney King won a civil suit and received 3.8 million dollars with which he began a record company. The irony is that the leader of the original prosecuting team was Terry White, an African American district attorney. The leader of the prosecutor's team for the second legal process was Steven Clymer, a white district attorney.

In economic terms there was some progress in the city's "rebuilding efforts." In some areas progress has been greater than in other areas. In cities like Lynwood, 85% of buildings damaged or destroyed were rebuilt. But in the City of Angels itself only 17% of the buildings that received major damage had been rebuilt by 1994. Also, the polarization that pervaded race relations in the city remains. The problems raised at a national level by the Kerner Commission in the 1960s and the California McCone Commission are still present in Los Angeles. While there are improvements and important advances in some areas, in terms of police brutality, segregation and unemployment, financial and commercial practices all remain basically the same as they were decades before.

In fact, for all the publicity that the federal government received for its efforts in the "rebuilding" of Los Angeles, most of the funding has come from private sources, specifically the insurance companies. The Federal Emergency Management Agency provided about 125 million dollars in grants and other forms of aid. The Small Business Administration has provided about 318 million dollars although the insurance companies have paid out close to 775 million dollars for close to 8,500 claims. Rebuild LA's contribution, is more ambiguous, although officially stated at 500 million dollars many of the funds are actually pledges that did not materialize.

On the other hand, Latinos feel that their suffering has been compounded. Fifty-one per cent of the arrested were Latinos, 30% of those who died were Latino, 40% of the businesses destroyed were Latino and yet, according to a study by the Tomas Rivera Center in Claremont, California, denial rates for loans and grants to Latinos has ranged from 76% to 90% (Pastor, 1993). Latinos constitute the largest minority group in the city and in the state.

Still, some innovative efforts have sprung from various sources, including the religious sectors. One of them, called the "New City Parish," is the result of a coalition of inner-city Lutheran congregations that have incorporated themselves in order to better coordinate their efforts. Their efforts have ranged from food and clothes distribution immediately fol-

lowing the uprising to the development of a child care center, a tutorial center, and a business maintenance service.

Unfortunately, the kind of massive economic aid that would be needed to provide jobs for the thousands of young men and women of this city never materialized. These local community economic development efforts, while necessary, can only be effective as part of an overall economic development plan.

One business sector that is experiencing growth and that is a harbinger of things to come is gun sales. Los Angeles and Orange County (one of the adjoining counties to Los Angeles) were among the top three in handgun sales in California in 1994. Firing ranges were also doing some brisk business.

A Vision for the Future?

Whether or not there is another uprising in Los Angeles in the near future, confidence in the fairness of the nation's institutions has been given a respite. But this city is still an armed camp. Whites are either moving or arming themselves because of fear that those same institutions will not be able to protect them from the wrath of disgruntled communities of color. Journalist Dale Maharidge (1996) was able to capture in *The Coming White Minority* the fear and sense of being in a state of siege that is shaping the worldview of whites in California. What happens in Los Angeles is important, not only because it is the largest city in this state and one of the largest in the nation but because many "have come to regard Los Angeles as emblematic of our collective urban future" (Marks, et al 2003, quoting Dear 2000).

According to a comprehensive study of attitudes of Angelinos ten years after these events, "Fear and Loathing in Los Angeles?" (Marks, et al., 2003) indicates that 20,000 jobs were lost and 5,000 lost permanently. While the report cites a survey by Guerra and Marks (2002) that indicates a greater sense of community and tolerance than expected, contradictorily, but not entirely unexpected, "half of those surveyed believe another riot is likely to occur within the next few years" (Marks et al. 2003:4). Some 50,000 persons participated in the rebellion, causing damages that are estimated today to be at least 1 billion dollars (Marks, et al., 2003). The events touched off civil disturbances in thirty cities across the nation, and 3,700 police officers, 2,300 highway patrol personnel, 10,000 national guardsmen, and 4,000 army troops were used to quell the insurrection.

The United States will need to refocus the lenses through which it views its diverse communities. In the aftermath of the uprising one of the major television networks was advertising a program about the insurrection. A voice-over was saying "again black and white relations

lead to confrontation in our inner cities." In the meantime, the images that were shown were of young Mexican men waving the Mexican flag in front of the Parker Center, the LAPD headquarters during the early stages of the insurrection. The vision needs to be broader so that we can see the other actors in the American drama.

Richard Rodriguez, a Mexican American writer, said in an overly optimistic piece in the *Los Angeles Times* in 1994 that, "We are without a sense of ourselves entire." I agree with him. This idea of America was formed in the struggle and the oppression of Native Americans, of Mexican Americans in the Southwest, of African Americans, and of Puerto Ricans in the Northeast. We have wanted to deny a part of who we are and yet *it* comes back and shouts at us in the least expected places: Los Angeles, Washington D.C., San Antonio, Miami . . .

"Can't we all get along?" Yes, maybe, but we must first transcend the stage of denial before we can be stronger. That "other" is the marginalized part of "us," we can learn to know our authentic selves if we can open a true dialogue with each other. Otherwise, the alternative will be less democracy for all and less stability for all. It is chilling to read that in 1993 the Justice Department announced that 300 FBI agents whose jobs had become superfluous because of international changes would be assigned to the nation's cities. An internal "evil empire" perhaps? The continuing xenophobia against undocumented immigrants tends to spill over into the native-born sons and daughters of immigrants. But more dangerous is how divisions based on race are being replicated within communities of color. Native-born and foreign-born Latinos racialize each other in ways that hark back to how the dominant community racialized Latinos as a whole. In schools around the Southwest native-born and foreign-born call each other racial epithets that the dominant society used against them.

Hopefully we will embark down this path not because it is in our best interest but because it is right. Fortunately, the justice system did not "pursue a policy that strains social relationships" this time around. Hopefully, the next steps will be about justice. As Martin Luther King used to say, in freeing others we free ourselves, otherwise Robert Michels will have had the last word.

References ● ● ● ● ●

Bluestone, B. and B. Harrison. 1982. *The Deindustrialization of America*. Basic Books.

Bluestone, B. and B. Harrison. 1988. *The Great U-Turn: Corporate Restructuring and the Polarizing of America*. Basic Books.

Bobo, L. 1992. "Ethnic Antagonisms in Los Angeles," UCLA Research Paper.

Bonilla-Silva, E. 2003. *Racism Without Racists: Color Blind Racism and the Persistence of Racial Inequality in the United States*. Oxford, UK: Rowman and Littlefield.

California Department of Finance. "Race and Ethnic Population Estimates: Components of Change for California Counties, April 1990 to April 2000."

Clifford, F. 1992. "Rich-Poor Gulf Widens in State" *Los Angeles Times* May 11, p. A1.

Coughlin, Ellen K. 1992. "Following Los Angeles Riots, Social Scientists See Need to Develop Fuller Understanding of Race Relations," *The Chronicle of Higher Education (36)* May 13, pp. 10-11.

Crawford, J. 1992. *"Hold Your Tongue": Bilingualism and the Politics of "English Only."* New York: Addison-Wesley.

Dear, M. 2000. *The Postmodern Urban Condition*. Oxford: Blackwell Publishers.

Dunn, Ashley and Shawn Hubler. 1992. "An Unlikely Flash Point for Riots" *Los Angeles Times* July 5, p. 1.

Guerra, F. J. and M. A. Marks. 2002. "Survey of Public Opinion a Decade After the Los Angeles Riots." Center for the Study of Los Angeles, Loyola Marymount University.

Haney Lopez, Ian F. 2003. *Racism on Trial: The Chicano Fight for Justice*. Cambridge: Harvard University Press.

Hobsbawn, E. *Primitive Rebels. Studies in Archaic Forms of Social Movement in the 19th and 20th Centuries*. New York: W. W. Norton & Company, 1965.

Hubler, S. 1992. "Tears, No Love for Inner City LA" *Los Angeles Times* August 9, p.1.

Jacobs, J. *Cities and the Wealth of Nations: Principles of Economic Life*. New York: Random House, 1984

Katz, M. B. 1989. *The Undeserving Poor: From the War on Poverty to the War on Welfare*. New York: Pantheon Books.

Le Bon, G. 1946. *The Crowd: A Study of the Popular Mind*. New York, Macmillan, 1946.

Lewis, J. M. 1972. "A Study of the Kent State Incident" *Sociological Inquiry* 42 (1972) pp. 87-96.

Lovelace, D. and G. Welty. 1992. "Community Policing in Dayton: More Flash Than Substance" *Dayton Daily News* May 28, 15.

Maharidge, D. 1996. *The Coming White Minority: California's Eruptions and America's Future*. New York: Random House.

Mandel, W. 1994. "What Los Angeles Means: "Negroes Are Lynched in America" in NCIPA Discussion Bulletin, Summer Bulletin.

Marks, M. A., M. A. Barreto, and N. D. Woods. 2003. "Fear and Loathing in Los Angeles? Race and Racial Attitudes a Decade After the 1992 Riots." paper prepared for the Annual Meeting of

the Western Political Science Association, Denver, Colorado, March 27-30, 2003.

Marmor, T. et al. 1990. *America's Misunderstood Welfare State*. Basic Books.

Michels, R. 1966 (1911). *Political Parties*. New York: Free Press.

Pastor, M. 1993. *Latinos and the Los Angeles Uprising: The Economic Context*. Claremont, CA: Tomas Rivera Policy Institute.

Rodriguez, V. M. 2005. "The Racialization of Mexican Americans and Puerto Ricans: 1890s-1930s" in *CENTRO* Journal XVII (1) (Spring): 5-40.

Rosenblatt, R. A. and J. Bates. 1991. "High Mortgage Rejection Rates for Minorities Found" *Los Angeles Times* October 22, p.1.

Rothmiller, Mike. 1992. *LA Secret Police: Inside the LAPD Elite Spy Network*. New York: Pocket Books.

Rude, G. 1959. *The Crowd in the French Revolution*. Oxford University Press.

Smelzer, N. J. 1962. *Theory of Collective Behavior*. New York: Routledge Kegan and Paul. Sage.

Stein, K. and R. Laila. 2003. "Who Really Gets Home Loans? Year Ten: Mortgage Lending to African Americans and Latino Borrowers in 5 California Communities in 2002." San Francisco, CA: California Reinvestment Committee.

Turner, M. A. et al. 2002. "All Other Things Being Equal: A Paired Testing Study of Mortgage Lending Institutions." Washington, D.C.: Urban Institute.

U.S. Bureau of the Census. Current Population Reports, Series P-20. *The Hispanic Population in the United States: March 1991*. Washington, D.C.: U.S. Government Printing Office.

Utley, G. 1997. "Volunteers lead rebuilding after L.A. riots" CNN Web posted April 28, 1997 http://www.cnn.com/US/9704/28/volunteerism/

Endnotes ● ● ● ● ●

1. This analysis is rooted in decades of involvement in anti-racist training and organizing in the United States. The experiences as Associate Director for Racial Justice Advocacy at the National Offices of the Evangelical Lutheran Church in Chicago 1988-90 and as a core trainer and Board member (until 2004) of Crossroads Ministry, an anti-racist organizing and training organization, shaped my understanding and analysis of race in the United States. A version in Spanish of this paper was read at the V International Conference on Hispanic Cultures in the United States, 6-10 of July, 1992 at the Universidad Alcalá de Henares, Madrid, Spain. Journalistic versions

of this article in English have appeared in the last years in *International Report* and in Spanish in *Deslindes*, Colombia, *Claridad*, Puerto Rico and *El Carillon* from Andover, MA. This version was updated (2005) but the analysis was left as close as possible to its original intent, to emphasize the racial character of an event where race and class intersected and where Latinos were invisible to the media.

2. In the period immediately after the Mexican American War, which ended with the signing of the Guadalupe Hidalgo Treaty of 1848, the newly conquered community of close to 100,000 Mexicans living in the Southwest, engendered the phenomena of social bandits. Social bandits were people who engaged in illegal activity as a form of social protest against social and economic oppression (Hobsbawn, 1965).

3. Because the Civil Rights movement gained the higher moral ground, race-based discourse became tabu unless it was used to remedy the consequences of racism. But today, an ideology of "blind racism" has developed where race has been erased from public discourse and a coded language to talk about race has substituted the old racist discourse (Bonilla-Silva, 2003). In fact, legal discourse now argues that unless race is explicitly the purpose of an act of discrimination, in other words, unless "intention" to do racial harm can be proved, the courts have determined no racial discrimination case can be supported. At a time when the cultural consensus does not require the use of racial categories to indicate the target group, this new legal perspective will exclude communities of color from being able to effectively use the legal system as protection of their civil rights.

4. At least until 1998, when the voters of California approved Proposition 227 that began the dismantling of bilingual education program in the state. This proposition and others that preceded it are indicators of the political racial polarization that marks California, the majority of communities of color voted against Proposition 227, majority of whites voted in favor. For an interesting historical look at the debate around bilingualism and "English Only" politics see Crawford (1992).

5. See Clifford (1992) good source article for the levels of social stratification experienced by the city of Los Angeles. Most of the article's focus is on socio-economic/class issues.

6. Le Bon (1946) attempted to understand the violence that followed the French revolution.

7. The events that led to the rebellion follow a pattern very similar to the one detailed by the "Structural Strain Theory" or "Value Added Theory" of collective behavior by Neil Smelzer (1962).

8. In fact, in a study done by George Rude in 1959 of the "criminal riff raff" that participated in the riots that preceded the French revolu-

tion of 1789, he found some interesting facts. Of the 662 persons that were killed in the attack of the Bastille prison, all had regular occupations and places of residence.

9. Similar patterns have been found in Boston, Detroit, Denver, New York, etc. See "Mortgage Lending in Black and White" in *Dollars and Sense* April, 1990. For Los Angeles see Rosenblatt and Bates (1991). Recently the California Reinvestment Commission (Stein & Laila, 2003) found a similar pattern in California for African Americans and Latinos.

10. Police forces in general, and the LAPD in particular came under additional public focus with the publication of former LAPD detective Rothmiller (1992). This book reveals the inner workings of the Organized Crime Intelligence Division, a unit that became a spying agency of the LAPD. Under its surveillance were Robert Redford, Connie Chung, Rock Hudson, Tom Lasorda, etc. The surveillance net was extended even to the city's luminaries.

11. See an interesting critique of "Community Policing" by Dean Lovelace, a community activist and Gordon Welty, a sociology professor at Wright State University, Ohio in "Community Policing in Dayton: More Flash Than Substance" in the *Dayton Daily News* May 28, 1992.

12. A classic and clear summary of the debate about the "welfare system" in the United States is Marmor (1990). This book also debunks the idea presented by neo-conservatives during the late 1980s that "Great Society" programs "created" poverty. Especially helpful are its pointed critiques of Charles Murray's neo-conservative classic *Losing Ground*. Unfortunately, President Clinton's administration in 1996 fell to the ideological influence of the neo-conservatives and dismantled the decades old social support net when the 1996 Welfare Reform Act was approved. The war against welfare was concluded.

13. One early good study on these processes are Bluestone and Harrison (1982) analysis of de-industrialization and their more recent updated analysis (1988).

14. An interesting description of the kinds of jobs the "Reagan Job Machine" was creating is provided by this study by Barry Bluestone and Bennett Harrison "The Great American Job Machine: The Proliferation of Low Wage Employment in the U.S. Economy," prepared for the Joint Economic Committee, U.S. Congress, December 1986.

15. There is a serious need for research about the nature of racism in post-industrial society. The neo-marxist bent of some approaches has been blamed for its failure to look at race as an "economic" force and more as epiphenomena, but in fact, even within this perspective there is room for a contextual understanding of race. There is also a need to break with the black/white model to achieve a true

understanding of race relations in the United States today, any effort that does not include the particular experiences of Latinos, Asians etc. will provide a flawed perspective. Bonilla-Silva (2003) begins to lend a focus to a new perspective.

16. Since the number for whites include a certain proportion of Latinos, in order to get to an approximation of the non-Latino white, I deducted Latino and black central city poor from the total of central city poor. Most of the "residue" should be white, Asian, and Native American poor.

17. This despite the evidence and wisdom that cities can be productive places for the national economy see Jacobs, Jane, *Cities and the wealth of nations: principles of economic life.* New York: Random House, 1984.

18. Despite the hoopla over the well publicized efforts at "Rebuilding LA" the mood in suburban Southern California has been very cool to linking with the inner-city communities in a circle of life. All of Orange County's Congress representatives, a suburban adjoining county to L.A. voted against massive federal aid to Los Angeles. Ironically, most persons outside of southern California make no distinction between Orange County cities such as Irvine or Anaheim and Los Angeles. The failure to link with Los Angeles will affect the whole region economically. See Hubler (1992).

19. After September 11, 2001, the fear of Islam and Muslim terrorism has replaced the "evil empire" as a divisive and uniting image for the United States. It has served to fan the flames of nationalism, while it has polarized the United States between those who struggle to maintain civil liberties and those who seem willing to give them up in exchange for the false security of the national security state.

20. The recent literature on multiculturalism evidences this concern for national unity. Unfortunately, the issue of justice is not a clearly articulated concern even in the liberal perspective of Schlessinger. See Dinesh D'Souza *Illiberal Education* and Arthur Schlesinger's *The Disuniting of America* as examples of early concerns for the disuniting effects of cultural diversity. More recently, Samuel Huntington from Harvard University in a Foreign Policy article in 2004 and a later book and Victor Davis Hanson, a Fresno State University professor of classics writing a book on sociology of assimilation have blamed Mexicans for their presumed inability to assimilate into Anglo-Saxon culture.

21. By 1997, despite the fact that 500 corporations had promised they would invest more than 1 billion dollars in riot-torn South Central Los Angeles few actually delivered on their financial commitments. (Utley 1997).

22. Chief Williams left amidst another racially stigmatizing scandal in the Ramparts division of the LAPD. An anti-gang units had used

the power of their badges to railroad dozens of Latinos and African Americans into false convictions with fabricated evidence. Ironically, but not surprising, the lead police officer was a Puerto Rican. This confirmed the community's sense that the LAPD while more "colorful" was still an instrument to perpetuate white supremacy.

Boricuas, African Americans, and Chicanos in the "Far West": Notes on the Puerto Rican Pro-Independence Movement in California, 1960s–1980s[1]

Abstract

From the late 1960s through the 1980s Puerto Ricans developed a movement in California in support of Puerto Rico's political independence that allied itself with Anglos, African Americans, Chicanos and other Latinos. These alliances were strategic in extending the influence of the movement in solidarity with Puerto Rico's struggle beyond the relatively small and geographically dispersed Puerto Rican population in California. These implicit and explicit political alliances with other sectors led to an interesting ideological and cultural exchange between radical Puerto Rican organizations and  these groups. These notes pretend to initiate an exploration of this period, through the oral histories of some of the participants in this movement. The focus of the initial exploration is on those who were in positions of leadership and influence in northern and southern California with the radical politics of the Puerto Rican Socialist Party, at the time the main Puerto Rican socialist organization in Puerto Rico and the United States.

Introduction

Radical politics in the United States have historically benefitted from the skills, traditions, and perspectives that immigrants have brought with them as they create a space for struggle and survival within this society. In fact, radical politics within the United States were energized and shaped by the contributions of Russian, Jewish, Italian, Polish, Irish, Mexican, Puerto Rican, and other immigrant groups who for various reasons found themselves as part of the flow of labor this nation has attracted from all over the world.

Latinos, and specifically Puerto Ricans, have made significant contributions to U.S. popular struggles that have yet to be recorded in the history of U.S. social movements. For Puerto Ricans who became part of the *diaspora*, participating in political struggles in a nation that was foreign and hostile to them represented just one more tool for material and spiritual survival.

Within the anthropology and sociology of social movements, movements of cultural reaffirmation and resistance are usually categorized as revitalization movements. Whenever these movements have a religious character or expression they are called religions of the oppressed. These movements tend to be considered pre-political expressions of resistance against the encroaching colonialism of expanding empires.[2] The struggle of Puerto Ricans for independence, is neither a revitalization movement nor a religious movement; it represents a clear example of an explicitly political struggle against oppression both as a colonized people and as oppressed minorities within the complex mosaic of U.S. racial and ethnic groups.

This political struggle influenced and is itself influenced by the nature of California's regional history and struggles of working people in the United States, by the complex dynamics of the relationship between Puerto Rico's struggle for independence and by the political and demographic makeup of Puerto Rican populations in the United States. What makes this political struggle unique and widely misunderstood is that there is widespread ignorance about the continuing relevance of anti-colonial democratic struggles today. Most people assume that anti-colonialism is an anachronism, that somehow we live in a post-colonial world. Most of our models for understanding these struggles hark back to pre-industrial societies or the post-World War II decolonization process in Africa. Puerto Rico and the United States are in an anachronistic colonial relationship similar and dissimilar to the classic colonial experience. In one sense, Puerto Ricans are struggling a nineteenth-century battle against a twenty-first century superpower. Most victorious anti-colonial struggles were facing declining empires, not a still vital global power.

In the Southwest, and particularly in California, Puerto Ricans developed a movement between the late 1960s and the early 1980s that generated solidarity with the liberation struggle of *Boriquén*. At the same time, these struggles were shaped by specific linkages and alliances they entered into in their respective communities. These alliances with African American and Chicano/Latino organizations reveal much about racial and ethnic dynamics in the United States, particularly in California, and also reveal some interesting patterns about the limits and strengths of radical political ideologies within communities of color.[3]

Puerto Ricans in California

The history of Puerto Ricans in California provides an interesting contrast with the stereotypes developed in U.S. popular culture. While the New York *barrio* image dominates the understanding United States has about Puerto Ricans, this portrait has very little to do with the reality lived by Boricuas in the west. One important factor among many others is that Puerto Ricans in California are part of a social milieu that has a history of Latino presence and influence that is more significant than in the Northeast. From Texas to California, a significant Mexican/Latino presence extends itself back into the sixteenth century.

At the time of the Mexican-American War (1846-1848), Mexicans had developed a small but significant presence in what today is the Southwest of the United States. As a result of the war, almost overnight, and despite the Treaty of Guadalupe Hidalgo, Chicanos became foreigners in their own homeland.[4]

Like Puerto Ricans, Chicanos developed independent political organizations to achieve the objectives of community empowerment. Two of the most interesting political projects among Chicanos were the Raza Unida Party (in Texas and California) and the Centros de Acción Social Autónoma, Hermandad General de Trabajadores, (CASA-HGT), a Marxist-influenced organization that developed strong relations with the Puerto Rican Socialist Party, itself a Marxist-Leninist organization.[5]

African Americans were not newcomers to California, despite the image that their presence in the West was initiated during World War II as labor-hungry defense industries opened their doors to African Americans. In fact, African Latinos were among the founders of "Nuestra Señora de Los Angeles" which is the original name of the city of Los Angeles. But it is true that the great demand for labor as a result of the war effort attracted large numbers of African Americans to California. A significant community developed in a number of places, but the largest were in the Bay Area of San Francisco and in Los Angeles. The most extensive relations between Puerto Ricans and blacks took place in the

Bay Area, both in San Francisco and Oakland. These relations included some joint work with the Black Panther Party (BPP) and other black radical and progressive organizations.

The Puerto Rican presence is relatively recent in California.[6] According to Carmelo Rosario Natal, the first recorded presence of Puerto Rican immigrants took place in 1900 when four to five workers destined for the sugar plantations of Hawaii got off at the train station in Ontario and fled into the lemon and orange groves.[7] Later, in December of that same year, another group of approximately fifty Puerto Ricans also refused to be sent to Hawaii and disembarked in the port of San Francisco. By 1906, Puerto Ricans founded the first "Club Social Puertorriqueño" in the city of San Francisco and one of the oldest Puerto Rican socio-cultural organizations in the nation. Carey McWilliams in his classic *Factories in the Field* about California's agricultural labor struggles, mentions the assassination of a Puerto Rican worker during a protest in 1913 over working conditions in Wheatland, California.[8]

Other Puerto Ricans came from Arizona where they had been involved in migrant agricultural labor and then followed the job demand into California. More recently, Puerto Ricans came as employees of military federal installations in the state; enlisted personnel (including many who retired from service and stayed in California) until the 1960s-1970s when the population was augmented by a significant immigration from the Northeast.

But the story of Puerto Rican migration to the West remains to be told, as most of the research on Puerto Rican communities in the United States has focused on their experiences in the Northeast, Midwest, and more recently in Hawaii. One reason for its relative obscurity is the relative invisibility of the community in a region of the country that is heavily populated by Mexican Americans. Also, this invisibility continues today because there is no particular region that serves as a cultural center of the community.[9] This Latino/Mexican regional culture and other factors impede the development of a strong ethnic identity that provides the foundation for a political organization and at the same time it makes the presence of Puerto Ricans in California imperceptible. This "invisibility" also makes Puerto Rican political organizations in this state rather unique and rare.

Other impediments, however, are linked to the powerful impact of Mexican American culture in this region. Interesting processes of assimilation into the Mexican American culture and experience are patterns that are yet unexplored and that form part of the cultural dynamics of Puerto Ricans and other Latinos in the diaspora. Important Mexican cultural traditions are effectively incorporated into the region's popular

culture. Dia de la independencia, Cinco de Mayo, piñatas, and venera-
tion for the Virgin of Guadalupe are all part of a cultural milieu that
influences both Anglo and other Latino cultures.

Also, the positive socioeconomic experience of Puerto Ricans in this
region has permitted their integration into local societies. This in turn
has placed obstacles to the ethnic maintenance mechanism so common
in Midwest and northeast Puerto Rican communities. This becomes a
powerful factor that creates the conditions for the need of political alliances with other organizations, particularly those of people of color. Most
organizations that have worked on solidarity with Puerto Rico's struggle
for independence are multiracial and multiethnic in character.[10]

The Demography of Puerto Ricans
in Southern California

A crucial factor in political organization among communities of color in
the United States is the strength of ethnic identity. Ethnicity is ironically strengthened by such factors as segregation (increasing social interaction within the community), poverty, discrimination, lower levels
of formal education, and by the kinds of conditions that tend to isolate a
group from the majority and that are part and parcel of the "minority"
experience in the United States. Puerto Ricans in the northeast and Midwest have historically supported the development of a significant number of political institutions, including those supportive of Puerto Rico's
struggle for independence.

In the West, political institutions of any kind among Puerto Ricans
are rare. Ethnic identity seems to be lower than what is experienced in
places like Chicago or New York. Another limiting factor for radical politics at least, is the seemingly larger assimilation of individual Puerto
Ricans into a "white" status and away from ethnic-centered politics.[11]
What also needs to be further explored is whether this very common
individual experience is becoming a pattern for the entire group. While
there are counter trends whose indicator is language use, there might
be a process that may be similar to that experienced by the Irish who
before becoming "white" underwent a process of racialization, being
considered non-white.[12] The Irish, who initially had engaged in some
instances of liberal politics as they became upwardly mobile vis a vis
blacks, later became increasingly entrenched in racist ideologies, particularly tinged with strong anti-Black sentiment. Among Puerto Ricans
in California, however, while the overt racist character is absent, the
Puerto Rican community is a very politically conservative community;
this conservatism is rooted in the material conditions of their existence
in this state.

One glaring trait of this community is the significant rate of intermarriage among Puerto Ricans in California, both with Anglos, Mexican Americans, and other Latinos. In 1970, nationally, only 20.5% of
Puerto Rican males were married to non-Puerto Rican spouses while
48% of California Puerto Rican males married outside their group. For
females nationally, only 15.9% married outside their group although for
California Puerto Rican females it was 44.6%.[13]

A recent study indicates that the process of intermarriage of Puerto
Ricans has increased dramatically in California.[14] According to 1992 U.S.
Census data, Puerto Ricans tend to marry Mexican origin persons almost as often as whites. In fact, with the exception of Native Americans,
Puerto Ricans have the highest ethnic intermarriage rates with 58.2%
married outside of the group. For Cubans the rate is 34.2%, for Mexicans it is 14% and for whites it is 6.6%. For Puerto Ricans who are married persons under the age of thirty-five, 69.4% are married outside of
the group.[15]

Another factor that has a bearing on limiting a strong sense of Puerto
Rican ethnic identity is that, in general, Puerto Ricans have fared better
economically in California than in other states. While historically Puerto
Ricans have suffered high rates of poverty, Puerto Ricans in California
have fared better. In 1975, the Census Bureau report indicates that in
the United States 1.7 million persons were of Puerto Rican ancestry,
with 33% experiencing poverty.[16] The national poverty for Puerto Ricans
continued to increase and in 1994 it rose to 38.7% for an estimated population of 2.8 million persons.

The average national household income for Puerto Ricans in 1993
was $27,917, only 14.5% hold managerial/professional occupations, the
median age is twenty-six years of age, and only 9.7% hold a college degree or more. The median household income for California Puerto Ricans
in 1990 was $30,000 although for Mexicans it was $29,160, for Central
Americans it was $28,000, and for Cubans, it was $30,000. In terms of
professions, 25.4% of Puerto Ricans are employed in professional and
managerial occupations compared to 23.9% for Mexicans, 15.8% for
Central Americans, and 5.8% for Cubans.

Puerto Ricans in California have a higher median household income,
are older, have a higher educational background and lower levels of segregation than Puerto Ricans in the Midwest and the Northeast. In fact,
Puerto Ricans and Asian Indians in Southern California are the least
segregated (from whites) group. These latter characteristics are more
closely associated with the majority white population than with Latinos
in general.[17]

For example, California Puerto Ricans have higher educational
achievement than the national average for Puerto Ricans. In 1990, 14.9%
of California Puerto Ricans twenty-five years or older were college graduates; only 4.9% of Mexicans, 11.3% of Central Americans, and 16.1% of

Cubans were college graduates. In general, Puerto Ricans exhibit some of the most socioeconomic advantageous characteristics that traditionally impede the development of a strong ethnic identity. For example, in the 1970s, during the time period of this study the percentage of Puerto Ricans in California born in Puerto Rico was lower than in the traditional communities of the Northeast.[18] However, many of the participants in radical politics in California from 1960-1980 were predominantly college graduates or college students and many of them were from the island. Other important differences from Puerto Ricans in the Midwest and Northeast are high levels of language assimilation and racial identity.

In terms of Southern California, according to Turner and Allen (1997) at least 77% of Puerto Ricans in California expressed in 1990 that they spoke English only or very well, compared to 42.6% of Central Americans, 48.7% of Mexican Americans, and 49.5% of Cubans. This level of language use provides some evidence for their lack of segregation when compared to Puerto Ricans in the Midwest and the Northeast.[19]

In terms of race, Puerto Ricans appear to be lighter-skinned (or perceive themselves as such). Few Puerto Ricans live in African American neighborhoods, contrary to a more widespread practice in places like New York and Chicago. Only 3% of Boricuas identified themselves as black.[20] The hegemony of Latino culture seems to serve as a buffer for a greater identification with "whiteness," however, Puerto Ricans have a strong "Hispanic" identification when asked to identify ancestry. Only 49.1% chose white, while 95.1% chose Hispanic (including those who chose white). In contrast, 64.5% of Cubans chose white, and a smaller number, 94.8% chose Hispanic.[21] In this region the "Hispanic" category has become racialized to such an extent that despite its being an "ethnic" category, people perceive it indistinctly as a racial category.

Today, despite California's Puerto Rican population reaching more than 131,998, its organizational political reality remains the same.[22] However, these numbers are held suspect by many observers. A study done by the Western Regional Office of the U.S. Commission on Civil Rights in 1980 indicated that Puerto Ricans are undercounted. This obviously may contribute and/or may be an effect of the community's invisibility. The report also stated its geographic dispersion as a factor limiting a public presence for this community.[23] Some reports have argued that in reality the population of Puerto Ricans around 1977 was about 350,000, but these figures are considered too high.[24]

In summary, the region's culture, and the Puerto Rican population's demographic characteristics (including socioeconomic status) all have contributed to a very geographically dispersed pattern of settlement with no clearly defined center. These are the kinds of social factors that place clear obstacles on the ability of an ethnic group like Puerto Ricans to reproduce their ethnic identity, organize, sustain, and develop political

organizations. However, despite these structural factors, at least during the period of 1960s to 1980s, a small but significant movement in support of Puerto Rico's right to self-determination and independence developed both in northern and southern California. The social basis for these efforts will be explained in the last section of this chapter.

"La Lucha" (The Struggle) for Puerto Rican Independence in California

Contrary to the experiences of Puerto Rican pro-independence movements in the Northeast, particularly in New York, the history of the Puerto Rican solidarity movement in California is quite recent. New York, since the second half of the nineteenth century, was the place where many efforts and organizations worked to promote Puerto Rico's freedom from Spanish colonialism and then U.S. colonialism. There are no records, oral or written of any organizational attempts in California before the decade of the 1960s to support the rising movement for Puerto Rico's freedom.

In 1971, the Pro-Independence Movement (PIM) formally transformed itself into the Puerto Rican Socialist Party (PSP). The PSP, a Marxist-Leninist organization focused significant efforts into organizing Puerto Rico's working class (particularly trade union leadership) and developing party branches among U.S. Puerto Rican communities. The PIM had built a presence in some communities around the nation as a result of some previous work done by the Nationalist Party in earlier decades. While the PSP did not always have a consistent political perspective toward its relationship with Puerto Ricans in the United States, it was the first Puerto Rican political organization to explicitly focus attention on developing a political constituency in the metropolis. The organizing among Puerto Ricans by the PSP also led to some of the first analysis and reflection (later brought into the academic world) of the relationship between the United States and the island Boricuas. Initially, most of the organizing efforts were limited to the Northeast and Chicago, traditional centers of Puerto Rican migration.

The Bay Area in northern California is the site of the longest and most effective efforts in support of the island's liberation efforts. At least since the late 1960s, there were groups connected with the progressive nationalist Movement Pro-Independence (MPI), the organization that preceded the PSP. This region of California is also the site of other effective Puerto Rican organizations that are mainly social service providers. The Puerto Rican presence in northern California used to be the largest until very recently; the initial population was made up of people who returned from Hawaii's sugarcane fields during the first decade of this century.

Another characteristic of the Bay Area is its progressive political culture that harks back to its strong trade union history and presence. This regional culture provided an environment where many progressive movements have developed various efforts to effect social change. It is within this social AND cultural milieu that the initial efforts to support the growing Puerto Rican liberation movement took hold.

The organizing efforts in Southern California took place during the early 1970s, and while relatively effective for a while are no longer in existence today. However, in university campuses in northern California and in San Francisco there are still organizations (e.g., Casa Puerto Rico) involved in solidarity work and in support of the freeing of Puerto Rican political prisoners.

In the following section the history of both centers of solidarity will be briefly detailed using interviews of leaders involved in these efforts during these years. The name of some of the participants are disguised for reasons of personal security. These notes do not intend to be an "objective" historical account but a political perspective about the efforts of a group of Boricuas to struggle against colonialism in the "belly of the empire."[25]

"La Lucha" in the Bay Area

Previous to the organization of the (PSP) unit in San Francisco, Gilbert Rodriguez, a Puerto Rican Vietnam veteran, born and raised in New York, came in contact with the Puerto Rico Solidarity Committee (PRSC).[26] The PRSC was an organization with branches across the United States whose goal was to support Puerto Rico's liberation. It was a multiracial organization of Puerto Rican students, mostly of working class background, and middle-class white/Anglo leftist activists. The organization's leadership was primarily white/Anglo.

Around 1973-1974 Gilbert came in contact with the PRSC, after being radicalized by his experience in the U.S. forces fighting in Vietnam. He was already a supporter of independence, and particularly issues of racism led him into the pro-independence struggle. It is also through the PRSC that another Puerto Rican activist, Aurora Levins-Morales, became part of the cell of the PSP in the Bay Area.[27] Gilbert Rodriguez had been involved earlier in the founding of the party unit in San Francisco. Aurora arrived in San Francisco around 1976 when the PSP cell was already functioning.

Melba Maldonado, a Puerto Rican born in Guayanilla, Puerto Rico, but who lived for many years on the East coast also formed part of the PSP cell during these years in San Francisco.[28] Melba had been an activist since her high school days on the island. In 1966 she moved to Newark, New Jersey where she continued her involvement in a local

organization. Her activities were focused on civil rights issues around Puerto Rican empowerment. She came into contact with African American organizations, the Young Lords Party, but was not involved with any specific political party. Eventually she became involved with the MPI which was the political precursor of the PSP. When she came to California in 1977, Melba was already a member of the PSP and she was able to link with the already established PSP cell in San Francisco.

Gilbert Rodriguez was one of only two of the Puerto Ricans born and raised in the United States. Aurora Levins-Morales, born in Puerto Rico, had been involved in pro-independence activities for some time. Her father, Richard Levins, is a North American progressive who married a Puerto Rican. He has been deeply involved in the island's liberation struggle for many years. Despite Aurora's long involvement in the movement she explains how difficult it was for her to get in contact with the PSP unit given the geographic dispersion of the Puerto Rican community in California.

> "I arrived in February 1976 in the Bay Area and tried to get in touch with PSP and it took forever to find them."[29]

One organizational challenge for any group in California is the great geographical distance between population centers; this added to the geographic dispersion of the community makes organizing difficult. There was, particularly at that point in time, little communication between the dispersed Puerto Rican communities of this state.

The PSP unit was organized in San Francisco as a result of efforts from the PSP New York branch, which contacted Gilbert Rodriguez and another Puerto Rican, Pedro Perez, who had been active in the Bay area. The organizing efforts (1974-1975) were focused on organizing a study circle to develop a nucleus for a party cell in the Bay Area. This study circle later became a full-fledged party cell in a few years. Its membership was made up of students: Puerto Ricans who arrived from the East coast and Chicanos. Many of its members at one point or another were women, Melba, Aurora, Mayra, Maria (born and raised in California), Esther and Hilda. The others like Alex Ramirez and Pedro, grew up on the East coast. Gilbert is the only member who was a constant participant in the group for an extended period of time. The fluidity in group membership is a result of the migratory flows prevalent among Boricuas in the United States and Puerto Rico. Some changes in membership, however, are also due to ideology and/or the demands of membership in a militant Marxist organization.[30]

The cell was mostly engaged in organizing events for expressing solidarity with Puerto Rico's struggle for independence. However, no systematic grassroots community organizing efforts were carried out. There was a strong reliance on relationships with organizations and in-

dividuals to do this solidarity work. Women had a significant role in terms of party tasks, but were not in positions of formal leadership.[31] One exception was Melba Maldonado, who at one point led the cell for some time. But this was true, particularly, in the ideological realm. The "theorists," a significant position in an organization, which gave primacy to theoretical work in "party-building" were mostly men. Significant political education efforts took place in order to develop politically savvy "cadres," but these efforts also laid the ground for abstract ideological debates that did not contribute to strengthening the local organization.

It seems that the tight reins the U.S. party leadership had on its cells limited their potential for developing a more developed local analysis. In other words, most of the work, including the coalition or alliances with other groups was focused on supporting Puerto Rico's right to independence and self-determination. The issues of racism, unemployment and poverty, although present in the internal dialogues were not consistently woven into a local political analysis that could serve as the foundation for grassroots community organizing. For Aurora Levins-Morales, the strong reliance on a party leadership thousands of miles away was an obstacle:

> "One of the things I remember...was in fact how little we did, there was way too much reliance on the word coming down from Puerto Rico or from New York and not that much attention placed to what the political situation actually was around us . . ."[32]

Aurora left the organization to join the PRSC because she felt the cell was ineffective in doing outreach in the local community. The PRSC had a Marxist study group that also worked with the Chicano community but seemed to be more passive about community outreach.

One of the obvious reasons for this lack of community-centered organizing is that there was a not a geographically centered Puerto Rican community. Other reasons were the social background of the participants and unstable membership, but primarily that the PSP's ideological control implicitly led away from a grounded local analysis. The ultimate outcome of such an effort would be the subsuming of solidarity with Puerto Rican liberation as one of many other tasks in a multiracial, multi-issue Latino organization. According to Gilbert Rodriguez, much energy was spent on ideological debates and struggle:

> "A great deal of our work at that time specifically revolved around political discussions, ideological struggles, the reading of Marxist-Leninist texts, trying to understand the "National Question," trying to come up with good theory about what's proper political activity within the body of the beast.

What are the real political, economic ties between Puerto
Ricans in the U.S. and Puerto Rico. I would say that we tried
to study theory and argued and discussed a great deal in the
attempt of coming up with a program that was relevant to
Puerto Ricans around Puerto Rican independence in the U.S
that could also be directly linked with the independence movement in Puerto Rico. We realized that the conditions in the
U.S. were different than in Puerto Rico."[33]

This does not mean that there was no effort to work on local community issues, but that the focus on solidarity work consumed most of
the cell member's energies. The cell participated in solidarity with Chile,
workers' struggles, Gay Rights, etc., but these were ancillary activities
that were not central to the party's organizing strategy in the United
States. Significant relationships were developed with groups like the
San Francisco Mime Troupe, Casa Chile, and other local organizations
but although these relationships developed mutual solidarity they did
not result in increased organizational effectiveness.

In response to a question about work in the local Puerto Rican community, Gilbert says:

"We never recruited (in the community) any actual "folks." I
look at the time as a time where we spent so much time and
energy in discussions and arguments and study and meetings for a...producing leaflets and distributing them having
activities that we didn't do the kind of grassroots organizing
that you asked me about a little while ago. We just never did
that. It was not a conscious effort, it was not a conscious decision it was a matter of a small group of people who basically
looked so much inward that we never got it together to look
outward."[34]

With hindsight it is easy to say that in the long run the organization
could have been strengthened; obviously scarce resources (both human
and material), and ideological factors impeded a strategy that would
have led to a deeper grounding of this organization within the community. These Boricuas were working with the only tools at their disposal,
there were no precedents to build on, no body of theory to transform
and adapt except the obscure writings of early nineteenth-century socialist writers whose experiences were distant, not only geographically,
but politically to the reality of building an organization to empower
Puerto Ricans. Building a political organization in an advanced capitalist colonial metropolis was a task for which there were no models to
follow.

However, the cell was able to build on its own weaknesses to de-velop relationships with local organizations that multiplied its presence and augmented its propaganda on behalf of Puerto Rico's struggle for independence. Crucial to these efforts were the experiences of some of its members in other Chicano and African American organizations. These organizations included student, community and political organizations. Members of the cell were active in Non-Intervention in Chile, NiCh, a group supporting the Chilean resistance to dictator Augusto Pinochet. At San Francisco State University, Puerto Rican students developed alliances with Chicano and Pan-African student organizations. Also, fundraising events were held for the Nicaraguan Sandinistas, Chileans, and other Latino groups in the Bay Area.

The organizational efforts with Chicanos, although considerable, were limited by the nationalistic ideology of Chicano organizations like La Raza Student Organization at San Francisco State. Nationalist Chicano ideology considered Marxism an eurocentric ideology that had no bearing on the Chicano/Latino struggle. The reconstitution of Aztlan could not be guided by a perspective and theory they considered to be part of the oppressive European apparatus.[35] The uniting factor between the PSP cell and Chicano organizations was anti-imperialism and nationalism. However their support for Puerto Rican independence was peripheral, and limited to support for some cultural issues. Individual Chicanos, however, were involved in many of the cell's activities. The Pan-African Student Union and the Chicano organizations did not have a good relationship with each other because of mutual racial prejudice. In addition, Chicano nationalist ideology on one side and the Nation of Islam ideology among African Americans separated these potential allies.

The other important alliances were mostly a result of the relationships of one of its members (Gilbert) with African American organizations. Gilbert, as a black Puerto Rican student in Oakland at a time when the BPP had been decimated by repression from COINTELPRO, the FBI's counter-intelligence program, was involved in joint student work in 1973 with African Americans. Gilbert shared a position in the student

government with members of the BPP in a local college. The focus of the joint work was in developing an affirmative action program to increase black faculty on that campus.

The organizing efforts included direct pressure on the university's chancellor by the student organization. The university's chancellor responded to the student pressure to hire more black faculty by firing six male faculty members, one Asian, five whites and all leftists, and hired two conservative black Southern women. This pyrrhic victory led to the demise of the movement because the nature of the university's response led to the undermining of the progressive foundations of the movement.

"'La Lucha' in Los Angeles"

Los Angeles is a megalopolis that is usually defined as a city without a center. Los Angeles is actually a network of cities and neighborhoods with a very loose sense of identity but with a strong network of local progressive organizations. It is within this region that the PSP developed its second significant cell in California.

Placido Rodriguez, Ivan Gutierrez, Zoilo Cruz, Sandra Ortiz, Hector Albizu, Antonio Gonzalez, Olga Perez, and others were at various times part of an organization, the PSP local cell, with significant alliances with the Chicano/Latino community. Placido, born in Puerto Rico and a resident of California since 1957 had a long experience in socialist and pro-independence struggles as a young World War II veteran in New York. He had attended courses offered by the school of the Communist Party in New York. He was a student of Jesus Colon, the veteran Puerto Rican community and labor organizer who was one of the instructors in the school. For Placido, the experience in the armed forces was a defining moment in his transformation into a radical pro-independence activist. Ivan Gutierrez, another significant member of the Los Angeles group was also a veteran, having served in Vietnam.

The Los Angeles group was organized with the aid of a New York branch representative who led the organization of the cell. Among the initial members were Sandra Ortiz who was married to a wealthy Anglo from Beverly Hills and Placido, both of whom remained quite active for some years. The members of this cell were mostly students, workers, and local residents.

The role of Puerto Rican students, particularly in the University of California at Los Angeles (UCLA) was clearly essential. In the early 1970s, with the arrival of Olga and Jose Perez the cell received a boost in activity. Initially, most of the activity was in the area of political education. The PSP weekly *Claridad* was distributed in Latino communities, and other educational materials were received that gave organizing goals and theory to the new members of the cell.

The level of meetings was intensive at the beginning; usually there were meetings every night and they went late into the night.[36] Initially there was a strong sense of democracy that pervaded the group, which extended their meeting into long dialogues. In addition to these meetings, members had tasks assigned to them: some were assigned to trade union work, propaganda, finances, etc. The task of selling the weekly *Claridad* was one of the most difficult tasks, because selling a paper in communities that were very conservative and non-Puerto Rican was an almost impossible task.

Olga Perez was one of the most active leaders of the Los Angeles PSP unit. As a UCLA student she became an intellectual leader of the cell and provided some leadership in developing demographic data on the Los Angeles Puerto Rican community. However, the membership became more diverse when the group recruited Latinos and Anglos into the organization. Frank, an Italian American, and Rosa, his Chilean partner, Pedro Ramirez, a Venezuelan, Martin Soto, a Chilean, John MacBride, an Anglo (later it was discovered he was a member of the Los Angeles Police Department intelligence unit) and others who at various times joined the organization.

Later in the mid 1970s, Zoilo Cruz joined the PSP cell after being involved in the Civil Rights movement and the antiwar movement in New York. Zoilo was born in Manhattan and had developed relationships with the BPP in New York. When he arrived in Los Angeles, cell membership was rather diverse although still led by Puerto Ricans.[37]

The initial external activities of the cell were its participation in a demonstration with the support of Chicano and Salvadorean organizations against the actions of the conservative New Progressive Party (NPP) a pro-statehood party in Puerto Rico. These actions led to very positive and cooperative relationships with a significant number of Latino organizations. The main factor that brought people together according to Zoilo Cruz, was "cultural identity." MacArthur Park was a neighborhood in Los Angeles were many Latinos, including Puerto Ricans gathered. Music was played, picnics were organized, and political recruiting took place among the crowds.[38]

One important source of financial funds for the cell, in addition to the members' dues, were "salsa" dances. Salsa became a glue that united various Latino constituencies, with Puerto Ricans as connectors between the various groups. Most of the relationships at this time were with Chicanos, including the Brown Berets, because of the fact that African American organizations in Los Angeles were in disarray because of government repression. Later in the 1970s, strong relationships were established with Nicaraguan and Salvadorean organizations.

The cell was able to have its own storefront office in east Los Angeles, which led to the need for a source of financial support. A significant number of persons in Los Angeles, Puerto Ricans and non-Puerto Ricans

alike, were financial contributors on a regular basis. Also, study circles were organized to politically educate the party members on various themes from the "national question" to history and theory. Among the issues discussed was that of immigration, which concerned everyone in the Latino community. Activists like Nativo Lopez and Antonio Rodriguez, leaders of the Hermandad Nacional de Trabajadores (CASA), developed a relationship with the cell through these exchanges.

CASA was a Chicano organization that attempted to influence immigration policies, a crucial issue for Mexican Americans. The organization was an outgrowth of "Hermandad Nacional Mexicana" (National Mexican Brotherhood), which had been organized in 1951 with the purpose of empowering undocumented immigrants.[39] CASA members were mostly young Chicano middle-class professionals.

In fact, the PSP and CASA members shared a similar class extraction. Both were middle class or in the case of students, aspiring to be middle class. The analysis of Bert Corona of CASA really applied to the PSP:

> ""Despite their inexperience, these young activists were highly idealistic and motivated. In the end however, they just couldn't do everything. They couldn't operate the service centers while at the same time trying to organize a mass movement and build a revolutionary party."[40]

The first relationship between CASA and the PSP took place in 1973 when the Movimiento Estudiantil Chicano de Aztlan (MECHA) chapter at California State University at Long Beach organized an "International Conference of the Americas" with speakers that included Alfredo Lopez, a leader of the U.S. PSP branch and Carlos Feliciano, the pro-independence leader who had just been released from jail. Alfredo Lopez stayed in Nativo Lopez' home in Norwalk.[41]

This early relationship with Nativo Lopez and his brother (who served as security for Carlos Feliciano) served to create good rapport between the PSP and CASA. Later, during the summer of 1973, Jorge Rodriguez (Antonio Rodriguez' brother) and Nativo Lopez were delegates to the World Festival of Youth and Students in East Berlin, Democratic Republic of Germany (socialist). There they again met with PSP members and developed contacts that took Jorge Rodriguez and Nativo Lopez to Puerto Rico in 1973. This trip also strengthened relationships between the PSP and CASA. Conversations were initiated about party-to-party relationships including a follow-up trip to New York where relationships with the U.S. branch were established.[42]

According to Nativo Lopez there was a strong sense of comradeship and identity, given the similar experiences of Boricuas and Chicanos. "Us, as well as those who studied with us saw in the PSP experience

very similar things to what we were dealing with, identity, the "national question," were we a minority within the U.S. working class or from the Aztlan nation, or part of Mexico? The debates never ended. This fed the interest in maintaining a relationship with the PSP comrades."[43]

CASA members participated in a major event in New York's Madison Square Garden in 1974 in support of Puerto Rico's independence. In part, through the support of CASA, a mass gathering was held before the "Bicentenary Without Colonies" event held in Washington D.C. in 1976 and was held in a Los Angeles auditorium where more than 3,000 persons attended. Juan Mari Bras, the PSP General Secretary came at the behest of the PSP cell and CASA to Los Angeles to aid in the mobilization for the national event in Washington D.C.

This linkage developed and matured until later a formal agreement between CASA and the PSP was reached in July 1976.[44] Bras visited Los Angeles and in a private meeting with Antonio Rodriguez developed some formal principles for the CASA/PSP alliance.[45]

The alliance with CASA was probably the closest political relationship the PSP established in California. The foundation for this alliance was the common ideological perspective (CASA was a Neo-Marxist organization), top-level relationships between both organizations and good social rapport between its members. The CASA activists, particularly the Rodriguez brothers were strong supporters of Puerto Rico's liberation struggle and had some knowledge of Puerto Rican cultural identity. The social bond between the organizations was the result not only of political dialogue but also of social interaction in political and social events.[46]

This relationship enabled the PSP to extend its image and influence beyond what its small number of cadres could achieve on their own. CASA sold copies of the weekly *Claridad* in Chicano communities and increased understanding and support for the Puerto Rican liberation struggle. The organizations shared speakers in their respective events, creating a public image of mutual support. Also, both organizations experienced a decline partly because of their joint espousal of a doctrinaire ideological perspective.

In the late 1970s and early 1980s, the shift of politics changed to the Nicaraguan and Salvadorean struggles. During this period the PSP cell was weakened but was able to maintain a significant presence in a new organization in Los Angeles, which attempted to provide a center for Latin America's national liberation struggles. This organization, the Latin American Coordinating Committee ("Coordinadora Latinoamericana") provided significant support not only to Latin American struggles in Chile, Nicaragua, and El Salvador, but also worked to publicize and educate people about Puerto Rico's colonial situation.

The Nicaraguans had a center, "Casa Nicaragua," which served as a homebase for many political and cultural activities. In the early 1980s,

PSP leaders like Pedro Grant, an influential trade union leader, were brought to Los Angeles to participate in activities sponsored by the Latin American Coordinating Committee. Ivan Gutierrez, a PSP cell leader was instrumental in representing the PSP and becoming a leader within the coordinating organization. This alliance extended the organizational life of the cell, which at that point was stagnant, given its inability to transform its relatively successful public activities into an expanded membership base. There never was a clear strategy of how to systematically utilize the relationships and activities as an organizing tool. There was no explicit process for assessing whether the cell's participation in events or activities strengthened or weakened the organization as decisions were arrived at in an informal fashion.

However, as in San Francisco, the PSP's Achilles heel was its bureaucratism, petit bourgeois social base, inexperience, and its lack of a strategy for grassroots politics as Ivan Gutierrez puts it:

> "It was very interesting because the solidarity group with Puerto Rico continued doing solidarity with Puerto Rico but not really doing political organizing work in the community. While the PSP was more involved in direct political issues, it is amazing because the majority of the members who were in the solidarity committee were students who were at People's College of Law. Those individuals tended to gravitate toward the PRSC. While the members of the PSP were from different backgrounds and those different backgrounds were reflected in the political discussions of the organization. There was always a turmoil about achieving goals how to go about organizing the Puerto Rican community naturally because the working class members would focus on a different focus than students. Students were transients; they really at the end did not care whether the work was done or not, and those of us who where here to stay were looking for more stronger bonds with the community."[47]

The internal debates that took place in the PSP about national issues (in Puerto Rico) tended to have a distorted effect on the PSP's units in the United States. Because some of the members had been active in island cells their focus was not on the U.S. branch but on the dynamics in the island. In some sense many still saw themselves as "sojourners" with no long-range plans to establish themselves in California but return to a middle-class status in Puerto Rico.

> "I never thought I would be still living in the United States. My original plan was to study, get a degree and return home to continue my involvement in the struggle with a middle-

class profession that could sustain me and my family financially. Farthest from my mind was that I would establish roots
in the US. Remember, this was the 'entrails of the empire' as
Jose Marti called the U.S., I did not want to be a 'minority.'"[48]

Hector Albizu and Ivan Gutierrez became involved in an effort in
the early 1980s to revive the PSP cell and initiated political education
with some local intellectuals who supported Puerto Rican independence.
Ivan Gutierrez continued his leadership in the Coordinating Committee while Hector Albizu became the cell's theorist. Albizu was a student
at one of the UC campuses in southern California. Albizu placed most of
his focus on solidarity with Puerto Rico and refining political theory to
guide the cell's political practice.

The cell became involved in a very conflictive 1982 PSP internal
debate about the nature of a socialist party. The issues of Eastern Europe were brewing, and the cell asked Melba Maldonado to represent
the cell in the party's congress in Puerto Rico. The outcome of that congress resulted in the defeat of what was considered the "left opposition"
and to the resignation of all Los Angeles (and some San Francisco) members of the party. This ended the role of PSP in California after more
than ten years of political practice. It was not until the late 1990s when
the Viequense solidarity movement to stop the U.S. Navy bombing in
Vieques began to re-energize Puerto Rican communities around the
United States. This social movement's focus on the return of the lands
expropriated by the navy in 1941 and the end of naval bombardment on
the island, struck a chord in many Puerto Ricans who resided in the
mainland (Rodriguez, 2004). The smaller diaspora of Viequense residents,
resonated in the Puerto Rican community who also felt they had no
choice but to leave their homeland in search of better economic opportunities. In Los Angeles, the *Alianza Puertorriqueña de Los Angeles*
(Puerto Rican Alliance of Los Angeles) was formed by a new generation
of Puerto Rican activists. Some of the early PSP militants were involved
in the initial stages of organizing. As of today (2005) it remains as the
only radical Puerto Rican organization in southern California with a
very small membership.

While the Los Angeles activists resigned from the PSP, discontent
continued among the island militants. A significant number of prominent party activists also resigned, which initiated the process of decline
of the PSP and its eventual decision to disband.[49]

In some sense, the abstract theoretical perspective espoused by some
of the members led to the eventual demise of the Los Angeles unit. They
reorganized as the "Circulo Luisa Capetillo" of Los Angeles but lacking
larger organizational ties and support they disbanded during the mid-
1980s. Today, besides the small *Alianza Puertorriqueña* there is no significant organizational practice in support of Puerto Rico's independence.[50]

However, there are a significant number of cultural, professional and civic Puerto Rican organizations, most of whom represent conservative, middle and upper middle-class values. During the 2002 elections, Bonnie Garcia, the first Puerto Rican state assembly representative, was elected; she is also the only Latina Republican in the California State Assembly.

Conclusions

The experience of these two organizational units of the PSP in California provide some important lessons about progressive political organizing in communities of color in the United States. First, organizations that have a weak community base like these two in California can benefit from explicit and implicit alliances with other like-minded ethnic organizations. In fact, the efforts and achievement of these two PSP units would not have survived had it not been for these relationships. Second, and most important is that one must know intimately the social terrain on which one does political organizing.

Despite some attempts to gather data about the nature of the local Puerto Rican communities and despite being led by "scientific socialism" both organizations failed to understand the nature of the communities they wished to organize. Puerto Ricans in California then and now were demographically different from the Northeast experience and lived in a state of geographic dispersion. This conspired against the traditional community organizing efforts that were prevalent in New York or Chicago. The root of much organizing is based on the ethnic identity of a group, and this identity in California, given the powerful assimilationist trends, presents an obstacle to efforts among Puerto Ricans in this state.

Third, the social background of a significant number of participants led the groups away from consistently and strategically developing a long-term practice and strategy to develop deeper roots in the local Latino community. Students and other members who were sojourners did not have the inclination to develop the kind of organizing practice necessary to develop an organization that would withstand the impact of membership changes.

Fourth, the social background of many participants limited their ability to develop a concrete practice to link the organization with the communities around them. The excessively theoretical, abstract debates and theorizing tended to disarm and overwhelm members with less formal education who were ironically some of the most important and consistent resources of the groups. However, the role of some members like Gilbert, Ivan, and others served as bridges between various constituencies of people of color. But these had more to do with the character of these individuals than with the political practice or theory of the groups.

Fifth, the centralization and bureaucratization of the PSP, its inflated sense of itself and its "Stalinist" authoritarian practice also tended to alienate members and dissuade many from joining the organizations. These practices were not carried out consciously but were an outcome of following the PSP party line developed in Puerto Rico and applied in California in spite of a vastly different social, cultural, and economic context.

Finally, with the demise of a larger network of social movements in the United States and California that nurtured a progressive culture, organizations such as the PSP could not survive. With the rise of Reagan's 1980s "conservative revolution," progressive politics such as the one developed by Puerto Rican pro-independence activists withered on the vine.

Also, the groups' inability to develop a clear understanding of racial dynamics in the United States and nurture in a more explicit, proactive fashion the leadership of women also hindered the organizations' effectiveness. With so many resourceful women members these organizations could have developed a practice that could have rooted them deeper into the community. However, like many organizations then and now patriarchy was embedded within them. Even while the surviving group was called "Luisa Capetillo" after its split from the PSP, and although it spent a considerable amount of time in political education, it failed to deal explicitly with a feminist/*mujerista*/womanist analysis of gender relations or issues.[51]

What was significant about these organizing efforts was not their weaknesses, but that despite all the odds against them (including counterintelligence efforts) these organizations, thousands of miles away from *Boriquen* were able to develop important relationships, educate thousands of persons about Puerto Rico's colonial situation and keep hope alive for hundreds of Puerto Rican patriots.

In the words of Placido Rodriguez about the character of these militants:

> "What I learned in my PSP experience in California was that among leftists, socialists, revolutionaries, radicals are people with a higher moral character higher than those who are not revolutionary. I came to understand the potential of a human being when he truly believes in an idea. Of what he is able to achieve by his belief in an idea! I understand how the Soviets were able to defeat Germany during World War II and Vietnam defeat the U.S. All of this still leads me to believe that socialism is the solution."[52]

References • • • ● ●

Acuña, R. 1988. *Occupied America: A History of Chicanos*. Harper Collins, New York.

Albizu, H. 1997. Interview. Santa Ana, California. (June 6).

Allen, J. P. and E. Turner. 1997. *The Ethnic Quilt: Population Diversity in Southern California*. Northridge, CA: Center for Geographical Studies, Cal State, Northridge.

Allen, T. W. 1994. *The Invention of The White Race: Racial Oppression and Social Control*. London: Verso.

Cruz, Z. 1996. Phone Interview. New York, N.Y. (January 15).

Fernandez , R. 1996. *The Disenchanted Island: Puerto Rico and the U.S. in the Twentieth Century*. New York: Praeger.

Garcia, I. M. 1989. *United We Win: The Rise and Fall of La Raza Unida Party*. Tucson: University of Arizona.

Garcia, M. T. 1994. *Memories of Chicano History: The Life and Narrative of Bert Corona*. Berkeley: University of California Press.

Gutierrez, I. 1997. Interview. Irvine, California. (June 6).

Haney-Lopez, I. 1996. *White By Law: The Legal Construction of Race*. N.Y.: New York University.

Ignatiev, N. 1995. *How the Irish Became White*. New York: Routledge.

Hart, S. 1996. "The Cultural Dimension of Social Movements: A Theoretical Assessment and Literature Review" *Sociology of Religion* 57(1): 87-100 (Spring).

Hernandez, Jr., E. 1994. "Puerto Ricans: One of LA's Best Kept Secrets" *Los Angeles Times* October 30, b14.

Levins-Morales, A. 1995. Phone Interview, Berkeley, California (December 5).

Lopez, N. 1997. Personal interview, Santa Ana, CA. (November 5).

Maldonado, E. 1979. "Contract Labor and the Origins of Puerto Rican Communities in the United States. *International Migration Review* 13(I):103-21.

Maldonado, Melba. 1996. Phone Interview, San Francisco, California (July 9).

Melendez, H. 1984. *El Fracaso del Proyecto PSP de La Pequena Burguesia*. Rio Piedras: Editorial Edil.

Pulido, L. 2002. "Race, Class and Political Activism: Black, Chicana/o and Japanese-American Leftists in Southern California, 1968-1978" in *Antipode* 34 (4):762-788.

Roberts, R. and R. M. Kloss. 1974. *Social Movements: Between The Balcony and the Barricade*. St. Louis: C.V. Mosby Co.

Rodriguez, G. (Pseudonym). 1996. Phone Interview, San Juan, Puerto Rico (June 29).

Rodriguez, Placido. 1996. Phone Interview. Los Angeles, California (July 31).

Rodriguez, V. M. 1997. "The Racialization of Puerto Rican Ethnicity in the United States" in Juan Manuel Carrion, Ed. *Ethnicity, Race and Nationality in the Caribbean*. Rio Piedras: Institute of Caribbean Studies.

Rodriguez, V. M. 2004. "'¡Ni Una Bomba Mas!': Racialization and Memory in the Vieques Social Movement" paper read at the Sixth Biennial Conference of the Puerto Rican Association of Puerto Rican Studies, Graduate Center, C.U.N.Y. October 21-24.

Roediger, D. 1995. *The Wages of Whiteness: Race and the Making of the American Working Class*. London: Verso.

Rosario Natal. C. 1983. *Exodo Puertorriqueno*. San Juan, PR.

Santiago, A. M. and G. Galster. 1995. "Puerto Rican Segregation in the United States: Cause or Consequence of Economic Status?" in *Social Problems* 42, (3):361-389.

Souza, B.C. 1984. "Trabajo y Tristeza—'Work and Sorrow': The Puerto Ricans of Hawaii, 1900-1902" *Hawaiian Journal of History* 18:156-73.

U.S. Bureau of the Census. 1970. *1970 Census of Population and Housing*.

U.S. Bureau of the Census. 1990. *1990 Census of Population and Housing*.

U.S. Bureau of the Census. 1975. *Persons of Spanish Origin in the U.S.: March 1975, Series P-20, No. 283*.

United States Commission on Civil Rights. "Puerto Ricans in California." A Staff Report of the Western Regional Office. United States Commission on Civil Rights.

Zentella, A. M. 2004. "*Aqui no hay guaguas*: Language and Identity of Boricuas in Califas" presented at the Sixth Biennial Conference of the Puerto Rican Association of Puerto Rican Studies, Graduate Center, C.U.N.Y. October 21-24.

Endnotes • • • ● ●

1. These notes present a perspective that is part of a broader effort to look at alliances that Puerto Rican independence activists entered with other racial/ethnic groups in their organizing practice in the U.S. and to the role of culture and identity in these struggles. (See Hart, S. 1996. "The Cultural Dimension of Social Movements: A Theoretical Assessment and Literature Review" *Sociology of Religion* 57(1):87-100. The oral interviews provided much insights into these dynamics but the particular interpretation, and errors arising out of these are entirely my responsibility. Thanks to Gilbert, Ivan

Gutierrez, Placido Rodriguez, Nativo Lopez, Melba Maldonado, Aurora Levins-Morales, Zoilo Cruz, Hector Albizu, and others whose names need to remain undisclosed.

2. My former professor at Louisiana State University Professor Roberts spoke about how anti-colonial movements were at times perceived as pre-political. The ideology of white supremacy and imperialism represented rebellion as non-political expressions of the natives. See R. Roberts and R. M. Kloss. 1974. *Social Movements: Between The Balcony and the Barricade*. St. Louis: C.V. Mosby Co., pp. 81-90.

3. I will use the term Chicano and Mexican Americans to refer to people of Mexican descent who are citizens of the United States. The term "Mexicanos" will be used to refer to foreign-born Mexican residents of the United States. The term Boricuas refers to Puerto Ricans, it is derived from the Taino Indian name of the island, Boriquen. Boricua is very commonly used among Puerto Ricans in the United States.

4. For a radical history of the subordination of Chicanos see R. Acuna's *Occupied America: A History of Chicanos*. Harper Collins, New York, 1988.

5. For information of La Raza Unida Party, see I. M. Garcia's *United We Win: The Rise and Fall of La Raza Unida Party*. Tucson: University of Arizona, 1989; M. T. Garcia's *Memories of Chicano History: The Life and Narrative of Bert Corona*. Berkeley: University of California Press, 1994 and L. Pulido's "Race, Class and Political Activism: Black, Chicana/o and Japanese-American Leftists in Southern California, 1968-1978" for some recent analysis of the Hermandad General de Trabajadores (CASA) history.

6. The role of labor brokers in attracting Puerto Rican labor to the United States was made easier after Puerto Rico's economic debacle caused by U.S. policies following the Spanish-American War of 1898 see E. Maldonado (1979) "Contract Labor and the Origins of Puerto Rican Communities in the United States" *International Migration Review* 13(1):103-121 and B.C. Souza (1984) "Trabajo y Tristeza— 'Work and Sorrow': The Puerto Ricans of Hawaii, 1900-1902" *Hawaiian Journal of History* 18:156-73.

7. See C. Rosario Natal, *Exodo Puertorriqueno*. San Juan, PR, 1983, pp. 74-76. However, a *San Francisco Chronicle* article (December 7, 1900) indicates the train stopped in Pomona and that the workers fled to Los Angeles.

8. See Rosario Natal, p. 85.

9. See E. Hernandez, Jr. "Puerto Ricans: One of LA's Best Kept Secrets" *Los Angeles Times*, October 30, b14, (1994). Fortunately, writer and historian Aurora Levins Morales served as curator of a historical photographic exhibition of Boricuas in the west and is develop-

ing other historical resources of the Puerto Rican diaspora in the west of the United States.

10. Recent work by Ana Celia Zentella (2004) indicates the problematization of Puerto Rican identity development in California, Puerto Ricans develop a sense of self as "not being Mexican." This may be an underlying cause for the failure of explicit, proactive, contemporary Boricua and Chicano joint political alliances. The support for the struggle in Vieques from 1999 to 2003 was more the exception than the rule in Chicano and Boricua solidarity. See article on Vieques in this collection.

11. See my article on the counter-trend to this process of "whitening" in "The Racialization of Puerto Rican Ethnicity in the United States" in J. M. Carrion, Ed. *Ethnicity, Race and Nationality in the Caribbean*. Rio Piedras: Institute of Caribbean Studies, 1997.

12. For recent historical literature on the sociological and cultural formation of "whiteness" see T. W. Allen. *The Invention of The White Race: Racial Oppression and Social Control*. London: Verso, 1994.; I. Haney-Lopez. *White By Law: The Legal Construction of Race*. N.Y.: New York University, 1996; N. Ignatiev's *How the Irish Became White*. New York: Routledge, 1995; D. Roediger, *The Wages of Whiteness: Race and the Making of the American Working Class*. London: Verso, 1995.

13. U.S. Bureau of the Census (1970).

14. J. P. Allen and E. Turner. *The Ethnic Quilt: Population Diversity in Southern California*. Northridge, CA: Center for Geographical Studies, Cal State, Northridge, 1997.

15. Allen and Turner (1997), p. 249.

16. U.S. Bureau of the Census, *Persons of Spanish Origin in the U.S.: March 1975*, Series P-20, No. 283 (August 1975).

17. Allen and Turner (1997) p. 231. This pattern is not unusual except it is more intensified (not being segregated from whites) than in the Northeast. See A. M. Santiago and G. Galster "Puerto Rican Segregation in the United States: Cause or Consequence of Economic Status?" in *Social Problems* 42 (3):pp. 361-389, 1995.

18. Allen and Turner (1997) p. 113.

19. Allen and Turner (1997) p. 113 In their analysis of census tracts only nine have more than 2% of the residents identified as Puerto Ricans. In the tract where the greatest number of Boricuas live they are only 66 among 3,540 residents (Sun Valley, eastern San Fernando Valley).

20. Allen and Turner (1997), p. 113.

21. Allen and Turner (1997), p. 85. Only 85% of Panamanians chose Hispanic, while 36% chose black. For Panamanians, Hispanic and black seem to be both racial and mutually exclusive. This group is further along the racialization pattern.

22. U.S. Bureau of the Census (1990).

23. "Puerto Ricans in California," A Staff Report of the Western Regional Office, United States Commission on Civil Rights.

24. *The Third World Population in California.* Council of Intergroup Relations, cited in "Puerto Ricans in California," p. 6.

25. The participants in the interview were Ivan Gutierrez, Zoilo Cruz, Nativo Lopez, Melba Maldonado, Aurora Levins-Morales, Placido Rodriguez, and Gilbert Rodriguez (pseudonym), Hector Albizu, (pseudonym). These individuals are located in various parts of the United States and Puerto Rico. I appreciate their generosity, particularly because they provided me with time and patience for this project. Other participants whose first names are used are also pseudonyms since I did not have their authorization for using their full names. Given the extensive history of political persecution against Puerto Rican patriots it is necessary to protect their identity. For a recent incisive description of anti-independence persecution and covert actions see Ronald Fernandez' *The Disenchanted Island: Puerto Rico and the U.S in the Twentieth Century.* New York: Praeger, 1996, especially Chapter 8.

26. Rodriguez, G. (Pseudonym). 1996, Phone Interview, San Juan, Puerto Rico (June 29).

27. Levins-Morales, A. 1995, Phone Interview, Berkeley, California (December 5). Levins-Morales is a writer, historian and a speaker on feminist, cultural and historical issues throughout the United States and the Caribbean. She is the daughter of Richard Levins, a radical scientist who spent a considerable part of his life involved in Puerto Rico's left.

28. Maldonado, M. 1996, Phone Interview, San Francisco, California (July 9).

29. Levins-Morales, A. Phone Interview, Berkeley, CA.

30. Since it is outside of the scope of this paper I am not detailing the organizational and ideological issues that were paramount in leading to the PSP's demise as an effective political organization. The cycle of ideological and organizational crises affecting the PSP in the island migrated to the PSP's branch units in the United States. These debates led to many divisions in the party including one in 1982 in which the entire Los Angeles cell resigned from the party. For a passionate, particular perspective on these debates se Hector Melendez' *El Fracaso del Proyecto PSP de La Pequeña Burguesia.* Rio Piedras: Editorial Edil, 1984.

31. Levins-Morales, A. Phone Interview, Berkeley, CA

32. Levins-Morales, A. Phone Interview, Berkeley, CA

33. Rodriguez, G. Phone Interview.

34. Rodriguez, G. Phone Interview.

35. Rodriguez, G. Phone Interview.

36. Rodriguez, P. Phone Interview. 1996, Los Angeles, California (July 31).
37. Cruz, Z. Phone Interview. 1996, New York, N.Y. (January 15) Cruz was at the time a special aide for a progressive New York city council member.
38. Cruz, Z. Phone Interview.
39. M. T. Garcia. 1994. *Memories of Chicano History: The Life and Narrative of Bert Corona*. Berkeley, CA: University of California Press, pp. 293-297.
40. Garcia, M. T. (1994), p. 312.
41. Lopez, N. Personal interview, 1997, Santa Ana, CA. (November 5). Lopez shares the position of National Co-Director with Bert Corona of la Hermandad Nacional Mexicana.
42. Lopez, N. Personal interview.
43. Lopez, N. Personal interview.
44. Lopez, N. Personal interview.
45. Rodriguez, P. Phone Interview.
46. The extra-political social relationships included intermarriage between Chicanos and Boricuas. Ivan Gutierrez was married to a Chicana activist and Nativo Lopez married Noemi, a Puerto Rican PSP activist.
47. Gutierrez, I. Interview. 1997. Irvine, California (June 6). Ivan Gutierrez is an intellectual historian and visiting professor at Pomona College.
48. Albizu, H. Personal Interview. 1997. Santa Ana, California (June 6).
49. Later during the 1990s, the PSP disbanded and a small organization the New Movement for Independence (NMI) returned to its progressive nationalist roots. It did not condemn marxism but it became a pluralist organization with a small, diverse membership. Today this organization merged with the *Congreso Nacional Hostosiano* (National Hostosian Congress) and have formed the Movimiento Independentista Nacional Hostosiano (Pro-Independence Hostosian Movement). Eugenio Maria de Hostos was a Puerto Rican patriot, educator, sociologist, and a highly respected intellectual in Latin America and the Caribbean.
50. Albizu, H. Interview.
51. Albizu, H. Personal Interview.
52. Rodriguez, P. Phone Interview.

¡Sí Se Puede! The Mobilization of Naturalized Latinas/os in Santa Ana, CA: 1990-2003[1]

Abstract

In the late 1970s, Santa Ana, California became the largest city in the state in which Latinos were the numerical majority. But, despite being the numerical majority, Latinos in this Southern California city have lived in a state of "apartheid" for almost a century, with little access to social, economic, or political power. In the early 1980s, a series of grassroots community organizations in conservative Orange County, led by the Hermandad Mexicana Nacional, were able to mobilize naturalized Latino voters, elect the first Latina congresswoman in this county's history, elect the first majority Latino school board in the history of Santa Ana, and increase Latino representation in the city council. But more important than cosmetic changes, for the first time in the last 100 years, a progressive Latino majority led a multiracial coalition that began dismantling the system of apartheid in this city. This was the first major effort to challenge the subordination and racialization process of Latinos in this county since the end of World War II. The uniqueness of their political and cultural strategy contributed to increasing the electoral participation of naturalized voters to even higher rates than those of native Latino voters. This article explores Chicano/Latino politics in Orange County, California using oral history evidence and secondary data to describe the origins of the recent rise of Latinos to political office in the city of Santa Ana. It analyzes the historical origins of this political development and places it within a historically relevant context and theory of racialization although pointing at the contradictory forces at work in the Latino community that produced the mobilization of naturalized citizens. It highlights the role of labor and community organizations as important mechanisms for the interplay and mediation of race, ethnicity, gender, and class in local political movements. Finally, this article develops a historically grounded antiracist theoreti-

cal perspective about the role of race, ethnicity, gender, and class in mobilizing a predominantly working-class Latino community.

"All politics is local"

Thomas "Tip" O'Neill

Introduction

Santa Ana, Calif.—On the eve of Martin Luther King Jr.'s birthday in
January 1997, dozens of Latino immigrants huddled beneath a pound-
ing rain outside the Santa Ana headquarters of Hermandad Mexicana
Nacional (HMN), one of Southern California's most important immigrant advocacy groups. Inside, agents of the Orange County District
Attorney's office were confiscating "evidence," including most of the
organization's computers and bank records, to indict the organization
for allegedly engaging in a conspiracy to commit vote fraud in order to
elect the first Latina member of Congress from Orange County in
California's history, Loretta Sanchez. Earlier, the House Oversight Committee, had supported Congressman Robert Dornan's request for an
investigation of his allegations of voter fraud in Orange County's congressional election. Weeks later, in March, California's Secretary of State
Bill Jones, a Republican, in another attempt to find voter fraud opened
up an investigation of all 1.3 million Orange County residents registered
to vote in that election. The power structure was in full gear and HMN
and its leader, Nativo Lopez, was its target.

This election had been a historical watershed for Latino political
efforts to achieve a voice in the political arena; Congresswoman Loretta
Sanchez was able to oust Congressman Robert Dornan, a notorious and
powerful right-wing Republican, in the November 1996 elections. During this same election, Nativo Lopez, the HMN national executive director, was elected to the Santa Ana school board. Congressman Dornan
blamed HMN in particular, and Mexican immigrants in general for his
loss, and then managed to convince his powerful friends in Congress
and Sacramento to investigate the immigrant rights group.

A few months after they began their investigation, Secretary of State
Bill Jones in a letter to the House Oversight Committee revealed that
the number of "unlawful" votes, 303, was not enough to change the result of the election, which Sanchez won by 984 votes (Warren, 1997). A
year after the search of HMN (today the Hermandad Mexicana Latino
Americana) headquarters in Santa Ana, the House Oversight Committee voted to end a fourteen-month investigation they had conducted on
vote tampering. Sanchez was basking in glory and had become a very
effective fundraiser for Democratic party politics (Wilgoren, 1998;
Cleeland & Martelle, 1998). The following week, the full House also ended

its investigation. Earlier in December 1997, Orange County District Attorney Michael Capizzi announced that their year-long investigation had not produced sufficient evidence for the grand jury to press charges against any staff member of the HMN (Wagner & Cleeland 1997). More than 300 interviews by forty investigators, and 33,000 documents had been reviewed for this investigation on voter fraud. Loren Duchesne, chief of Capizzi's investigative section said: "This was easily the most complete and objective investigation anyone could ask for..." (Union Hispana, 1997).

The outcome was not a surprise for Latinos. Every Latino activist knew very well there had not been any Latino-organized vote tampering conspiracy. Sanchez won because of the kind of innovative mobilization strategy Latino organizations like the HMN had developed in order to shift the pivot of South Orange County politics. For a century, Latinos experienced segregation in their neighborhoods and their schools, overt and covert efforts were made to dissuade them from actively participating in the electoral process and Latinos were effectively excluded from entering the economic mainstream of one of the wealthiest counties in the nation. But since the late 1990s, a growing number of Latino voters in Orange County began to enter the political process and began to challenge the white political and economic structure and wrest political inclusion.

Contrary to the experience of Latinos in cities like San Antonio, where despite the election of a Latino mayor, Henry Cisneiros in 1981, no major changes in the city's power structure took place, the election of Latinos in Santa Ana and other parts of south Orange County was supported by a social movement and a network of Latina/o organizations and individuals who were poised to make real changes in power relations in this region. In San Antonio for example, despite the election of Henry Cisneiros from 1981 through 1989, no major fundamental changes took place in the correlation of power between a rising Latino majority and the Anglo power structure (Rosales, 2000). Since the shift from at-large electoral systems to single-member districts in San Antonio, Latinos had been able to increase their electoral representation throughout the political structure (Rosales, 2000:182). In 1997, for example, six of the ten members of the city council were Latinos and Latinos began to rise to various positions within the city government. However, as Rosales has clearly shown, the Anglo-dominated business agenda was still (and still is) in control in San Antonio.

Rosales describes how a rising community empowerment movement can fail to significantly change power relations in a racialized political and economic structure, and cites Ira Katznelson who discovered in his structural analysis of New York's Long Island community mobilization that:

> "...political empowerment in a very practical sense is more
> about the dilution of community power over a broader urban
> landscape, at the expense of any radical challenge to the domi-
> nant business-oriented policy status quo" (Rosales 2000:184).

The lack of a broader community agenda and a coordinating network led these efforts at empowerment to be subsumed by the prevailing political structure. In cities or regions that are becoming more racially
and ethnically diverse, "coloring" the various strata of political, economic,
or bureaucratic power does not always lead to a challenge of the status
quo but in fact could lead to its perpetuation by veiling the racialized
nature of the power hierarchies. The new "gatekeepers" whether they
are people of color or not, could find themselves operating under the
rules of a game that was created to benefit the white power structure.
Here the "opaqueness" of society becomes substituted by a multicultural
facade that hides the real nature of racialized and gendered class oppression.

The incredible amount of repression the Latino social movement in
South Orange county experienced is highly indicative of its potential
for disrupting business as usual in those cities where it organized and
mobilized. Also, the pervasiveness of the attacks on an organization like
the HMN (today the Hermandad Mexicana Latino Americana) indicates
that the elite conspired to destroy a threat to their power and hegemony.

In 1998, U.S. Rep. Stony H. Hoyer, D-Md, told the *Los Angeles Times*
that the congressional investigation was part of "a much broader agenda"
designed to undermine the Latino vote (Warren & Wilgoren, 1998). Nativo
Lopez, leader of HMN agrees. "In the mentality of Republican conservatives, the empowerment of a disenfranchised group like Latinos, and
the role of immigrants, (meant) something had gone wrong" (Lopez,
1998). What went wrong was that this social movement found the Achilles heel of the system of white supremacy in South Orange County.[2] The
Republican Party became the political organization that coordinated,
for the political and economic elite, the efforts to subdue, manage and
re-subordinate a rising Latino power. These efforts, more than just the
outcomes of individual choices are part of a systemic process that has
been in place for the last 150 years. Ironically, Republicans today are in
an all-out national battle to gain a portion of the Latino vote.[3] If Republicans achieve their objective of capturing a sizable segment of the Latino
vote they will relegate the Democrats to a minority for some time and
will contribute to maintaining white supremacy uncontested in the
United States. The experience of Latinos in Santa Ana is a window into
what the world of local politics would be like if Republicans achieve
their goal. Since the HMN's Santa Ana chapter was founded in 1982,
they have helped more than 120,000 Latino immigrants to gain U.S. citi-

zenship and aided the mobilization of this vote in the electoral process. In return, they have undergone congressional investigations that have attempted to demonize the organization. In 1997, U.S. Rep. William M. Thomas, R-Bakersfield, CA, who chaired the house investigation labeled HMN as "one of the most corrupt organizations that has ever existed" (Cleeland, 1997). Later, in June of 1998, the California Department of Education ordered HMN to repay 4.3 million dollars in educational grants they had been granted to provide English and citizenship courses to immigrants alleging that the HMN had failed to properly account for the money. In February of 2002, the California Department of Education dropped its lawsuit against Lopez in exchange for HMN and Nativo Lopez agreeing not to sue the state. The effective political and grassroots work by HMN also led to some fairly ugly immigrant-bashing and death threats against Hermandad's leader, Nativo Lopez.

There were efforts led by various conservative organizations to lead a right-wing offensive against the Latino social movement in order to demobilize the more progressive sectors of the Latino community, although at the same time capturing its more conservative elements. This offensive had a real and concrete impact on its members, including emotional and health costs.[4] What follows is an attempt to contextualize the Santa Ana social movement in a historical and theoretical framework and to reconstruct this history by using the memories of strategic participants in this process. Also, a theory about mobilization of Latinos at the local level within racialized and gendered class social structures is also being proposed. Politics are local and it's precisely at the local level where a political praxis leads to Latino empowerment.

Historical Context and Racialization

Efforts to place Latino politics within a broad theoretical framework have failed to provide an understanding of racialization in the Chicano and Latino experience. Early foci on Latino political behavior were strongly embedded in the black/white paradigm of the Civil Rights movement, which failed to account for the cleavages that exist within the "Latino" racialized category. Even the concept of "Mexican Politics" was in practice, seen as an oxymoron since most of the foci on the political practice of Mexicans were shaded by the ideology of the "Mexican Problem," which described Mexicans (and by extension other Latinos) as incapable of independent political behavior (Gonzalez & Fernandez, 2003). This ideology constructed Mexicans as passive, apolitical, and of having a dysfunctional culture. The cluster of social science literature of the 1960s that studied oppressed communities revolved around the idea of a "culture of poverty." Anthropologist Oscar Lewis, author of *The Children of Sanchez* and *La Vida* provided a body of concepts and theory,

which validated, from a liberal perspective, the "Mexican Problem" ideology that had been part and parcel of Latino representation since the beginning of the twentieth century. This new social science discourse provided an avenue into popular discourse for a way or normalizing a "commonsense" understanding of the subordination of Chicanos in the racial, social, and political structure of the United States. Until the last decades, Latino political behavior was seen as dependent on their manipulation by others, like the historical experience of the Santa Fe or San Antonio political machines (Gomez, 1990).[5]

For liberal political analysts the solution for the dilemma of Latino empowerment was "Mexicans could improve their lot if they would band together and elect their own people to office" (Gomez, 1990:18). The ideology of American pluralism pervaded the liberal perspective and was unable to explain why many elected Latino politicians came to be subsumed in the elite politics rendering them as "gatekeepers" despite good intentions. Liberals also were unable to explain the perpetuation of subordination of Chicanos and their uneven, nonlinear patterns of political participation (Gomez, 1990). Most of the foci were on structures of domination, like discrimination and electoral obstacles to full participation without a connecting strand that would link these to issues of identity and agency. How is it possible for a community that produced insurrectionary movements and leaders into the early part of the twentieth century to be then conceptualized as passive, indolent, and malleable? In order to answer this question it is necessary to understand the dialectic of racialization and the way it interweaves class, race, and gender in a political praxis. It also becomes necessary to delineate a theory that elucidates and clarifies the way racism works in our present societal context.

First, as Omi and Winant argue in their 1996 classic, race is a fluid concept that changes with respect to what they call racial formations. Race and racial formations that legitimate and sustain racial categories are basically constituted by state systems that support the interest of a ruling group or class. Race, is probably better understood as "a sociobiological concept constructed to assign human worth and social status, using Europeans as the paradigm" (Karenga, 2005). Race was constructed as part of an ideology that developed during the period of world colonization and conquest, this ideology serves to justify and legitimate colonialism and imperialism as mechanisms to ensure the subordination of groups. This period is also the period in which capitalism developed as a global system so that capitalism and racialization are interwoven processes. The birth of capitalism is marked by race and race is intricately tied to the reproduction of capitalism. The race construct is then supported by racism, which is defined as "a system of denial, deformation and destruction of a people's history, humanity and human rights based exclusively or primarily on the specious concept of

race" (Karenga, 2005). Racism then becomes not a problem of individual attitudes or of personal relationships but becomes a systemic reality that demands a politics of transformation, not a politics of reform. Politics then does not become an exercise of how can we develop better and more civil relationship between racial groups, dominant and nondominant, but, instead, how can we *all* dismantle the architecture of racism in the nation? In order to understand how race was created and how racism operates we need to understand the mechanics of the social construction of race and racism. By focusing on racialization we can understand the way in which the various hierarchies, race, ethnicity, class, and gender became woven together in a basic architecture designed to provide a foundation for a system of white supremacy. Mexican Americans, as a group that was "incorporated" into the United States after white supremacy was embedded in the social fabric of the United States, represents a good opportunity to reveal the hidden process of racialization.

Since the Mexican American War (1846-1848), Mexican Americans experienced a process of racialization that has led to their cultural, social, and political subordination in the United States' racialized social hierarchy. Racialization is defined as:

> "Racialization is the social and historical process of assigning individuals and groups a socially constructed racial identity and status. As populations compete for land, status and resources, they build hierarchies based on clusters of phenotypical biological factors which are then assumed to represent archetypes for members of a particular racial group. Those who become the dominant group interpret those presumed phenotypical biological differences as indicators of essential differences and assign a negative meaning to them, subordinating the contending group and limiting their access to those things their society values. The process of racialization in modern societies, is historically specific, and is carried out by its basic social institutions: economy, education, family, religion, government, criminal justice system, media etc." (Rodriguez, 2002:7).

Historical Processes of Racialization

There is at least four identifiable processes or "moments" in the racialization process (Rodriguez, 2002:9). The four moments and outcomes of racialization are:

Primary Processes	Outcomes
Limiting access/control of land	Imposition/Subordination
Ideology/Cultural Racism	Institutional Arrangements
Negotiation/Contestation Acceptance and participation in discrimination by ethnic groups	Placement in Racial System/ Hierarchy
Assimilation/Americanization, homogenization ("lumping"), internalized racist oppression etc.	Crystallization of a Racialized Identity

Rather than being dichotomous and mutually exclusive these processes overlap each other and do not necessarily follow a specific sequence. Each of these processes contributes to the social construction of a "cultural" group (in Rosaldo's terms) a group that becomes a racial group in the perception and experience of the dominant white power structure and in the group's own sense of self (Rosaldo,1989). The main focus of this analysis will be the ideology that contributes to how the dominant white elite understands itself and Chicanos, the institutional arrangements that perpetuate racial hierarchy and how structures and ideology are challenged and internalized by Mexican Americans.

Imposition/Subordination

The first stage is a process of subordination entailed limiting the collective control and /or access to land. This process may imply some degree of violence and/or coercion whose function is to limit the range of responses to subordination. In the Mexican American experience this process includes the colonial conquest and racialization of Mexicans in Mexico's former northern provinces (the Southwest of the United States today) and the neocolonial experience of Mexico that followed its defeat in the Mexican American War that ended in 1848. This process of land expropriation renders Mexicans as subjects of the racializing forces of United States' social institutions. These basic social institutions, government, education, state, economy, etc., all manage and produce a new racialized subject that is then positioned in its proper place in the racial hierarchy of the historical moment.

This stage also sets the scene for the migration of millions of Mexicans who are then transformed into racialized subjects in the United States. These series of events excluded millions of Mexicans from having control and/or access to land, both in their homeland and in the diaspora. In the Southwest, this process included the legal and illegal ways in which the white/Anglo power structure took control of the millions of acres of lands that were in the hands of the Mexican landed elite (Acuña, 1988). These ways included laws that eased the expropriation of the landed elite, outright theft (squatters) and through the intermarriage between Anglo men and the daughters of the landed and lighter skinned Mexican elite (Acuña,1988:89).[6] Although the United States signed the Treaty of Guadalupe Hidalgo with Mexico (1848), which included protection for the religious, civil, and land rights of the Mexican community in the United States, U.S. legal institutions did not impede the almost complete expropriation of the Mexican community. In the words of Mexican American historian, Griswold del Castillo: "The promises the U.S. government made with respect to the conquered Mexican populations, however, have remained largely unfulfilled." (Griswold del Castillo, 1990:173).

If political, economic, and cultural dynamics are examined, rather than limiting the focus through a cultural model, like traditional Chicano historians, the history of the Mexican American/Chicano community is revealed, not as a continuous history beginning in 1848, but as a discontinuous process with an early phase of expropriation, disenfranchisement, and conquest leading to a second phase where a racialized, proletarianized immigrant Chicano population is formed. While it was true that the racialization process began earlier, it did not "produce" a racialized subject until this last period described by Gonzalez and Fernandez (1998).

It is for this reason that the forms of Mexican American political resistance to racialization assume various forms in different historical periods and regions. Despite traditional Chicano history portrayal of Chicano politics as an even journey from insurrection into the Chicano Civil Rights movement of the 1960s, the reality is that discontinuity is more prevalent in this narrative than continuity. For example, from 1848 to 1880, throughout the Southwest, the nature of resistance against Anglo encroachment and domination took the character of an anticolonial struggle. The prevalence of insurrectionary efforts like Juan Nepomuceno (Cheno) Cortina in Texas, the Gorras Blancas in New Mexico, or those of social bandits like Juan Flores and Joaquin Murietta in California and later, Gregorio Cortez in Texas, and ending with the Plan de San Diego in 1915 all begins to fade away as the Mexican American population is racialized, proletarianized, and pigeonholed into its new racial identity.

The intensity and biological character of the racialization of people of Mexican descent is illustrated by the level of violence used to subordinate the community. Violence against groups is made more palatable when the objects of violence are dehumanized in the culture. When social groups are constituted as racial groups, as "other," it facilitates the commission of acts of violence. While institutional forces were more prevalent that violence and coercion at times, in different regions, violence was utilized as a means to control the Mexican population. Levels of violence against a group become good indicators of the degree of racialization that group has experienced. The practice of lynching, often associated with the African American experience was also pervasive in some regions like Texas. But in California, the Mexican community was not immune to its effects. Haney Lopez (2003:67) cites Carey McWilliams' report in his book *Southern California* of eleven Mexicans being lynched in Los Angeles in 1857 and four additional victims in the neighboring community of El Monte. Violence seems to have intensified as the Mexican community grew and became increasingly subordinated and proletarianized. In counties like Ventura, north of Los Angeles, Martha Menchaca (1995:46) details how the Ku Klux Klan, police brutality, and violence against Mexicans while in labor strikes contributed to the oppression of the community.

As U.S. monopoly capital begins to develop its hegemonic control of world markets, it creates a demand for labor in U.S. industry and agriculture that is met by the streams of Mexican peasants "freed" from land attachments by U.S. investments in Mexico. These immigrants become proletarianized and racialized in the emerging social, economic, and political structure of the United States. The receiving communities are not the spaces that existed before the Mexican American war and that gave rise to the California culture but have become racializing spaces. In Los Angeles, for example, Mexicans experienced deep declines in the ownership of property, from 1850 to 1870 the percentage of Mexicans owning property declines from three-fifths to one-fifth (Haney Lopez, 2003:67).

Parallel to this expropriation process is their isolation from the emerging Angeleno social and economic structure, particularly their spatial segregation around the old Los Angeles plaza and south of the center of the city, "By 1880, 83% of the property held by Mexicans was located in this area and 70% of the Mexican population resided there" (Haney Lopez, 2003:67). These new segregated and subordinated spaces were the entry gates for Latino immigrants migrating to Los Angeles. In the meantime, since the latter part of the nineteenth century a segregated school system sprang up here and there for Mexican children. In Ventura County the segregated system began in the 1880s (Menchaca, 1995). These segregated, racialized neighborhoods become labor pools for the local economies while at the same time are maintained separate

from each other to avoid miscegenation. Mexicans as a social group, are gradually transformed from a dominant to a subordinate group in their own homeland. Their new status and social and economic position in the racialized structure of southern California also shapes the form of the contestation of the dialectic of racialization.

The proletarianized and racialized Mexican communities develop a political praxis that begins to revolve around community-based, legal, "civil rights," modes of attempting insertion into the excluding society. In other words, during the early stage of racialization (pre-twentieth century), the resistance is from the "outside," although in the latter stage the resistance is from the "inside." The partial incorporation of Mexicans into the emerging social and economic formation shapes the form of their struggle against racialization. The fact that they were becoming an urbanized community, not having access to land influences their political responses to those methods and means that are available to them.

In this latter period, resistance to racialization becomes then more local and takes the form of "mutualistas" (mutual aid societies), labor unions, and community cultural groups. While other forms of resisting racialization do not disappear entirely, they are no longer as prevalent as in the period following 1848. The mode of integration of Mexicans into the social and economic structure of the United States, particularly in the later decades of the nineteenth century, is rooted in their transformation into proletarians, workers within the expanding industrial capitalist economy of the United States. It is within these processes that race, ethnicity, class and gender become woven together in the Mexican American experience. This is the economic context for their racialization and what begins to shape the forms of resistance. This is also the context for the contemporary social movement efforts to challenge political and economic systems and their role in perpetuating the subordination and control of Mexican Americans.

Challenging Ideology and Institutional Arrangements: Education

After Mexican Americans experience the outcome of the historical process of imposition and subordination, by being excluded from access and control of the land in Mexico and in the Southwest, they face another process of racialization. This process includes an ideology that legitimates subordination and provides cultural racism with its power to perpetuate, through institutional arrangements, the inferior social, political, and economic status of the Mexican American population. This process is one that continues and expands today in the form of a racist educational system, the racist media portrayal of people of Mexican descent and the manner in which white political elites respond to Latinos

because whites feel increasingly threatened by the demographic shift being experienced by the United States. Census Bureau projections indicate that by 2050, one in four U. S. residents will be Latino and one in three births will be Latino children (Day, 1996). In California, by 2050, Latinos will be 54% of the state's population and will be the majority ethnic group by 2040 (State of California, Department of Finance, 2004).

Today, this racialization and subordination of Latinos, and specifically, people of Mexican descent, continues in a more subtle, institutionalized fashion than during the period of segregation de jure. The overt mechanisms of yesterday, are no longer visible or easily discernible. The Ku Klux Klan or the White Citizens Councils are quaint remnants of the past and are not seen as a threat to Latinos today. The Civil Rights movement and the legal artifice built against racial discrimination are seen as having all but eliminated institutional exclusion of people of color. This is particularly evident in California where the popular culture has erased from its historical memory the powerful role that racial discrimination had before the Civil Rights movement.[7] Race in white popular discourse has become irrelevant in a new "nonracial society." Latinos and African Americans are represented in the highest levels of the federal government. However, the prevalence of racial inequality persists and the dilemma revolves around how to account and explain the racial gap.[8]

Today, a new racial ideology, "color-blind racism" has developed to explain the assumed non-racial nature of contemporary racial inequality (Bonilla-Silva 2003). This allows whites, when confronted with the reality of contemporary racial inequality, to exculpate social, economic, and political structures that continue to exclude Latinos and other people of color while providing power and privilege to whites. This ideology permits whites to blame individuals without feeling they are racially prejudiced. This new ideology allows for a new version of the "culture of poverty" theory to blame Mexican culture for any gaps between the economic performance of whites and Mexicans. The large unemployment rate among Latinos, for example, can be explained away by believing there is a lack of a work ethic among Latinos, like a top officer of a cart transport company in Chicago said: "the Hispanics are 'mañana, mañana'—tomorrow, tomorrow" (Wilson,1996:112). These notions about Mexicans are not validated by labor participation rates (LPR) which evidence that people of Mexican descent have one of the highest levels of engagement with the labor force. In fact Mexicans, have even higher labor participation rates (LPR) than whites. In 2004 whites had an LPR of 66.3% compared to 68.9% for people of Mexican descent (U.S. Department of Labor, 2005). Mexicans have the highest LPR of any Latino subgroup. But color-blind ideology obfuscates the facts and allows the same stereotypes of the past to be used without the baggage of seeming racially charged.

This ideology builds on the historical antecedents of the ideology of the "Mexican Problem," which overtly permeated pedagogical thinking during the first decades of the twentieth century and which continues to insinuate itself in more subtle and covert forms in contemporary educational practices (Gonzalez & Fernandez, 2003). These educational practices are reflected today in the inadequate educational facilities provided for Latinos, and in the general disinvestment in education that has taken place in California. The educational system, in a postindustrial society like the United States becomes a strategic tool for liberation and empowerment or can contribute to the continued subordination and racialization of Latinos. Local school districts, are not only educational institutions but also economically powerful institutions in local settings. Their function, at the local level can challenge local structures of power, not only as knowledge institutions but also as sources of political and economic power.

Education in California Today

The state of education today in California is the outcome of a series of political decisions made by California voters that have led to the rise of an educational system that is failing millions of children who are part of the rising Latino majority. Ironically, the contemporary state of economic disrepair arose out of a progressive effort to equalize the system for financing schools in California. A lawsuit, *Serrano v. Priest,* was brought in 1968 by the Western Center on Law and Poverty, this case is in some ways a fore-runner of *Rodríguez v. San Antonio 1971,* an attempt to address the unfairness of the school aid system in Texas (Sonstelie, Brunner & Ardon, 2000). As the authors of this study of school finance reform in California describe, in the late 1960s, a study by Arthur Wise, *Rich Schools, Poor Schools: The Promise of Educational Opportunity* provided the inspiration for attempts by Latino activists to use the legal arena to challenge institutional racism in education financing (Sonstelie, Brunner & Ardon, 2000). What they found was the tool of the equal protection clause of the U.S. Constitution as a means to challenge the racist way some Latino schools were treated by institutionalized financing practices. Unfortunately, as Arthur Wise later described in another study, *Legislated Learning: The Bureaucratization of the American Classroom*, bringing the state into the process of financing education led to centralizing power on the state and facilitated the increased bureaucratization of the educational system that we have inherited today.

One of the reasons that contributed to the derailment of the social movements of the 1960s and 1970s was their increased reliance on legal processes that contributed to the shift of the locus of struggle from community organizing to the courtroom. The Chicano and Puerto Rican social movements, just like the African American civil rights struggle

became increasingly bureaucratized and weakened by state repression and the good intentions of rising Latino middle-class leaders, groomed in some of the best white educational institutions, who began to utilize legal remedies for social maladies. The combination of state repression and the shift from the streets into courtrooms, made lawyers and middle-class professionals the leaders and pivots of the movement and diminished the role of working-class and community leaders. For example, the Chicano student movement in Los Angeles led the 1968 "blowouts" where thousands of Latino students protested against a racist educational system that condemned them to an inferior status. Later in 1969, as a result of the Chicano community's political agitation, the state of California felt pressured to respond to the issues raised by the movement with an educational conference during the spring of 1969 at the Biltmore Hotel (Haney Lopez, 2003). Both events, the "blowouts" and the protests at the Biltmore conference ended with a significant number of the movement's leadership having to defend themselves in the courts. Some of the charges leveled against the young leaders ranged from conspiracy to disturbing the peace with respect to the "blowouts" in May 1968, and burglary and arson for protests carried out during the 1969 Biltmore Hotel conference where then Governor Ronald Reagan spoke. The "East LA Thirteen" and the "Biltmore Six" became legal cases that bogged down the Chicano leadership in the courts and away from the organizing and agitation that the movement needed to maintain the momentum. Increasingly, the legal arena became the battleground for the antiracist struggle during this period.

In 1971, the California Supreme Court agreed with the plaintiffs in the *Serrano v. Priest* case and ordered the state to bring the financing of K-12 education in California in conformity to the equal protection clause of the fourteenth amendment of the U.S. Constitution (Sonstelie, Brunner, & Ardon, 2000). Unfortunately, many agree that the eventual outcome of this change was that the system for financing became so bureaucratized and gave so much power to the state that gradually, it made matters worse. Because the dynamics of institutionalized racism were not understood, because there was not a strong social movement to demand accountability from the state, institutionalized racism permutated instead of being dismantled. Because of the particular nature of the Latino racialized experience, many Latinos lived in both high-spending districts and low spending school districts. But the effect of the changes in financing basically equalized inequalities across districts but did not, specifically, direct resources to the students of color who needed them the most (Sonstelie, Brunner, & Ardon, 2000). Also, in 1978, Proposition 13 enhanced the racialized inequalities that existed before and led to a dramatic decline in per pupil spending in California at a time when Latinos were becoming the largest proportion of California's school population.[9] As Sonstelie, Brunner, & Ardon, 2000 note, spend-

ing reduction led to a decline in the hiring of teachers and a dramatic increase in teacher/pupil ratios. It is interesting to note that previously to the full effects in the way that changes in the financing of education occurred in California, students were performing at or above national standardized tests in the 1970s and 1980s (Sonstelie, Brunner, & Ardon, 2000). This decline, according to this study is not uniquely related to the increase in limited English students, since even after controlling for this demographic effect the decline is still substantial.

Just like the anti-Latino/antiminority propositions that have plagued California politics in the last decade: Proposition 187 (exclusion of undocumented aliens from social services), in 1994, Proposition 209 (dismantling of affirmative action), in 1996 and Proposition 227 (dismantling of bilingual education), in 1978, Proposition 13 was voted with the overwhelming support of whites. In 1978, whites were an overwhelming proportion of the electorate and the "populist" character of the measure hid its eventual racist outcome and its contribution to the continued subordination of Latinos (Maharidge, 1996). It is quite striking that at a time when the Latino student population was growing and dramatically rising as a percentage of the student population, the state begins a secular decline in its per-pupil spending in such a way that it almost corresponds perfectly with the change in population demographics. Irrespective of whether one is "caused" by the other, the reality is that the association of both processes led to a racist outcome.

For example in Los Angeles, with 746,831 students from K-12 in 2002, and the largest district in the nation where Latinos are a majority (71.4% in 2001), of nine districts studied around the nation by Rothstein (1997), Los Angeles had the largest decline in per-pupil spending from 1991 to 1996. Spending dropped by 6.5% and while the author ascribes the decline to the recession, per-pupil spending has not reached, even today, any level comparable to a few decades ago. This decline in spending is compounded given the nature of the student population today which includes a larger proportion of students categorized as having limited English proficiency (LEP). This period of investment decline included events like the Los Angeles insurrection of 1992, the antiimmigration wave that climaxed with Proposition 187 and the series of anti-Latino initiatives that were approved by California voters in subsequent years. To posit that these events are unrelated challenges any reasonable interpretation of the facts.

According to the National Education Association, California's national ranking in terms of investment in public school education declined from being ranked number twenty-seven in 2000-2001 to an estimated ranking of thirty-fifth in 2001-2002 (Ed Source 2003). During the earlier period, in 1996-1997, the state had dipped to forty-one in terms of public investment in public education K-12. The early 1990s were a time of great xenophobia and antiimmigrant feeling that shaped the electorate's sense

of detachment from investing in public education. During 1990-1991 and 2001-2002, the Latino percentage of the K-12 student population increased from 34.3% to 44.4%. The proportion of Latino children from K-12 is expected to rise to 48% in the 2005-2006 school year. Since the summer of 2001, 50.2% of all births in California are Latino children (Hayes-Bautista, et al., 2003). To talk about investment in public education in California is to talk about investing in educating Latino children. In 2004, thanks to a strong Latino caucus in the state legislature the per-pupil investment climbed to twenty-five among the nation's states. These numbers, while still very low, are a significant contrast to years before when Latinos where not the majority in the school system.

In 1976-1977, when the majority of the public school children where white and California was nationally ranked number seven in income per capita, California's investment per pupil was close to 98% of the national average (Ed Source, 2003), or $1,320 per-pupil, which led to a national rank of twenty-four (U.S. Census Bureau, 1976). By 1995-1996 it had declined to about 80% of the national average and in 2001-2002 it "climbed" to 90% (Ed Source, 2003). Although California in 2003 was third among the ten most populous states in terms of per capita income (by comparison Texas was number ten), it was number nine among those same states in terms of expenditures per K-12 student per $1,000 of personal income (Texas was number eight) (Ed Source, 2003). The problem of disinvestment is not a lack of resources in California, but it is a problem of political will. Latinos have not been able to develop the political muscle to lead the state to invest in public education and whites do not feel invested in the education of Latinos. The white population in California is aging and is producing a smaller number of the kids who attend the public educational system. Increasingly, Latinos have a larger proportion of the childbearing age population (15-44 years of age) (Hill & Johnson, 2000). In 2000, there were more than 900,000 more Latino children (less than eighteen years of age) than white children in the state (Census, 2000). This disproportion of Latinos and whites in the reproductive ages is projected to expand:

> "Current projections for California assume continued high levels of fertility for Hispanics, with the result being that the vast majority of the state's population growth through natural increase is projected to be among Hispanics. Whites are expected to experience natural decrease (more deaths than births) within the next few years because of their older age structure and lower fertility rates" (Hill & Johnson, 2000:7).

Local politics, especially around issues of educational policy are instrumental for achieving Latino empowerment in California. Although a downward revision in population projections for California was ex-

pected, due to a decline in Latino fertility, this will reduce the absolute numbers of Latinos in the public school system, but Latino children still will become a larger and larger proportion of those attending California's public schools (Hill & Johnson, 2000).[10] Organized Latino constituencies at the community level can effectively shape educational policy in school boards, can nurture Latino leadership, and can maintain lines of accountability with Latino and other politicians elected to compel them to represent Latinos interests. But more strategically, local politics can be an effective instrument to challenge the perpetuation of racialization and the ideology that pervades our popular culture and particularly the racializing ideology that is infused throughout the current educational system.

Ideology and Latino Education

Because of the homogenization that Latinos experience as they are racialized, this ideology of the "Mexican Problem" that has permeated Latino education in this state, becomes, in fact, the "Latino Problem" ideology. The various Latino subgroups, whether Salvadorean, Guatemalan, Puerto Rican, or Colombian are perceived through the "Mexican Problem" ideological lenses. Ideologies, tend to provide paradigms that provide basic rules to "understand" certain social phenomena. The "Mexican Problem" ideology assumes that Chicanos, and by extension all Latinos, are unassimilable. Contrary to previous immigrant groups, Latin American culture is understood as ingrained or innate in Latinos. This "commonsense" understanding, rooted in history and the large immigration flows that replenish immigrant cultures, renders Latinos, in the popular culture as incapable of fully performing to the expectations of mainstream white society.

The notion that people of color have an innate inferior culture is accompanied by the belief that whites have an innate superior culture and this notion has had an almost uninterrupted presence in American popular culture. After the colonization of the Americas a racist ideology developed as a way to make sense of the European experience in the newly conquered territories. These ideas also allowed Europeans to distance themselves from the dominated, and this distance allowed the exploitation of the "other" with minimal moral consequences. As Durkheim, the French sociologist described in his *Elementary Forms of Religious Life* (1912), humans create social boundaries that define membership. The social groups created by these social boundaries, whether tribes, nations, families, or racial groups, also create moral boundaries that define what kinds of behavior are acceptable in endogamous or exogamous terms. In other words, membership defines and labels behavior such as sex within the family as incest and morally wrong, yet sex with partners outside of the family group carry less of a moral stigma.

Killing a member of a tribe is usually an unforgivable act unless sanctioned by the tribal authorities, yet killing another human being who is not a member of a tribe carries with it less moral sanctions. All of these boundaries are social constructions yet they tend to frame what is acceptable within and without the boundaries. In some sense, these boundaries are myths that we collectively create and later perpetuate through cultural processes.

Stephen Jay Gould in his classic *The Mismeasure of Man* (1996) tells a story from Plato's *Republic* in which Socrates explains to Glaucon how in his ideal society he will have a hierarchy for people (laying the foundation for inequality). In order to have people accept their position or social status in this society he decides that a myth will be used. He will tell people that god has created those differences and that they are immutable. When Glaucon asked how would they be able to believe the myth, Socrates responded that maybe not in their generation but with the passing of time, after the myth is studied, taught, and believed it would become an unquestionable truth (Stoskopf, & Alan, 2002). What the belief basically does is it "normalizes" some social phenomena and makes it part of the "common sense" we learn through culture. The existence of poor people becomes in the mind of acculturated citizens not a social construct, a product of societal inequalities and inequities in the distribution of resources and opportunity, but becomes a natural outcome of individual human differences. Believing that individuals reject assimilation and choose to self-segregate shifts the focus away from institutional processes and lays the blame on the victims (Ryan, 1996). The structures that produce the inequality then can escape social inquiry and are assumed to have no role in reproducing inequality among the citizens of a society. If the myth is based on religious teachings then the social status becomes not only divinely ordained but it also becomes a coded way of reading moral status in a society. Poor people are not only innately inferior and therefore deserving of their status, but they are also morally defect and doubly deserving of their lowly status. This myth is then perpetuated by institutional processes, which embed these paradigmatic frames into popular culture. The educational system and all other systems who participate in socialization and acculturation instill these frames of thinking into the worldviews through which each individual understands the world around him.

In the classic book, *Killers of the Dream* Lillian Smith details her southern upbringing as a white woman. In her book she explains how this paradigm shaped her socialization leading her to accept as "normal" and not discern the meaning of the contradictions her life confronted in the Jim Crow south:

> "The mother who taught me what I know of tenderness and love and compassion taught me also the bleak rituals of keep-

ing Negroes in their 'place.' The father who rebuked me for an air of superiority toward schoolmates from the mill and rounded out his rebuke by gravely reminding me that 'all men are brothers,' trained me in the steel-rigid decorums I must demand of every colored male.... From the day I was born, I began to learn my lessons.... I learned it is possible...to pray at night and ride a Jim Crow car the next morning and to feel comfortable doing both. I learned to believe in freedom, to glow when the word democracy was used, and to practice slavery from morning to night. I learned it the way all of my southern people learn it: by closing door after door until one's mind and heart and consciences are blocked off from each other and from reality" (Smith, 1963:17, 18-19)

This "normalization" of the subordinating myth was also present in how Mexicans were represented in California. The most powerful institutions in the state operated on never questioned paradigms that justified and affirmed the inferior status of Mexicans. The ideology, constructed in the nineteenth century became "commonsense" during the latter part of this century and stabilized during the twentieth century. In the 1920s, the nation was pervaded by xenophobia and nativism, immigration was at an all time record and Congress debated legislation to control the "invasion" of the foreigners. In 1924, the U. S. Congress approved the National Origins Act, which effectively curtailed immigration into the United States. In the course of the debates between March and April, California congressman Clarence F. Lea said in discussing the "assimilability" of some racial non-white groups:

"True assimilation requires racial compatibility. Nature's God has given the world a brown man, a yellow man, and a black man. Whether given to us by the wisdom of a Divine Ruler or by our own prejudices or wisdom we have a deep-seated aversion against racial amalgamation or general social equality with these races. Members of these races may have all the moral and intellectual qualities that adorn a man of the white race. Many individuals of any race may be superior, by every just standard of measurement, to many individuals of the white race. Yet there is an irreconcilable resistance to amalgamation and social equality that cannot be ignored. The fact is it forms an enduring barrier against complete assimilation. The brown man, the yellow man, or the black man who is an American citizen seeks the opportunities of this country with a handicap. It may be humiliating or unjust to him. You may contend it is not creditable to us, but it does exist. It causes irritation, racial prejudice, and animosities. It detracts from

the harmony, unity, and solidarity of our citizenship. But to avoid further racial antipathies and incompatibility is the duty and opportunity of this Congress. The first great rule of exclusion should prohibit those non-assimilable. Our own interests, as well as the ultimate welfare of those we admit, justify us in prescribing a strict rule as to whom shall be assimilable" (Stoskopf, 2002:226).

Here we see how the problem that pervades the United States in the 1920s is not racial prejudice, that is considered almost a natural attribute of the "American" polity; the problem, as seen through the myth, are the people of color who pretend to enter the United States and create conflict. The irony is that because the National Origins Act effectively closed the door to southern and eastern European migration, whose 'whiteness" and assimilability was questioned, at a time of high labor demand, the labor was eventually provided by Mexicans entering the United States through the common border. The act, against the darker skinned and non-Protestant Europeans had the unintended consequences of opening the doors to a large flow of immigrants from Mexico to fill the labor needs of the United States economy. Then, when the Mexican population began to rise in California, the racial myth emerged strongly even in the most educated. In 1930, an economist, providing "expert" testimony in the House Committee on Immigration said:

"In every huddle of Mexicans one meets the same idleness, hordes of hungry dogs and filthy children with faces plastered with flies, disease, lice, human filth, stench, promiscuous fornication, bastardy, lounging, apathetic peons and lazy squaws, beans and dry chili, liquor, general squalor, and envy and hatred of the Gringo. These people sleep by day and prowl by night like coyotes, stealing anything they can get their hands on, no matter how useless to them it may be. Nothing left outside is safe unless padlocked or chained down" (Haney Lopez 2003:64).

This ideology constructed the Mexican as less than human, thus not deserving of respect or a space within a nation of immigrants. The characterization of Mexicans is a dehumanizing one that is rooted in a culture steeped in animalizing stereotypes and a "commonsense" understanding disguised as social science. This "commonsense" knowledge of Latinos harks back to Richard Henry Dana, one of the earliest travelers' account of Mexican California, a classic that shaped the popular culture's perception of Mexicans. In his classic *Two Years before the Mast* in 1835 (D. H. Lawrence called this a "great book") he described Californios as "an idle, thriftless people, and can make nothing for them-

selves" (Haney Lopez, 2003:63). This ideological foundation provided the justification for the expression of Manifest Destiny and the conquest of California, Mexicans were a disorder in need of the Anglo-Saxon order.

The normalization of this thought pattern was so steep in the consciousness of Californians that even the descendants of the early Californio ruling class shared these views. In the *Sleepy Lagoon* trials of the 1940s, the chief of the Los Angeles County Sheriff's Foreign Relations Bureau, Captain Edward Duran Ayres, a descendant of the Mexican landed class that ruled California, spoke about the nature of Mexicans in these terms:

> "All the Mexican element knows or feels is a desire to use a knife or some lethal weapon. In other words, his desire is to kill, or at least let blood...when there is added to these inborn characteristics that has come down through the ages, the use of liquor, then we certainly have crimes of violence" (Haney Lopez, 2003:74).

This social construction of Mexicans as innately depraved meant pedagogically, that education was limited in terms of what it could do to elevate their assumed degraded status. In a nation where education is such a valued principle, the Mexican was understood as outside of its potential for individual and collective transformation. But this ideology not only pervaded the political system and the criminal justice system, it also deeply pervaded the institution most responsible for perpetuating cultural norms in any society, the educational system. In the 1968 "blowouts," when an earlier generation of Chicanos walked out of schools in order to challenge the racist educational system, they confronted a deeply entrenched ideology internalized precisely in those who were supposed to contribute to the enlightening of Latino children. In response to the thousands of students who went out into the streets to protest inadequate educational facilities and resources that condemned Mexicans to the lowest rungs of U.S. society, a teacher from Lincoln High School, one of the schools involved in the walkouts, Richard Davis, in an open letter to the community said in 1968:

> "Most of the Mexicans-Americans have never had it so good. Before the Spanish came, he was an Indian grubbing in the soil, and after the Spaniards came, he was a slave. It seems to me that America must be a very desirable place, witness the number of 'wetbacks' and migrants both legal and illegal from Mexico. Yes, I agree that he sees himself as a 'passive object.' And therein lies the whole problem as well as the answer. When it comes to going to school—free and the best of the

world—he is passive. Absenteeism is his culture, his way of
life, always mañana; maybe he will get an education—mañana;
when it comes to repairing his home, controlling child birth,
planning for tomorrow, he is passive" (Haney Lopez, 2003:24).

Mexican were socially constructed as passive, fatalistic, violent, pro-
crastinating, promiscuous, unclean, unhealthy, and childlike, the products of both inheritance, culture and dysfunctional families not adequate
for U. S. society. Whenever they violated any of these stereotypes, and
like the students, demonstrated they were not passive or fatalistic, they
faced recrimination and repression. This process of racializing Latinos
did not arise out of the individual behaviors of bad versus good people.
Racialization was a systemic product fashioned by the coordinated efforts of societal systems and institutions. The culture those individual
whites brought into the educational system was also not an individual
product but the systemic outcome of the racialization process occurring
in all of the U. S. basic social institutions. The normative social tissue
that pervaded the educational system, for example, was independent of
individual will. In other words, liberal-minded teachers were not autonomous or independent in these institutions. Their worldview and
behaviors, even while rejecting racial prejudice was embedded in the
racist culture that contextualized their efforts to challenge racism. Individual teachers, for example, even while challenging the overall goals of
the racist educational system unknowingly contributed to the process
of racialization. In their earnest and honest commitment to stamp out
racism, they took leadership of antiracist processes and did not allow
Latino leadership to develop their own autonomous process. Good individual intentions did not exclude their actions from becoming part of
the machinery that perpetuated the racialization of Latinos.[11]

In addition to the educational system, the racializing ideology was
quite strong in the highest levels of the criminal justice system. From
1950 to 1966, the Los Angeles Police Department's culture was formed
by Police Chief William Parker who believed that law enforcement was
the "thin blue line" between "chaos" and "civilization" (Haney Lopez,
2003). White society represented civilization and Mexicans represented
chaos. In 1969, in an incest case where a young Mexican was the accused, Superior Court Judge Gerald Chargin characterized all Mexicans:

"Mexican people after 13 years of age, it's perfectly all right to
go out and act like an animal... You are lower than animals
and haven't the right to live in organized society—just miser-
able, lousy, rotten people. There is nothing we can do with
you. You expect the county to take care of you. Maybe Hitler
was right" (Haney Lopez, 2003:84-85).

Even today, in the "liberal" Hollywood culture, Latinos are absent from positive representation in the media. When there is some form of representation the most popular focus is on the Latino family (Marti-Orvella, 1997). It almost seems like there is a voyeuristic interest in understanding what are the family dynamics that engender the chaos in need of order. But also, the media (whether film or advertising) contributes to perpetuate the ideology even when it is attempting a caring portrayal of Latino characters. In order to reach markets, filmmakers seem to make an extra effort to appease white viewers. In the essay of Marti-Orvella (1997) he writes:

> "The problem of cultural stereotyping is at the very heart of the matter. In my view, it serves a double function. On the one hand, it helps Hollywood's purpose to flatten and/or assimilate cultural otherness in order to appease the fears of white Anglo-Americans; and, on the other hand, it becomes a narrative staple that helps to identify, and, therefore, to commercialize the Latino films as pertaining to a specific representational type, more often than not, labeled under the by now domesticated rubric of 'magical realism'" (1997:1-2)

So the media industry, instead of providing the masses with accurate social documents of the Latino experience, develop cultural products built on the already accepted myths. In order to capture markets these media commodities tap into the already established commonsense ideology pervading the popular culture and instead of challenging its tenets they contribute to their perpetuation. This process even leads to the distortion of media commodities whose original intentions were in fact to challenge the ideology:

> "Studios have yet to commit themselves to the grass-roots marketing strategies that ethnic and other specialty films require. And, more often than not, traditional saturation campaigns—especially the television trailers—have played into stereotypes that alienate the films' potential viewers. In their trailers, for example, *Zoot Suit* came across as a gang film, and *The Ballad of Gregorio Cortez* appeared to be yet another 'macho' western—the very expectations the films sought to critique and change (Noriega, 1992:147).

Individual efforts at challenging racialization tend to find themselves distorted by the social web of racializing institutions and the normative culture that legitimize them. The "intractability" of racism, as described by many antiracist analysts, comes from the efforts to deal with a collective and systemic problem with individualistic methods. Historically,

Latinos, and in particular Mexicans have used various strategies to challenge racialization, especially in the educational system. One of the most important challenges has been the ideology that pervades the education of Mexicans. A second and related problem has been the lack of local Latino community power exercised in the educational districts. This ideology has been perpetuated in the California educational system by school boards controlled by the white majority even in school districts where Latinos constituted the majority of the student body.

Resisting Ideology in the Educational System

It is within this context that the Mexican American community developed resistance to the role of the educational system in perpetuating their subordinate role in economy and society. Struggles around education have been a pivotal point around which Mexican communities have attempted to resist racialization and begin to challenge white supremacy throughout the Southwest. Education became, early on an arena of contestation of the white elite's attempt to keep Mexicans "in their place" that is, as a subordinate, cheap, obedient, and docile labor force. Some of the first Mexican challenges of white supremacy in California occurred in the area of educational segregation (Gonzalez, 1990). Since the nineteenth century, the state of California attempted to develop a segregated educational system for Mexicans. Initially, most of the challenges against segregation were carried out in the form of legal challenges. By the mid-1930s, close to 85% of the school districts in the southwest were segregated in one way or another (Gonzalez, 1990). For many whites, "the Mexican is a menace to the health and morals of the rest of the community" (Gonzalez, 1990:24). In some cases, the Mexican children were tracked into vocational or slow learner classes. In some Southwest schools like in Texas and Riverside, California children were tracked into educationally retarded tracks (Gonzalez, 1990; Mercer, 1973).

In 1931, the Mexican American community of Lemon Grove won a court case, *Roberto Alvarez v. The Lemon Grove School Board*, which mandated the dismantling of a separate school for children of Mexican descent. The local board was concerned about the impact illnesses that purportedly Mexican children had, and their alleged slow pace of learning could have on white children. Later in 1946, in *Mendez v. Westminister School Dist. of Orange County*, members of the Latino community again won a legal victory against segregation in Orange County. One of the four school districts that were segregating children was the Santa Ana school district. But despite the legal victory, segregation de facto continued until the present. This decision was supported by the U.S. District Court of Appeals in 1947. On this occasion, Thurgood Marshall, who would later lead the legal struggle against segregation in the *Brown v. Topeka Board of Education* in 1954 represented the National Associa-

tion for the Advancement of Colored People (NAACP) by filing a amicus curiae. Throughout this period, the Mexican community contested in the legal arena the attempts by institutional arrangements to perpetuate their social, economic, and political subordination.

School boards have become an important space to challenge racialization. From 1893-1913, the size of school boards in the nation's twenty-eight largest cities was cut in half. This led to the development of at-large city elections, which wrested the power away from neighborhood ethnic groups to have a say in educational policy (Applied Research Center, 2004). From then on the socioeconomic "makeup of school boards changes from small local businessmen and some wage earners to professionals (like doctors and lawyers), big businessmen and other members of the richest classes" (Applied Research Center, 2004). In addition to the class issue, the specter of continuing educational and housing segregation of Latinos creates both challenges and opportunities for Latinos as they become a growing proportion of those attending public schools.

In 1991, whites constituted 59% of all the students in western public schools, in 2001 they declined to 49.3% (Orfield & Lee, 2004:15). Today (2005), when Latino children constitute one third of all children in the national public educational system, and in California and Texas have surpassed whites in the state public school system they face the specter of segregation. Together with New York, they are also the states with the highest rates of Latino educational segregation.

> "The percent of Latino students in predominantly minority schools in the West has almost doubled from 42 percent in 1968 to 80 percent in 2001. It is fast approaching the level in the Northeast, previously the most segregated region in the nation. In addition, the share of Latino students in 90-100% minority schools has more than tripled during the same period, from 12 percent to 37 percent. Overall, in all regions of the country, Latino segregation has increased fairly consistently since 1968." (Orfield & Lee, 2004:20).

This national trend is reproduced in the city of Santa Ana in which Latino children comprise 91.3% of the 63,000 students in the Santa Ana Unified School District. Only 3% of the students are white. The majority of school board members until very recently were white and for many years no Latino sat on the board. Its members are elected in an at-large election. It is precisely this at-large election of school boards and how they have historically excluded Latinos that propelled organizations like the HMN to engage the political system. It is around contesting the educational policy and practice of the white political and economic elites in Orange County that a social movement emerged.

This social movement's goal was to effect the changes that were necessary to provide Latino children with a quality education and aid them in the process of integrating into society, not as subordinated subjects but as citizens. The role of Latinos influencing educational policy indicates that when at-large systems exist, Latinos have a subordinated role in influencing educational policy (Fraga, Meier, & England, 1997). The presence of Latinos in school board was found to be a catalyst for an increase in Latino teachers and for greater educational achievement for Latinos students (Fraga, Meier, and England 1997). However, the presence of Latino individuals alone will not insure continuing and radical changes in the power structure that controls school districts. These Latino individuals have to be accountable to a social movement in order to maintain a momentum in the transformation of educational policy. If there is not a social movement to whom these individuals are accountable, they more likely will end up being coopted and transformed into colorful cogs in the institutionalization process of white supremacy and the continued racialization of Latinos. The Achilles heel of white supremacy lies in the local grassroots organization of working-class Latinos. In Santa Ana, for a brief moment, there was a glimpse of real Latino power exercised, a power that would contribute to the democratization of life for every citizen.

Mobilizing Latinos in Santa Ana

Santa Ana is located in Orange County, which is one of the nation's wealthiest counties and until recently, the recipient of a large number of upper-middle class whites who were part of the "white flight" emigration leaving Los Angeles after World War II. Suburbanization after World War II was a racialized process that occurred parallel to the nation's efforts to fight racism. While Congress was enacting antidiscrimination legislation and federal agencies were implementing them, other public policies contributed to the modern de facto racial segregation we experience today (Massey & Denton, 1993). While the federal legal system was providing protection against housing and job discrimination, economic forces led by federal public policies shaped the building of freeways, gave rise to the more subtle practices of redlining, block busting, and federal subsidized mortgage financing, which favored whites and contributed to the spread of black and brown urban spaces and vanilla suburbs across the nation (Massey & Denton, 1993; Avila, 2004).

Although Latinos and blacks were finally able to legally enter most urban spaces, whites were driving out of the city on the new freeways toward the suburbs. The suburbs became the new sites for the new industrial development of the emerging post industrial society. Orange

County represented this new postindustrial white society. Although early on cities such as Los Angeles increased its white population, other cities like New York experienced an increase in African Americans and Latinos. Later, when Los Angeles began to "brown" itself through the increased immigration of Latinos in the 1960s, Orange County became the place for white pioneers. It also became the birthplace of a new conservative white culture counterposed to the white "New Deal" liberalism of the previous decades. Former President Ronald Reagan, as governor of California became an icon for the transformation of the white political culture (Avila, 2004). Orange County with its Disneyland, new freeways, and its white suburban spaces also became the fertile space that spawned the Reaganites and Barry Goldwater fans reconstituted out of the former John Birchers and California segregationists.

In the 1950s, Orange County was wealthy and overwhelmingly white, its population increased by 226% from 1950 to 1960. While it has become more racially and ethnically diverse today, whites still constitute the largest majority of the residents of the county. However, Orange County has come to mirror California's demographic transformation. In 1980, only 14.82% of Orange County residents were Latinos (U.S. Bureau of the Census, 2000). By the year 2000, Latinos rose to more than 30% of the population of the county. In the state as a whole, from 1900 to 1980, the white population of California dropped from 90% to 78% but in 1970, the percentage of whites dropped almost as much as it had declined in the previous seven decades, or 66.6% of the state's population (Maharidge, 1996). In 2000, whites only made up 46.7% of all Californians while Latinos rose to 33% of all Californians. For a state that had considered itself to be the inheritor of the white heritage vis a vis the urbanized Northeast, a heritage projected to the nation through Hollywood, this dramatic change laid the basis for an identity crisis. This demographic shift challenged California's sense of self and gave rise to a series of political movements including those related to education in Orange County. The "English Only" proposition of 1986 was the first warning salvo to Latinos that a cultural war was about to be waged.

One important battle in the empowerment of Latinos and the democratization of California took place in the City of Santa Ana. The demographic changes that took place in the state and Orange County were magnified in Santa Ana. In 1990, 64% (U.S. Census Bureau, 2000) of the 293,742 residents of Santa Ana were Latino while whites accounted for 23.1% of the total. In the 2000 census, Latinos rose to 71% of the 337,977 residents of Santa Ana although whites declined to only 12.4% of the population. Whites also declined in absolute terms, from 67,897 residents in 1990 to only 41,984 residents of Santa Ana. Santa Ana was the largest city in California where Latinos were the majority. In many ways, the white minority of Santa Ana lived in the "white islands" described by

Maharidge (1996), gated communities, or separate neighborhoods where the class boundaries made it difficult for working-class Latinos to cross. Only the small number of affluent Latinos lived in these white spaces and also shared the white worldview and politics. The cultural context for these whites created a siege mentality out of which a racialized brand of conservative politics arose. In the words of Dale Maharidge:

> "First, whites are scared... They fear the change that seems to be transforming their state into something different from the rest of the United States. They fear losing not only their jobs but also their culture. Some feel that California will become a version of South Africa, in which whites will lose power when minorities are the majority. It is an ill-founded fear because most nonwhites have the same economic and social interests of whites, but in an interview across the state I found this fear permeating the thinking of many whites" (1996:11).

Santa Ana, contrary to cities such as Tucson, Arizona did not have a political infrastructure or a local leadership such as Arizonan Congressman Raul M. Grijalva, who recently became a congressman but was already active organizing during the 1980s (Palacio, 2002).[12] Arizona's Mexican Americans were mostly native-born and had already developed a pattern of political participation and had elected Chicanos to the city council. Tucson had a district electoral system, not an at-large system, which enabled the election of community representatives. According to John Palacio (2002), Santa Ana received a large number of Mexican immigrants while Santa Ana began experiencing a process of gentrification during the 1980s.[13] Palacio had worked in the city of Santa Ana in the area of public works assisting the city manager. He had the opportunity to observe city politics and the process of urban development in Santa Ana during the early 1980s. Just like in many urban areas of the nation, housing segregation of communities of color did not take place through restrictive covenants or other legal mechanisms used during the period of de jure segregation, racism operated in a more institutional, subtle way.[14]

This is an area that needs further exploration because beyond anecdotal information there is not much research about how Santa Ana became one of the most segregated cities in California. The north side of Santa Ana became the most white and affluent sector of the city and the place where most of the political and public policy decisions were made. Just like in California as a whole, despite the increased political participation of Latinos, their influence on public policy issues is still not evident (Fraga & Ramirez, 2003). At least in Santa Ana, one of the reasons for this inequality is that the at-large electoral system in the city gives

this small affluent white group a power beyond their numbers. Planning decisions made by public and private groups shaped the landscape of the city of Santa Ana in a racially significant pattern. City policies promoted the building of condos, which expanded the white population while the low-income housing stock continued to diminish.

Even today, the white power structure that controls the economic and political life in Santa Ana has created a new process of gentrification in downtown Santa Ana. The renovation of downtown, the building of an Art Village with artists' lofts has brought white upper-middle class persons into the area and has created a powerful interest group. This group, which ironically includes politically active members of the liberal gay and lesbian community has on various occasions taken stances against the Latino community. A coalition of various conservative groups and the Gay and Lesbian network that has developed around the Art Village were against the building of a Mexican business, Northgate Supermarket, which serves the Chicano community. This alliance also has been very active in city elections and in the support of candidates who support the pro-growth, gentrification policies that are gradually "whitening" the Santa Ana downtown area. In general, many Latino merchants were not included in the decision-making process about developmental plans for the downtown area (Palacio, 2002). In response to this exclusion, local businessman Manuel Peña created the Hispanic Chamber of Commerce (Palacio, 2002).

In other urban areas of the United States, financial institutions have used "redlining" as a way to shift investment away from the neighborhoods of people of color. These practices assume that people of color, whether Latinos or African Americans are financial risks for these institutions. These practices result in a deteriorating housing stock that tends to perpetuate the stereotype that poor people don't keep up their homes and devalue real estate values. In fact, the problem is that poor people, mostly people of color, cannot get the financial support they need to renovate and maintain the older and deteriorating homes. Another practice used, this time by city planners is "red curbing," which is a practice designed to reduce the number of parking lots available to the neighborhood. This seemingly racially neutral practice makes a Latino working-class community less viable since many Latinos, given their low salaries, share apartments and own cars. If parking is constrained by this practice, apartments with multiple tenants who drive are unable to find a place to park their vehicles. Also, another tactic is that of reducing the number of city parks, a feature of the urban landscape that Latinos use intensively. For example, in 2002, a city of more than 300,000, the largest in Orange County, and with a predominantly Mexican American population has only four parks for playing soccer or "futbol" a national Latin American pasttime (Palacio, 2002). All these seemingly

"color-blind practices" are in fact how institutional racism operates in contemporary post-civil rights society. These practices serve to diminish the quality of life for Latinos and other communities of color. In Santa Ana, Latinos did not have a voice in the circles of power where these decisions were made. John Acosta, a Latino Republican, was the only Latino in the city council until Miguel Pulido was elected in 1986.

It is within this context that Latinos have lived and struggled in Santa Ana for decades. Before they became a numerical majority, they had to cope with the system and struggle against its most egregious abuses. Before the 1980s, given that their numbers were still quite small, they relied on legal means and the support of liberal whites when oppression became intense. Most of the great strides in mobilizing Latino voters took place in the last decade, especially from 1990 to 2002. Most of these efforts were attempting to develop an autonomous political process to empower working-class Latinos and to build on community networks and resources provided by ethnic cultures. In other words, ethnic culture in a racialized society such as the United States, has the potential to provide a bond and a tool for survival in a society that is at times hostile against Latinos.

Mexican Americans in Watsonville, California, for many years were unable to elect political candidates to represent them. Fourteen Mexican Americans ran from 1971 to 1985 to no avail (Cruz Takash, 1999). Even in 1980, when Latinos were close to half of the population, not one Latino sat in the city council. Latinos went to the courts in *Gomez v. City of Watsonville*, under the Voting Rights Act to request political representation. The at-large system that had served to exclude them was overturned in 1988 (Cruz Takash, 1999). The at-large system for political representation was replaced with one based on electoral districts. For years, Anglo prejudice failed to support Latino candidates and Latinos were unable to have any representation in the city government. In 1989, Watsonville elected the first Latino mayor and Mexican Americans sat in the city council. Today, five of the seven council members are Latinos.

Another important grassroots effort in Southern California is the history of the struggle of the "Mothers of East LA" a legendary group of women who decided to form a grassroots community organization to speak truth to power. With the support of the local Catholic church and community activists with training in community organizing, the Latina housewives challenged the power structure and stopped a number of projects that would have polluted and contaminated the community even more (Pardo, 1998). All of these efforts relied on kinship, gender, and ethnic bonds and the kind of grassroots mobilization that was not initiated by mainstream political institutions. A similar effort, building on the Mexican culture and emphasizing on local grassroots community organizing had significant results in Santa Ana.

Organizing the Latino Community, 1980s

In 1980, Santa Ana, in which about close to 45% of the residents were Latinos, and a majority of the children in the public school system were Latinos did not have one Latino sitting on the school board or in any elected position in the city council. It was not until the election of Sal Mendoza in 1988, when the first Latino sat on the board since the incorporation of Santa Ana in 1886.[15] By 2001, 76% of the population of Santa Ana was Latino, predominantly Mexican American, and four of the five board members, including its chair, were Latinos. Also, the mayor and two members of the city council were Latinos.

This transformation and increased participation of Latinos in the decisions that effect their lives did not take place in a vacuum. These changes took place when a coalition of organizations and individuals, led by the HMN began to vigorously organize undocumented workers, a group historically marginalized and excluded by many mainstream and Latino community and labor organizations. During the 1870s and 1910, when large numbers of European immigrants were arriving to the United States, local political machines and local governments rushed to naturalize and mobilize the Italian, Irish, and Jewish vote. However, the role of local mainstream political organizations with respect to Latinos did not follow that model. The role of mobilizing Latinos in cities like Santa Ana was done predominantly by local Latino community-based organizations like the HMN.

The HMN, according to Bert Corona, Mexican American activist and labor organizer, was founded around 1951 by Phil and Albert Usquiano, two trade union leaders in San Diego (Garcia, 1994:291). Its constituency was primarily made of undocumented workers. The organization was formed to combat the anti-immigrant sentiment that pervaded California during those times and to protect the civil rights of Mexicans. Bert Corona, an organizer who had been involved with Saul Alinski's model of grassroots organizing, and Soledad Alatorre, a Chicana organizer, extended the organization to Los Angeles to continue their work with undocumented workers.[16] Unfortunately, many mainstream Latino organizations neglected the work with the undocumented workers and focused their work on achieving a middle-class status for their native born or naturalized members.

Traditional mainstream Latino organizations, like the League of Latin American Citizens (LULAC), founded in 1929, supported the empowerment of Mexican Americans, by promoting the assimilation of Latinos as whites into the racial hierarchy of the United States. Instead of challenging white supremacy and the excesses of capitalism like the Chicano movement of the 1960s, LULAC celebrated capitalism and promoted the individualist goal of moving Mexican Americans into the white

middle class (Chavez, 2002; Marquez, 2003; Rosales, 2000). Unfortunately, this goal of individual social mobility did not challenge a faulty democratic system based on race and tended to ignore the needs of working-class Mexican Americans who would be unable to experience social mobility in their lifetime. Previous to the 1960s, many Latino organizations courted the dominant white elite by claiming whiteness as a way of ensuring protection against discrimination and achieving social mobility (Chavez, 2002). Given the fluidity of race, at some historical junctures Latinos were formally considered white at other points they were considered non-whites; in fact, this "shifting, context-dependent experience is at the core of many Latinos' life in the U.S" (Rodriguez, 2000:5). However, for the majority of working-class Mexican Americans of mestizo heritage, the formal, bureaucratic status of "white" did not change their everyday life. Since the Guadalupe Hidalgo Treaty of 1848, the "white" status for Mexican Americans was at best an "honorary status," a status that was only fully enjoyed by the lighter skinned Latino elite and not by the majority of the Latino population.[17] This focus on achieving "whiteness" experienced a strategic transformation when in the 1960s, Chicano organizations developed a nationalist ideology that was rooted in the "non-white" status of Chicanos (Chavez, 2002). This new ideology, combined with the influence of Marxism led to a combination of strategies that included alliances with progressive whites, labor organizations, and cultural nationalists from other people of color communities.

HMN attempted to build on the Mexican American culture of struggle although incorporating a class-based organization that focused on the most exploited segment of the Chicano community. In order to achieve this, organizations like HMN needed to create independent structures that allowed them the option of creating an independent power base that responded to the needs of the Chicano community. It is only when oppressed people have an independent political base that they can begin to enter into alliances and coalitions. If a solid power base is not constructed, communities of color cannot speak with an independent voice that reflects their interest and aspirations. Historically, when people of color have become part of alliances without this independent political power base, they have become subsumed under the alliance and have lost their ability to articulate their unique needs and vision. This was the history of Latinos who joined mainstream political parties in the United States without being carefully grounded in local political or community organizations that provided them a relationship of accountability and an autonomous organizing base.

One thing that distinguished HMN was its structure as a mutual aid society, or *mutualista*, a traditional self-help society that provided help to its paying members while also providing an autonomous space for

Latinos. Since the nineteenth century, this kind of organization required a modest quota and aided many Latino members in a variety of ways, from providing life and burial insurance to eventually helping undocumented with legal and naturalization services. Later, as HMN grew organizationally, it founded in 1969 the *Centros de Acción Social Autónoma* (CASA) an organization that was developed to address the day-to-day legal and social services provided by the HMN (Garcia, 1994:297).[18]

CASA disbanded in the late 1970s because of internal ideological divisions as it became involved in Marxist Leninist party-building efforts and was unable to maintain its service-providing structure. A group of young Chicano radical revolutionaries wanted to use CASA to organize a Marxist Leninist working class party. Around 1974, when the group joined CASA, the membership of CASA had risen to 4,000 members (Chavez, 2002:106). By 1978, the membership had dwindled to a few dozen members. In the course of these years of radical organizing efforts, CASA developed fraternal relations with the Puerto Rican Socialist Party, a Marxist Leninist organization, which also had a branch in the United States and a number of cells in California (Rodriguez, 1999). The PSP and CASA developed a fraternal relationship based on a Marxist interpretation of a common anticolonial struggle and support and solidarity with international movements like the Cuban revolution. Nativo Lopez, who would later organize HMN in Santa Ana was involved in CASA and was mentored by Bert Corona.

In 1982, Nativo Lopez and Maria Rosa Ibarra, his wife and a Mexican community activist, went to Santa Ana to organize a chapter of the HMN in Orange County (Ibarra, 2004). Initially following the Alinski organizing methodology used by Bert Corona, the Catholic Church served as a strategic center for the organizing efforts. Given the legitimacy of the Catholic church in the Latino community, other organizing efforts like the Community Service Organization (CSO), also modeled on the Alinski community-organizing model, were quite successful in these communities. Although, the relationship between Industrial Areas Foundation (IAF) organizers like Alinski and the Catholic church was a tenuous one, in some instances the relationship worked (Marques, 1997). Father Allan Figueroa Peck, a local Jesuit priest who served the Latino community, was instrumental in the early organizing efforts in Orange County (Lopez, 2002-2003). Father Figueroa, sympathetic to "Liberation Theology" and the concept of the preferential option for the poor was able to provide an important bridge into the community for the organizing efforts of Nativo Lopez. Also, Maria Rosa Ibarra Lopez, who had been active in the student movement in Mexico during the late 1960s had training and taught public speaking as a professor in the *Universidad Obrera* (Worker's University) (Ibarra, 2004). Her skills were important in the development of a Chicano working-class leadership

base. Providing leadership skills was strategic because many working people were usually afraid or uncertain about speaking in public and Ibarra's work provided the workers with the tools to lead meetings, develop their human potential, and express themselves in ways that would empower them as workers (Ibarra, 2004). These skills Ibarra brought to her organizing work, would prove important among working-class Latinos in Santa Ana, particularly, among women, a strategic sector that would prove crucial to the empowerment efforts of the HMN. Making presentations, conducting meetings, and speaking in public are skills that have been historically associated with higher levels of political incorporation and participation (Garcia, 1997).

However, the Alinski-style model of community-organizing, while having a radical facade, its content never challenged the kind of economic structures that laid the basis for white supremacy. Not only because they operated on an issue basis, and were fundamentally a-theoretical, but also because they avoided taking clear antiracist stands. Their populism sometimes included supporting grassroots racist antibusing and anti-integration white activists under the guise of local community control campaigns (Marques, 1997). Their role in states like Texas, with organizations like the Texas-IAF was to shift their ideology away from the cultural nationalism of the 1960s, which was then prevalent within Mexican communities, and to emphasize in a class-centered a-theoretical populism. The Texas-IAF had a religiously grounded vision of the future, which guided their organizing practice (Marques, 2003). Because of their individualistic perspective and lack of a systemic analysis they believed that "building bridges would eventually eliminate racism" (Marques, 2003:116).[19] Unfortunately, they failed to develop an understanding of racism as a systemic phenomenon, as something that was woven into the fabric of our capitalist system as it operates in the United States. In order to challenge racism one needs to challenge society's social structures, including the economic and political system with a theoretical perspective that is grounded in a systemic understanding of racism. Racism is not a problem of individual attitudes for Latinos or African Americans, it is a problem of how societal structures operate to benefit whites at the expense of people of color. Challenging racism then does not become an exercise of holding hands or building bridges but of systemically challenging racist structures and white supremacy. Therefore, the particular issues that impacted Mexicans as a racialized group were never confronted in a direct fashion as the HMN eventually did in Santa Ana. What the HMN wanted to achieve was the building of a movement by developing coalitions of interests with community and labor organizations, and undocumented immigrants were a key piece of this strategy.

Mobilizing the Naturalized Latino Citizens

In 1981, President Ronald Reagan rescinded the authorization to stay in the United States provided by the "Silva Letter" to thousands of undocumented immigrants. The Silva letter was an authorization that arose out a class action suit decision in *Silva v. Levi/Silva v. Bell*, which successfully challenged the State Department's western hemisphere immigrant visa allocation practice between 1968 and 1976, resulting in orders preventing the deportation of tens of thousands of people and the recapture of 144,000 immigrant visas for natives of western hemisphere countries. Eliminating this protection created a tremendous fear among thousands of Mexican undocumented citizens in Southern California. Immigration and Naturalization Services (INS) raids during these days became pervasive in workplaces and in the communities. Since the election of President Lopez Portillo in Mexico in 1976, the economy of Mexico began to experience an economic crisis, forcing thousands of its citizens to come to the United States in search of economic survival. Although the Mexican economy grew by an average of 6% per year from 1977 to 1979, the purchasing power of the people over that period dropped by 6.5% in Mexico. The most deeply affected were the working-class and the poor. Now, without the "Silva Letter" protection, desperation pervaded the Latino community.

During this period, Congressperson Jerry Patterson was a Democratic Party representative in Orange County who supported the Silva letter. Congressman Patterson, who served in congress from 1975 to 1985 had also served as mayor of Santa Ana. Nativo Lopez was involved in political efforts to support his candidacy, and this was one of his first forays into local politics. During the 1980s, HMN focused its efforts in lobbying the Reagan administration for a program to legalize and naturalize the millions of undocumented workers that lived in the United States (Lopez, 2002-2003). Between 1984-1985 an estimated 3-6 million undocumented immigrants were facing deportation proceedings. Achieving some form of legalization program for these immigrants became a strategic goal for the HMN organizers. Santa Ana, had a substantially large undocumented population who could not vote or participate in any meaningful way in school board elections or in shaping public policies that affected them and their families. Their inability to fully participate in the political process and their predicament of having to live in the shadows of society served to perpetuate white supremacy in Santa Ana. Empowering Latinos basically meant providing them with the means to leave the shadows in which they eked out a living and with a legalized status and civil and economic rights.

In 1984, Robert Dornan, who would later become a Republican congressman in Orange County, moved from Santa Monica to Orange

County. In 1976, he had served in the U.S. Congress until the seat he held in west Los Angeles was reapportioned out of existence. Meanwhile, Orange County was experiencing a political transformation, during the late 1970s, a corruption scandal among Orange County supervisors began to undermine the political base that Democrats held in the county. Also, due to "white flight," an increasing number of white Los Angeles residents began to migrate to Orange County and the Republican Party began to establish a strong foothold in regional politics. Robert Dornan ran and won as a Republican for the thirty-eight congressional district in 1984 and served there until his defeat in 1996. However, during the initial stages of the organization of HMN, Nativo Lopez and other activists visited the Washington, D.C. office of Congressman Dornan and received his support for some immigrant's issues. The HMN continued its work of organizing local support for some programs that included amnesty, but also continued lobbying in congress for an amnesty program.

With the support of Congressman Edward Roybal and with other white allies, the 1986 Immigration Reform and Control Act (IRCA) was passed. This act, despite its employer sanctions section, had the merit of allowing hundreds of thousands Latinos to legalize their status and eventually naturalize as U.S. citizens. In 1987, people began to apply for legalization as a first step toward naturalization and U.S. citizenship.[20] Nativo Lopez continued developing a strategic relationship with Congressman Dornan, and in 1988, HMN activists were able to receive Dornan's support for extending IRCA. In 1992, Dornan's thirty-eight congressional district was reapportioned and became the forty-sixth[h] district, a more democratic district. Throughout this period Congressman Dornan supported a more moderate position on immigration issues, but beginning in 1994, he began to be held captive by the extreme right-wing xenophobic wing of the Republican party (Lopez, 2002-2003). The Los Angeles insurrection of 1992, and the large number of Latinos who participated in this protest, created a strong anti-immigrant sentiment in California that was utilized by extreme xenophobic sectors of the Republican party. Congressman Dornan had plans to run for president and had seen how white Californians had reacted positively to California Governor Pete Wilson's anti-immigrant propaganda. Bob Dornan then decided to join the xenophobic wave and ride it all the way to the presidency of the United States. He supported Proposition 187, which was considered an anti-immigrant racist proposition in the Latino community. As a result, many in the Latino activist community began to take a more critical stance on Congressman Dornan, a pastoral letter Father Allan Figueroa Peck wrote during the electoral process in 1996 was seen as an attack on Dornan (Lopez, 2002-2003).

During the amnesty campaign, and following the Alinski model, HMN provided leadership training to Latinos and provided various opportunities so that they could speak with their own voices and experi-

ence the political process. One of the tactics utilized by the HMN was to have workers speak for themselves in lobbying efforts that included local congressional field offices and in Washington, D.C. This allowed the immigrants to be humanized, seen as individuals (Lopez, 2002-2003). At one point, in order to expand the national campaign HMN founded offices across the nation (New York, Chicago) as the outcome of its urban-based efforts to organize the undocumented immigrants. This face to face experience with the political process developed leadership skills in many Latinos who today work as labor and community organizers, teachers and professionals throughout Southern California. But while the HMN used Alinski organizing methods it also built on the strength of Mexican American culture and challenged racism in its various forms.

But the white power structure saw the challenge that the HMN meant for its continued domination of Latinos. In Orange County, a network of organizations that included the Lincoln Club (predominantly white, Republican, exclusive upper-class membership), real estate and business organizations that funded candidacies and with the Republican party operatives worked intensely to block Latino organizing efforts that were perceived to challenge the status quo (Palacio, 2002). This network of organizations was the foundation for the maintenance of white supremacy in Orange County and particularly in Santa Ana. It was flexible enough that at times it included conservative, probusiness Latinos in their midst but just as junior partners. It wasn't until the 1980s when this elite began to feel the pressure from below.

In the 1980s, the threatened white power structure began to fight back in various ways. In 1986, Measure C was presented to the electorate of Santa Ana to introduce a ward system that would enable Santa Ana voters to directly elect city leaders. Historically, at-large systems have served to perpetuate the white elite domination of the electoral system and have effectively excluded Latinos from office, even in political districts where they constitute the majority of the electorate (Cruz Takash, 1999). The at-large system, although not inherently racist becomes an instrument of racial exclusion where the electorate is racially polarized. This was the case in Santa Ana, just like in Watsonville, white voters were not very likely to support Latino candidates. The racially coded way of not supporting Latino candidates was by labeling the candidates as "not qualified." Another strategy of effectively rousing the white vote against a measure to empower and democratize the electoral process was to associate the proponents of reforms with negative consequences. In order to agitate the white vote against a ward system, a racially tainted campaign was used to intimidate voters. Some of the flyers called Nativo Lopez the "radical leader of the gang of illegals" that wanted to take over Santa Ana. One of the flyers issued by the organization "Good Government Committee" was titled "Proposition C Would Turn Santa Ana into the Slum of Orange County"[21] The Santa Ana

Merged Society of neighbors (SAMSON), whose chair was a local community activist Rick Norton, called the campaign against Measure C the "most blatantly racist smear campaign that the Santa Ana community has ever seen." As Latinos began to increase their numbers in Santa Ana, the white power elite began to use stronger exclusionary tactics to intimidate Latino voters and dilute their electoral strength.

In the 1988 election the Republican party of Orange County placed security guards to intimidate Latino voters in Santa Ana polling stations. The uniformed security guards hired by the Republican party carried signs that read "Non-Citizens Can't Vote" and were posted at polling places in Latino Santa Ana neighborhoods prompting charges of racism and intimidation. In 1992, a political action committee related to the Santa Ana Police Department produced flyers characterizing Latino youth as gang members and criminals.[22] They juxtaposed a portrait of young two-year-old Mexican children holding rifles taller than themselves with photographs of armed teenage gang bangers. The caption read: "When their baby pictures look like these, this is how they grow up."

Even conservative Latino politician, Miguel Pulido, who is presently the mayor of Santa Ana (2005), jumped on the race baiting wagon. He supported Proposition 187, the infamous effort to deprive Latino undocumented children from access to education and other social services. In a brochure for his re-election campaign in the 1990s he characterized undocumented immigrants as "a public nuisance that illegal aliens bring upon us." His flyer, in an effort to attract the anti-immigrant vote then proceeded to ask voters to support him since he would "Stop Illegal Immigration Support..." Pulido, a Mexican American and a small businessman who rose to power waging a fight to preserve his business, gradually became subsumed into the white power elite control.

In 1996, a shift took place in the political role of Latinos around the country, put especially in Santa Ana. Thousands of newly naturalized citizens were mobilized and for the first time in the history of Orange County, a Latina woman was elected to congress. Loretta Sanchez a neophyte in politics, was able to defeat Congressman Robert Dornan, who had become one of the most conservative members of the California Republican congressional delegation. The shift occurred because HMN, together with a number of other organizations allied to it, began to canvass Latino neighborhoods using Latinos who were immersed in the culture of the community, who were culturally competent and imbued with a sense of vision about the need to democratize the political system. Nativo Lopez and Maria Rosa Ibarra Lopez, like many other HMN activists went back to old-fashioned door to door political campaigning while at the same time developing an effective program of education to naturalize and lead Mexicans into acquiring United States citizenship. One of the problems facing Latinos was that although they

constituted a significant majority of the local population, many of the residents were undocumented or not yet citizens. In addition to the exclusionary and discriminatory barriers Latinos faced in the political process, they also faced some structural barriers related to their demographic characteristics. Voters who are older, highly educated, and wealthy are more likely to vote in elections (Hajnal, Lewis & Louch, 2002). Those who most likely share those characteristics are white Californians. For example, although half of California is non-white, 72% of the registered electorate is white (Hajnal, Lewis & Louch, 2002). In a city like Santa Ana, for example, which in 2003 had a population of more than 340,000 inhabitants it had only 81,906 registered voters. A small block of active white voters can have a significant effect in local elections. This phenomenon is also true for California as a whole. A study by the Public Policy Institute in 2002 projected that if present-day citizenship rates hold steady, by 2040, whites will only be 31% of the population of California yet they will make 53% of the voters (Citrin & Highton, 2002:10). These dynamics pertain especially to Santa Ana politics. Latinos not only faced institutional racism they also faced the realities of the role of individual demographic characteristics in United States politics.[23]

In order to challenge the structural and institutional barriers that historically have excluded Mexican Americans from the political system, HMN based its organizing on what Agustin Gurza has called the process of "mobilizing naturalized voters" by relying on the cultural and ethnic networks that sustained the Mexican community.[24] Also, there was a strong reliance on the organizing efforts of women and the support and resources of labor unions. Nativo Lopez, who was mentored under the leadership of Bert Corona, was able to translate the radical goals of the 1960s generation in terms and a language that would be relevant to contemporary politics. Nativo Lopez, a charismatic leader, is described by David Amin, leader of Los Amigos de Orange County—a strategic Latino organization that has worked closely with the HMN—as a person with an "uncanny ability to lead" (Amin, 2001). Under Nativo Lopez' leadership, HMN was able to maintain the services needed by their constituency, although providing the leadership needs to forge a movement for Latino empowerment in the region. But also, under his charismatic leadership other Latinos, men and women, where able to hone their leadership potential. In addition to the leadership classes provided by HMN, they also provided naturalization classes sponsored by the Department of Education and English as a second language courses for HMN members. A significant amount of the work in this area was carried out by the women of the organization.

In addition, the HMN also worked in concert with unions like the Service Employees International Union (SEIU) and the United Food and Commercial Workers Union (UFCW). Rick Eiden, who is president of UFCW Local 324 and now serves also as president of the Orange County

Central Labor Council, has supported and has been a strong ally of the HMN. Some years ago he served as a member of the advisory committee of *Union Hispana*, an HMN newspaper led by Juan Garcia. Rick Eiden provided significant support to the newspaper and the organization's fundraising activities. Nativo Lopez, in turn, has also been involved in numerous solidarity activities with the Orange County labor movement. An Orange County forum for the discussion of social issues was organized by a number of labor unions and supported by the HMN. The relationship between HMN and labor organizations does not only come exclusively because of convenience but also because of the ideology of building on both the racial/ethnic dimension of the Latino experience and class, this has expanded the network of relationships that support HMN's work and its organizing in Santa Ana. It also has woven together their network of leaders, with allied institutions. For example, Maria Rosa Ibarra works as a labor organizer for the UCFW in Orange County.

The SEIU, which today is considered one of the most active labor unions in the United States, has also worked closely with HMN. This union, which has become a national leader in organizing janitors through their "Justice for Janitors" campaign, shares with HMN a commitment in organizing those with the least amount of power in the working class. Just like HMN, it has chosen to empower workers at the lowest rungs of the occupational structure, including undocumented workers, to provide them with a voice in shaping the social forces that impact their lives. In doing this, SEIU has been able to bring Latino workers out from obscurity. Reina Schmitz, an SEIU organizer came to work in organizational drives led by HMN in Orange County for the 1996 election of Congresswoman Loretta Sanchez. Schmitz, a Mexican American woman became involved in political organizing when she attended her first labor rally as a Bonaventure hotel worker in 1986. Today she has become an extremely respected and skillful grassroots organizer. "The contract as a vehicle to improve people's life" brought Schmitz into seeing the political process as essential for achieving a better quality of life for Latinos (Schmitz, 2004).

Today, she has an extensive record of political organizing including involvement in the electoral campaigns of Democrat Joe Dunn, for the state senatorial thirty-fourth district, Congresswoman Loretta Sanchez, the first Latina woman elected to Congress from California and who gained national recognition for defeating the powerful conservative, Robert Dornan, for Linda Sanchez, sister of Loretta Sanchez and former president of the Orange County Labor Council, who ran for the thirty-ninth congressional district, and for Lou Correa, who ran for the California state assembly, all winners in their respective races.

Strong leaders like Schmitz and Rosa Ibarra contributed to the rise of a large number of women who became involved in the political process, and many of whom became elected to public office. As Reina

Schmitz argues, Latina "women fight harder for the issues that they care about, their children, they care about safety in the workplace, they care enough to sacrifice a lot" (Schmitz, 2004). One of the reasons for the rise in the involvement of Latina women in the politics of Southern California, despite the stereotype of Latina as passive and domesticated beings, is precisely their experience of multiple oppressions. As Schmitz explains about her own involvement, "I am a woman, a Latina, an immigrant...." All of these levels of oppression provide women with a worldview and a motivation for a struggle of empowerment and justice. Reina Schmitz argues that women are easier to "convince to take a stand than men" (Schmitz, 2004). She also argues that their role of mothers gives them a focus on issues of justice that is quite unique and that builds upon the need to sustain the community as well as the family. Because women face the "double shift" of workers and mothers, they also are quite willing to work harder on behalf of the families and communities.

She recalls how during the election of Congresswoman Loretta Sanchez, hundreds of janitors organized by the SEIU invested a Saturday a week during the campaign to work the precincts and motivate voters to participate in the election. For workers who work as hard as janitors, and who earn low wages, to dedicate their limited free time to a political campaign indicates the extent of the motivation that organizers like Reina Schmitz and others were able to provide hundreds of Latinos. The election of politicians is usually celebrated in terms of the politician's ability to have a platform and project an image to the electorate, but it is the grassroots' organizing drive that ensures the "elector-ability" of a candidate. This is what organizations such as HMN were able to apply from the historical experience of previous immigrants groups and apply to the conditions and context of Mexican Americans fighting for empowerment.

From November 1996 to November 2000, more than 2 million Latinos became eligible to vote in the United States, 1.7 million Latinos naturalized as U.S. citizens during that same period. In 1976, Congressman Carl Albert from Oklahoma passed a bill that impeded native-born immigrants from bringing their parents or relatives until they reached the age of twenty-one. That created a bulge of undocumented immigrants who came to join their children and who were unable to naturalize or become legal residents of the United States. By 1986, when IRCA was enacted there were millions of Mexicans, who because of the change in the law had been unable to regularize their status. By 1996, a significant number of those immigrants and others were able to make the transition into naturalization and U.S. citizenship.

While Proposition 187 in 1994 provided the motivation in Latinos about how state institutions could hurt Latinos, it was the opening of the amnesty track and the organization of the newly naturalized citizens that made a difference in the political process. In 1996, and con-

trary to electoral trends, the "mobilized naturalized citizenry" had a higher rate of electoral participation than native-born U.S. citizens (Haberman, 1998; Rodriguez, 2004a). Most previous research on the political participation of Latino naturalized citizens had evidenced that naturalized Latinos had a lower rate of electoral participation than the native-born (DeSipio, 1996). HMN was able to place itself strategically to ride the crest of that wave of newly formed citizens, and form a movement to support progressive candidates committed to the working class and ethnic issues that mattered to Latinos. But more important, HMN and its allies had been able to connect these newly formed citizens with organizations that mobilized them and created a sense of belonging and entitlement in them. As Diaz (1996) found "organizational membership has a strong impact on Latino political participation, especially among Mexican Americans and Puerto Ricans" (1996:154).

Nativo Lopez' organization, with chapters all over Southern California aided the naturalization process of close to 120,000 Latinos, many of whom also were channeled into the electoral system.[25] In many ways, this organizing effort is crucial to the election of the next generation of Latino politicians who were able to break the "Orange County Curtain" that excluded Latino leaders from emerging as independent leaders. This surge of new leadership began with the Loretta Sanchez victory, owed, in a significant way to the work of HMN and Nativo Lopez. Nativo Lopez also was surrounded by a number of able Latinos whose advice and counsel he respected and who were, at times, crucial in designing effective political strategies. According to David Amin, John Palacio thought in those days that instead of focusing the organizing on the gubernatorial elections they should focus on school board elections. This idea was developed by Nativo Lopez and he began refocusing HMN energies into local grassroots organizing to elect himself the Santa Ana school board. While Lopez' allies in the California State Assembly such as Gil Cedillo had asked him about his political ambitions, Nativo Lopez thought the focus should be on creating grassroots organizations (Lopez, 2002-2003). For Lopez, Latinos elected into political office do not automatically translate in Latino empowerment; a significant number of the new Latinos being elected shared a pro-business ideology that allied them with the elite. In order to empower the community it was necessary to develop organizations that could keep politicians accountable and develop leaders that would keep themselves accountable to the community. Lopez was clearly aware of the ideological hegemony that the political elite had in southern California and he knew that only a cohesive strategy and relationship to politicians would impede their subsumption into the elites' ideological control. Just like Rosales (2000) found with respect to San Antonio, many elected Latino politicians ended up playing by the corporate elite's game rules. Initially, it almost seemed impossible for Nativo Lopez to run for office, particularly in Santa Ana.

In those days, given the hostility that the white elite and conservative sectors of Santa Ana felt for Nativo Lopez, it truly seemed unthinkable that he could be elected to any elected position in the city. But Santa Ana, had changed and the strategy of the "mobilization of naturalized immigrants" would begin to show success.

In June 1996, Nativo Lopez became the first of the new generation of Latino school board members who would soon become a majority on the school board by the 2001 elections. The new Latino voters, not only elected the first Latina from California to congress but it also led activist Nativo Lopez into the halls of power in the Santa Ana school board. By 1998, Nativo Lopez had been elected as chair of the Santa Ana Unified School Board, the first Latino ever to occupy that position (Rodriguez, 2003; Rodriguez, 2004b).

Santa Ana 1996-2002:
Educational Policy to Empower Latinos

As soon as Nativo Lopez was elected to the Santa Ana Unified School District (SAUSD) board, he began to face the city's power structure and its allies within the district's bureaucracy. The task that Lopez faced was a seemingly insurmountable one given that this organization, with a budget close to 400 million dollars was larger than the budget of the city itself. The entrenched district staff was overwhelmingly white, while the students served were overwhelmingly Latinos. A strategic district, SAUSD represented the fifth largest school district in the state of California and its 60,000 students, 92% Latino, 3% white, 1% African American and 4% Asian, with some exception were not receiving an across the board quality education. One of the concerns raised by Lopez was the fact that according to the district's own data 70% of the students had limited English proficiency (LEP), in other words, English was not their primary language. The majority of these students were poor and from working class families, close to 85% participated in the free or reduced meal program. The school system had experienced a dramatic growth rate, during the last decade when it had grown by 23%. The students were crowded in deteriorating classrooms, while California averaged 1,660 students per each forty-acre campus, Santa Ana averaged 3,000 on only twenty-five acres, this represented a 4:1 ratio. Many students were receiving instruction in "temporary" portable classrooms; in fact, according to the district's own data, there were as many students in the "temporary" classrooms as there were students in the entire neighboring, whiter Tustin school district.

Obviously, SAUSD was in a crisis, a crisis that had a deleterious impact on the lives of Latino children who were experiencing extremely high dropout rates and a teaching and administrative staff that was not culturally competent and at times unwilling or unable to address their

needs. The political will of the white elite was not invested in the public school system since most whites enrolled their children in private schools. The investment of public monies to resolve these problems seemed politically impossible. Whites still had a significant measure of control, not only of the economic activity in Santa Ana, but also in terms of the electorate. Many Latinos still were not naturalized and even those who were citizens were working class or poor and had lower rates of registration and electoral participation. The Democratic Party made no extraordinary efforts to incorporate the new members of the Santa Anas' polity as it had historically done with Irish and Italian immigrants in other urban areas like New York, Boston, or Chicago. This is the political, social, and economic landscape that Nativo Lopez and the HMN coalition encountered when he was elected to the SAUSD board in 1996.

Immediately, they set out to do the political work to expand the number of Latinos who supported a shift in educational policies in the district. Nativo Lopez understood that in order to effect changes in educational policy, he needed a strong social movement for educational reform. This movement, could serve as a way to keep the newly elected board members accountable to the community and not to the powerful networks that were actively involved in the institutional life of the district. In 1998, coalition member John Palacio, formerly director of an Orange County leadership training program for the Mexican American Legal Defense Fund (MALDEF) and Attorney Nadia Maria Davis were elected to the school board. In 2000, Sal Tinajero, teacher in the district and initially part of the HMN coalition was also elected to the school board. By the year 2000, for the first time in the history of San Ana, Latinos had a majority on the school board. The remaining member, Rosemarie Avila, also elected in the 2000 election, was a white woman who was born in Guatemala when her German parents were doing missionary work, she married a Latino and learned English in the school system. Very conservative, she was a trustee of Biola University, which is a fundamentalist, evangelical conservative higher education institution. One of the first tasks chosen by the coalition was to build and improve the infrastructure of the schools while simultaneously increasing the number and quality of the culturally competent staff and faculty that served the district and a process to empower parents.

In 1999, 71% of the voters of the district approved, for the first time in decades (since 1970), bond Measure C for 145 million dollars. These funds would then be matched with 185 million dollars matching state funds; this would sum a total of 330 million dollars for new school construction. For years, the previous white dominated boards had not mobilized the community as the present Latino dominated board did. They also were able in four years to double the number of students attending fundamental schools, from 3,000 to 7,000 students, these are schools that have been very successful in raising the academic achievement of kids.

They created an institute to develop leadership skills for Latino parents and required translators for the SAUSD board meeting. These changes made the board meetings truly participatory events where for the first time in the history of the city, Latinos and not only whites were able to participate in school board meetings and hearings. The changes began to provide a voice for Latinos in the educational policies that shaped their children's future. The coalition created a social movement that was actively engaged with the district leadership in transforming "business as usual" and challenging the old paradigms and practices in order to enhance the quality of education for Santa Ana's children. This coalition also, in accordance with Proposition 227, provided parents with the information they needed to make an informed choice over whether they wanted their children to receive quality bilingual education. The coalition made sure, contrary to other school districts, that information on how and where to file waivers was provided to parents who were interested in benefitting from bilingual education.

From 1998 to 2002, nine new schools were approved, two of them fundamental schools, they increased the number of high school graduates, implemented a comprehensive college preparation program to enable Latino children to attend college.[26] One thing the coalition found was that when they arrived on the school board, most of the teachers teaching LEP students were not certified in bilingual education or ESL. The board then began to require that teachers working with English learners had the appropriate skills and certification required to perform a quality task. Bilingual Education scores then began to rise in the district. They also approved/created charter schools in the arts, medical professions, science and arts academy, etc. Stanford Achievement Test-9 scores increased at every grade for five years (this trend began before Proposition 227) and English instruction was increased at all grade levels. Since the dismantling of affirmative action the proportion of Latinos at the California State University system and the University of California system have not kept up with their growing proportion of high school graduates who are Latinos.[27] While Latinos are almost half of all children from K-12, and increased 34.4% from 1995 to 2002, they only increased 21% in the University of California system. The previous boards were unable or unwilling to transform a system that did not serve the Latino community well (Palacio, 2002).

In terms of the district bureaucracy, new staff that was culturally competent, as teachers, principals, or in the district offices were hired. Before the coalition was elected, only 20 out of 400 district employees were Latinos, after a few years, close to 40% were Latinos. Before, only about 10% of the teachers were Latinos, after the reforms close to 30% of the teaching staff was Latinos. A racial audit that was performed before the passage of Proposition 209, pointed out the need for "culturally sensitive" staff throughout the district. Latino parents had quietly com-

plained for years about the perceived hostility they experienced when dealing with district staff, principals, and faculty. The culture of the district, like many white created institutions was designed to serve a white constituency, not a school district where 90% of the student body was Latino and not English proficient.

Pro-labor measures were approved, which required vendors and other contractors with the district to utilize unionized labor and/or required that labor was paid prevailing wages and benefits. Employees received salary raises that surpassed any trends in the previous decade, they were provided staff development days, health benefits were provided to part-time employees working six hours or more, and SAUSD became one of the few school districts in the state who provided stipends to teachers in year-round schools. More Latino and Spanish competent principals and teachers (regardless of racial or ethnic background) were hired so that Latino parents could communicate effectively with them.

But more strategic, and what may have been one of the crucial causes of the conservative white backlash that drove the recall movement, the Nativo Lopez coalition began to bring new players from the Latino community so they could bid and receive district contracts as vendors or service providers for SAUSD.[28] For decades, a "good old white boy network" controlled contracts with the SAUSD. The Lopez coalition began to open the system and break the racially discriminatory entitlement program for whites that the district had allowed in its midst for decades. Despite the conservative "free market" theory that pervaded the conservative elites, in practice, the free market was in actuality a free market for whites. Breaking into this network was almost impossible for most Latino entrepreneurs. The coalition began to create cracks in the system and began to truly democratize it bringing new blood into a rigid white control system. However, despite the numerous progressive reform agenda items that the coalition implemented, they still received attacks from a number of places, especially, from the conservative media. The *Orange County Register*, a powerful daily based in Santa Ana, is owned by conservative Libertarians who at times have allied themselves with the conservative, reactionary white elite. This newspaper would perform a similar role to the one performed by the City of Orange, *Foothill Sentry*, in supporting the white power structure and articulating the myths that legitimated attacks on the reformists while strengthening the conservative discourse. Just like in the City of Orange, bilingual education would be the "issue" around which most of the conservative organizing would coalesce.

"The Empire Strikes Back": The Recall

In 1998, the voters of California approved Proposition 227, which enabled the dismantling of bilingual education programs in the state. The initiative allowed children under the age of ten to continue in bilingual education if parents of 20 students in the same grade make a request in person each year. Interestingly, 63% of Latino voters voted against the dismantling of Bilingual Education while 67% of whites voted in favor.[29] Historically, Latinos have supported bilingual education when these programs are fully funded (de la Garza, et al., 1992). Many bilingual education programs around the nation are not the objects of the kind of controversy bilingual education experienced in California. In fact, the conservative state of Texas was interested in recruiting discouraged teachers from California after the passage of Proposition 227 (Seymour, 1998). The reason for the controversy is that some conservative elements see bilingual education as a conspiracy to aid the ascendancy of Latinos in this state. For some time, since the debate around Proposition 187, extreme right-wing organizations like American Patrol, a white supremacist organization, have talked about the conspiracy among Latinos to effect a *"reconquista."* In other words, that California Latinos, especially Mexican Americans are involved in a conspiracy to return California to Mexico.[30] The subculture represented by this fringe of extremists has received legitimacy by the involvement of key anti-immigrant activists, who in subtle ways subscribe to this ideology, in campaigns against Latino politicians in southern California. The most recent effort was the campaign to recall Nativo Lopez from the Santa Ana School Board in 2003.

But behind the struggle over educational policy lies another factor, a clash over control of the process of assimilation. In other words, the United States, as it faces the challenges of demographic change has experienced the rekindling of a cultural struggle over which cultural profile will represent the United States as it moves into the twenty-first century. California, is already in the midst of what the United States will experience as a whole by the fourth decade of this century: when one in two "Americans" will be people who trace their ancestry, not to Europe but to Asia, Africa, and Latin America. The United States, as a nation populated and constructed out of immigrants coming out of a diversity of cultures, has always relied on a strong, systemically enforced process of "Anglo-conformity." In other words, all immigrants, whether from Europe, Asian, Latin America, or Africa are expected to adopt the core Anglo-Saxon values upon which white supremacy and the nation's civic and political institutions were created (Williams, 1970). In order to create "Americans" out of a diversity of immigrants from a variety of cultures, a process to inculcate strong values that privileged Anglo-Saxon values was created. Early in the formation of the United States, the found-

ing fathers sent strong messages about the need to assimilate and perceiving those who failed to quickly assimilate as somehow disloyal. In 1750, the flow of immigrants from Germany was so great that strong anti-German feelings were generated across the colonies. Benjamin Franklin expresses what was in the mind of many Anglo Americans:

> "Why (should) the Pennsylvanians...allow the Palatine Germans to swarm into our settlements, and by herding together to establish their Language and Manners to the exclusion of ours? Why should Pennsylvania, founded by the English, become a colony of Aliens, who will shortly be so numerous as to Germanize us instead of our Anglifying them?" (Parrillo, 1990:141).

If one substitutes the Germans for Mexicans the parallel between today's situation becomes apparent. The basic difference is that although Benjamin Franklin asks European immigrants to "take off your European skin" and become "Americans" (that is, white), the melting pot never was intended for non-white groups. Most major American institutions were created at a time when their basic goal was to serve white Americans. From the educational system to the criminal justice system all of the basic American social institutions were created in a time when only whites were full-fledged citizens of the polity. The educational system, especially with the advent of universal education, has been encumbered with a major role in the process of assimilation and of inculcating Anglo-Saxon values in the emerging citizens. At the same time, just like when the Irish arrived in the second Irish immigration wave of the 1840s, their Roman catholic religion challenged the Anglo-Saxon Protestant foundations of white culture. Their immigration led to the rise of the Know Nothing Party, a nativist and xenophobic party that also was concerned with the cultural profile of the United States. Latinos, and particularly Mexicans, also tend to be the objects of fear because of how their culture is perceived to be "Mexicanizing" the United States instead of the complete, blank slate Anglo assimilation of Mexicans.

Unfortunately, moderate California conservatives like Ron Unz, an activist multimillionaire, have found a political strategy to strengthen the assimilationist ideology by adding a "compassionate" facade (Unz, 1999). Unz is probably the only well known conservative who preceded Bush's compassionate conservatism as a tool to impose on Latinos policies, which in the long run will lead to their disempowerment and to the strengthening and perpetuation of white supremacy in California. Part of the strategy includes using religion and well intentioned, highly visible Latinos to provide a degree of legitimacy and "color" to their racist strategy. It is here where the issue of bilingual education and religion tend to overlap.

In order to understand what took place in the politics of Santa Ana, the role of conservative religious groups must be examined. During the 2004 elections much was said about the political role of religious organizations such as the Christian Coalition in contributing to the election of President George W. Bush. Although nationally, and in some local issues, Catholics and Protestant conservatives work in concert on issues like abortion, the reality is that the role of Protestant groups and organization is more strategic in issues like bilingual education than the role of Catholic conservatives. Historically, Protestant groups have taken a leading role in protecting what they thought was the "integrity of American cultural values." In fact, the Ku Klux Klan (KKK), founded in 1866 in Pulaski, Tennessee, was not only an organization that struggled against African Americans it also struggled against the perceived pernicious Catholic and Jewish influence in a Protestant country like the United States. The KKK also experienced a rebirth during the early twentieth century as a result of the large immigration from south and central Europe. Many "white" immigrants from Italy and Russians Jews experienced the rejection of the nativists and other white nationalists who wanted to preserve the integrity of white, Anglo-Saxon America.

Although white Catholics and Jews have almost been thoroughly integrated into the social fabric of the United States, Protestants still have cultural and political dominance in the United States. Within the protestant branch of Christianity, fundamentalist and evangelical organizations and sects have become highly militant and visible in the rise of the new right in U. S. politics. After a period when Evangelical and Protestant Christian supported left and liberal causes—Civil Rights movement and antiwar movement during the Vietnam War—in recent decades they have lost the moral high ground and the vacuum is filled by the right-wing conservative Christians.[31] This right-wing also have served as a foundation, perhaps unwilling or unconscious, to the rise of what Unz (1999) calls white nationalism. As whites perceive themselves becoming a numerical "minority" they also perceive themselves as losing control of their own lives and neighborhoods and see the dream or myth of "America" being diluted and stained. During the white flight to Orange County in the 1950s and 1960s, whites were looking for a pristine, "white" space to raise their kids. These immigrants were imbued with a more individualistic and entrepreneurial culture than other whites (Matthewson, 2003). The spiritual nurturance and support they needed was not provided by the mainstream protestant churches they found in California. The kind of spirituality support they needed was provided by fundamentalist evangelical organizations rather than the social gospel theology and discourse still prevalent among the historical mainstream churches. The notion of a personal relationship with Christ made sense within the individualist ethos of these immigrants (Matthewson, 2003). Also, their evangelistic missionary zeal made them targets for

conservative political operatives who could provide them with a political vision of a good and moral society (the proverbial "house on the hill") where their values became operant in the basic institutions in their midst. One of those institutions, the educational system became in their vision the battleground where the forces of good (conservative) and evil (liberal, radical) fought for the souls of the new citizens (students).

During the 1970s, Ralph Reed created the Christian Coalition, which immediately focused on the educational system. In 1970, Ralph Reed said "We don't care who's in the Oval Office, we care who is in the principal's office" (Matthewson, 2003:16). Since the 1960s, conservatives viewed the emerging social movements as bringing about the decline of all that "America" stood for. Imbued in the radical free enterprise principles espoused by free enterprise economic theorist Milton Friedman they began introducing the concept of "vouchers" as a way of privatizing the educational system. During the forced integration of schools after the Civil Rights movements many of these Christian conservatives created private schools to avoid integrating their children in multiracial classrooms. In many instances, the ideological claim that they wanted to preserve their Christian values and culture was a facade for not expressing their true desire of maintaining their children in white schools. At a time when the antiracism movement had the moral high ground, expressions of outright racial prejudice were substituted by a coded language about individual rights and individual values. But underneath that language was a rejection of what a multiracial society could potentially mean in terms of culture and racial amalgamation. Later in the early 1980s, Democrats were trying to figure out why they were losing their white working-class base to Republicans. The Republicans never claimed to be the working man's party yet, increasingly, the "Reagan Democrats" were joining and voting for Republican candidates. In Macomb County, Michigan, the local Democratic party requested a research group to conduct focus groups to begin to make sense of this seemingly paradoxical reality. Stanley Greenberg, president of Analysis Group in a summary of his findings says, among other things, that for the white participants "not being black is what constitutes being middle class; not living with blacks is what makes a neighborhood a decent place to live" (Edsall & Edsall, 1992:182). In the context of California, and specifically Santa Ana, the absence of Mexicans and their cultural influence is what makes a neighborhood a "decent place to live."

The Christian Coalition funded an organization in California called the Education Alliance, which began to select and groom conservative political candidates, which also had a religious cultural agenda. In 1993, in the City of Orange, County of Orange, the Education Alliance allied folks gained control of the local school board (Matthewson, 2003). Previously they had similar successes in San Diego County and were hoping to extend their cultural and educational policies into Orange County.

The City of Orange, like the rest of the county, was also experiencing the kind of demographic shift taking place in the state. Latinos, especially Mexican Americans were becoming a significant proportion of the residents of Orange and their children were becoming a growing sector of the student population. For example, one of their first targets in the Orange Unified School District was the "Head Start" program. This program, highly recognized for its successful work with children throughout the nation was considered a tool of liberal "social engineers" that were creating dependency in its beneficiaries. They disallowed any request of federal grants for feeding poor children or providing dental care because "taking Federal money was like taking drugs" (Matthewson, 2003:21). Needless to say, the primary beneficiaries of these social support programs were young Mexican children. Their next target was bilingual education, which along with other aspects of the public school curricula was seen as "anti European and 'socialist oriented'" (Matthewson, 2003:23). Their extremism, was at times clearly racial, as when they successfully ended their busing of Latino children to white schools, they used coded language but the outcome was clear, de facto segregation was perpetuated.

In Orange, the conservative group had ties to local evangelical churches as well as to the local Republican party (Matthewson, 2003). It is a characteristic of suburbs like the city of Orange for citizens to have a fairly active organizational and religious life. Contrary to what is happening nationwide to the civic culture, many suburbs in individualistic California Orange County, have been able to maintain a semblance of the old voluntary membership organizations that built a political culture in the United States (Skocpol, 2003). But contrary to the old voluntary associations which were racist and gender exclusive, the 1970s and 1980s saw the rise of professional organizations where the active form of participation was through financial contributions (Skocpol, 2003). However, while many liberal organizations created new think tanks or advocacy organizations, the right continued to rely on these neighborhood local organizations. From the PTA to neighborhood associations, church and school activities, an "overlapping membership between church, school and neighborhood, and dense social networks" constituted the foundation for a worldview and a culture that sustained their conservative values (Matthewson, 2003:17). These strongly, unexamined assumptions about how the world works were deeply legitimated by strongly held religious faith. This sustained a culture that provided a strong citizen involvement in a movement that was more than political it was a movement for "traditional morals and values." The combination of the Education Alliance, funded by billionaire Howard Ahmanson, the Lincoln Club, a stalwart Republican party organization, a local for profit newspaper, *The Foothill Sentry*, and local evangelical churches

provided a social fabric for a powerful and replicable conservative social movement.

One of their favorite and successful strategies was the use of the "recall" process. The "recall" strategy is an effective strategy for a relatively small group of highly motivated activists to electorally "bring down" an "enemy." Given the low electoral turnouts in local elections, the turnouts in "recall" elections tends to be even lower. Particularly, if the electoral process becomes plagued by negative campaigning, many voters become confused and demobilized leaving the highly motivated group in control of the electoral outcome. If an individual in an elected position stands as an obstacle for the development of a policy perspective favored by the activist group, a highly stigmatizing campaign may effectively demoralize the targeted individual's supporters and motivate his or her opponents into greater participation. This strategy worked quite well when conservatives wanted to recall a "liberal" school board president in Anaheim during the 1960s. He was "accused" of being a member of the American Civil Liberties Union (ACLU) and was effectively and democratically removed from his post. This strategy, was effectively used in Santa Ana politics to remove one of the most effective and charismatic Mexican American leaders in California: Nativo Lopez.

"Unholy" Alliances: Santa Ana

Ronald Unz, the Silicon Valley millionaire, had been involved in California politics for some time and was later to become an active participant in Santa Ana politics. In 1994, Unz ran for governor in the Republican primary and spent $2,322,735 (more than 1 million dollars of his own money) in an effort to challenge Republican Pete Wilson in the primaries. His ideology was rooted on the belief that if California was going to avoid a "race war," conservatives had to avoid the anti-immigrant and xenophobic politics that had plagued California right-wing politics for many years. He blamed the increasing cultural and racial divide between the white and the Latino population, not to the experience of racial discrimination that Latinos had experienced since 1848, but to the advocacy politics of Latino political activists (Unz, 1999). Latino political activists, struggling against educational segregation and inadequate educational and economic opportunities were, according to Ron Unz, the main culprits for the racial divide widening in the state. Unz believed that the racially divisive politics created by whites and the Republican Party when they supported Proposition 187 (he did not support this measure), had to be avoided. In some sense he preceded President's Bush compassionate conservatism in California. He proposed the idea that reinvigorating the institutions that promoted assimilation was a pro-Latino policy (Unz, 1999). Therefore, he focused on the educational system that historically has been the most important system that has

racialized people of Latin American descent. Within Unz' ideological framework, Mexican culture and the Spanish language, rather than enriching or providing a shield from racism in the United States for Latinos, were in fact, creating a balkanizing trend expanding the racial divide. If only Latinos would "take off their Mexican skin," they would be gladly accepted into the American social and political social fabric. The problem wasn't a system of institutionalized racism that did not provide an even playing field for immigrants of color, the problem was that their seemingly persevering cultures fanned white nationalism and contributed to racial politics. In order to aid the assimilation process of Mexicans and other Latinos and provide them with the social mobility that previous European immigrant groups experienced, he began to focus on a strategy to dismantle processes that eased the transition of Spanish-speaking Latino children into English, programs like the various categories of bilingual education programs.

Mr. Unz, later created and funded the organization English for the Children as a political vehicle to support the movement against bilingual education. Because all political movements require a mythical narrative that legitimates their efforts, Unz found it in one instance of Latino parents in Los Angeles in 1995 who were disappointed with the underfunded bilingual education program their children were receiving. He created a myth about how most Latinos were against bilingual education and disseminated a narrative involving Sister Alice Callahan, a liberal Episcopalian priest who works in the "Las Familias del Pueblo" an advocacy organization in the Garment Sector of Los Angeles, and who became an ally in Unz' antibilingual education crusade. A group of parents in a local school decided to boycott their bilingual education program because they felt their children where not learning English. This story became a way of making the antibilingual education movement seem like a grassroots movement led by Latinos and as a way of empowering Latinos, although in fact it led to strengthening the same forces that have historically perpetuated Latino subordination and white supremacy in California. The political campaign about bilingual education politicized an issue of educational policy and took it away from the educational experts and placed the future of the education of Latino children in the hands of conservative politicians. Unfortunately, the well-intentioned efforts of some Anglos and Latinos contributed to the perpetuation of a system that has not worked in 157 years. In the end, the pre-election polls allegedly showing Latinos supported the proposition and the propaganda of the assimilationists turned out to be a lie, more than 63 per cent of Latinos voted against the measure despite allegations by its promoters that 60 per cent of Latinos supported the antibilingual movement. Ironically, upper-middle-class areas of southern California were able to maintain their highly popular double immersion programs, highly favored by many whites. Some of these

programs are seen by upper-middle-class whites as ways of providing their children another language that will enable them to be more competitive in a global society. Meanwhile, few working-class Latino children will have access to quality bilingual programs at a time when they are prevalent and seen as legitimate across the United States. Recently, Robert Slavin of the Johns Hopkins University and Alan Cheung of the Success for All Foundation (2003) published the most extensive study of the effectiveness of bilingual programs over English Only and found:

> "Calling for an end to ideological debates on teaching English language learners to read, a new report analyzing more than three decades of research finds that bilingual education programs produce higher levels of student achievement in reading than English-only approaches for this rapidly growing population" (Slavin & Cheung, 2003).

But even more insidious is that the California Department of Education announced on February 12, 2004 that it takes students 3.6 to 7.4 years to become fluent in English and yet the new law pushed children of special English immersion programs after a year. More than seven years after the enactment of Proposition 227, only 7% of the children have managed to become fluent in English every year. California's future is jeopardized if this 93% failure rate continues, especially, since the burden falls on Latinos, the largest growing portion of the state's population. It would not be far fetched to imagine in a not too distant future Anglos, in high level positions in import/export and high technology companies engaged in trade and speaking Spanish with their counterparts in the growing sectors of Latin America, while Latinos, the products of English immersion programs labor quietly in the factories as they see their jobs being outsourced to the third world. The antibilingual movement, after winning at the state level in 1998 focused its resources on the last remaining bastions of struggle in cities like Santa Ana.

Mr. Unz supported the efforts of a small group of conservative parents and teachers from Santa Ana in an effort to unseat the Latino majority on the school board who came in as a result of the 1996 grassroots organizing efforts. They were particularly focused on the leader of the HMN, Nativo Lopez, in order to dismantle the movement for Latino empowerment in southern Orange County. Gloria Matta Tuchman, a former teacher in the Santa Ana school district, and former member of the anti-Latino organization "U.S. English" was one of the co-leaders in the antibilingual education initiative with Unz and was also involved in the Unz' financed Santa Ana efforts to unseat Nativo Lopez.[32] Matta Tuchman also ran in November 1998, and was soundly defeated as a

candidate for the position of state superintendent for public instruction for the state of California.

The group financed by multimillionaire Ron Unz at the tune of hundreds of thousands of dollars, accused Lopez of subverting the dismantling of bilingual education in Santa Ana. They also made an issue of Mr. Lopez receiving campaign contributions from "outsiders" and people who do business with the school board. The reality is that 90% of the children are in English only programs. This is astounding given that, 92% of the 60,000 students are Latinos and 70% of the children are English learners, with Spanish being the most common language spoken by them. The group of conservatives funded by Unz allied with Education Alliance Santa Ana School Board members like Rosemarie Avila to unseat Nativo Lopez. The recall strategy had worked before, they were sure it could work again. Rosemarie Avila had acquired notoriety in the district for her extreme conservative views with respect to federally funded programs. She was against reduced food programs and health programs because of her conservative ideology. Her antiabortion radical stance led her to attack a health education program because it "promoted abortion."

The conservative coalition was able to use a group of disgruntled Latino parents, just like Unz had previously done in the statewide antibilingual education measure, to provide a Latino veneer to a white, conservative controlled social movement. Strategic to these efforts was the support of a large evangelical congregation, Calvary Church, one of the largest predominantly Latino churches in the nation, whose 6,000 members were tightly organized in Bible study cell groups, (ironically modeled on leftist Christian-base communities in Latin America) which created a dense social fabric. Its members spanned various generations and ethnic backgrounds, native-born and foreign-born Latinos since their multiple religious services were offered in Spanish and English. But also, this church was also the church of a number of the strategic participants in the conservative coalition, Al Mijares, school district superintendent, and Rosemarie Avila, a teacher and school board member. The church provided a powerful organizing center imbued with the religious cultural underpinning necessary to motivate Latinos to support an almost religious crusade against the "infidels." The role of the church in the politics of Santa Ana is an unexplored area that needs investigation, especially, its relationship to the Christian coalition and the Education Alliance.

Republican party operatives like Tim Whitacre, initially working behind the scenes, soon became the power behind the local Latino grassroots organization, leaving Latinos as a showcase to avoid the racial message ensconced in their efforts. They exploited delays in school construction, they agitated upper-middle-class residents of the north side of seventeenth street in Santa Ana who did not want a school built

in their midst. The planned school, Lorin Griset, was designed to aid the overcrowding existing in the nearby Santiago school where 1,150 Latino children attended a school built to house 650 students. But the white, upper-middle-class residents were concerned with the flow of Mexican children that would enter their predominantly white enclave. Bob Richardson, later elected to the Santa Ana school board after the recall of Nativo Lopez, Miguel Pulido, the conservative Latino mayor and owner of a million-dollar mansion, wealthy white members of the gay and lesbian community attracted to Santa Ana by the Artist Village, and Tim Whitacre, who overnight became the white knight in shining armor who led the oppressed Latino parents into freedom, all lived in the north of Santa Ana neighborhoods. Tim Whitacre, married to a Latina, portrayed as a "pull yourself by the bootstraps rugged organizer" was in fact a member of the Republican party Central Committee. He was one of the political operatives of the white conservative movement who fanned the flames of white nationalism by saying that Nativo Lopez was part of the "reconquista" conspiracy that wanted to return the Southwest to Mexico.

In the end, close to a million dollars were channeled into the school board recall campaign, mostly for the Conservative Coalition, this was the largest amount ever spent in a local school board election in California. The largest proportion of that money came from millionaire Ron Unz. Extreme negative campaigning was utilized, Al Mijares, the school superintendent who had backed many of the Lopez' coalition initiatives turned around and joined the opposition. In fact, the *Orange County Register* seemed like a propaganda newsletter for the conservative coalition in favor of Nativo Lopez' recall. Hours before the recall election the *Orange County Register* published an open letter by Al Mijares blasting Nativo Lopez' reputation and leaving him with little time to repair the political damage. Sal Tinajero, a member of the original HMN coalition who began to falter in his support of the Latino coalition, was later found to also be a member of "Templo Calvario" the Spanish-speaking branch of Calvary Church. Tinajero seemed to be concerned that being allied with Nativo Lopez would impede his aspiration to become a member of the state assembly.

Most of the local politicians such as Congressman Loretta Sanchez and state assemblyman Lou Correa, stayed out of the recall election and failed to support the one person that was probably most responsible for their political careers. Sanchez is eyeing running for the U.S. senate someday and Lou Correa had plans to run for county supervisor, a position he holds today (2005). The Democratic party, following its past practice also stayed out of the fray and left Nativo Lopez to fend on his own during the recall election process. Eventually, the recall election came on February 4, 2003 and Nativo Lopez lost. 69% of the voters voted to

recall Nativo Lopez. Only 22% of the electorate showed up at the polls, just like past experiences have shown, negative campaigning de-mobilizes voters and the massive mobilization of pro-Lopez voters failed. As predicted by electoral experts, a motivated group in a local election, with enough resources can win against a powerful candidate.

Conclusions: What Did the Recall Mean for Latino Empowerment?

So what was this recall about? Was it about quality education? Was it about bilingual education? This recall election was about dismantling an effective social movement that developed a mobilized citizenry that spoke truth to power in Santa Ana. This was an election that could turn the clock back to the time when the white power structure that maintained Santa Ana as one of the most segregated cities in southern California, was in complete control. For many years Latino activists have called Santa Ana's social and political system "apartheid." It may sound strong, but it is accurate. Fortunately, thousands of Anglos, Latinos, blacks, and Asians in Santa Ana have struggled to begin the process to change that. Unfortunately, some, unaware of the history of Latino empowerment are contributing to again try to teach Latinos "their proper place."

Following the defeat of the Lopez' coalition, John Palacio remained on the board as the only voice of the social movement. Newly hired Latino teachers, principals were fired. The contracting system went back to the good old boy network with a sprinkling of Latinos as showcases for the "color-blind" policy of the district. The Lorin Griset school was canned, the bilingual education waiver system was made even more rigid and inaccessible to parents who wanted access to it, and new, extreme "educational" programs were introduced to help Latino children end their promiscuous sexual behavior. Rosemarie Avila, concerned with the high teen age pregnancy rates proposed an "abstinence" program that was so extreme and rigid that even her Calvary Church allies rose against it 3-2. Sal Tinajero said in a response to the press that while he believed in abstinence, "But I believe there is a need to give knowledge because knowledge is power." Sal Tinajero was probably unaware that he was in fact saying that Rosemarie Avila's plan wanted to "disempower" the kids by failing to provide them the knowledge they need to make reasonable decisions (Bonilla, 2003).

But the experience of Santa Ana politics and the role of the HMN, Nativo Lopez and the allies that worked with him, indicates which is the ideological thought and practice that must inform post-Chicano movement empowerment politics. As Chavez (2002) argues recently, the

Chicano movement was a short-lived process that was unable to grow out of the contradictions that created it. Chicanos, in their struggle with systemic racism and the process of racialization rooted their struggle in the formation of a counter narrative that was rooted in the same racializing "commonsense" ideology they were trying to challenge. They were creating a racialized identity which was legitimated by the essentialist dominant racial discourse.

The most important contribution of the Chicano movement was not powerful grassroots organizations that still remain but the development of an identity, a politicized Chicano identity. This heritage created the ideological foundation upon which Chicano studies academic programs were founded across the nation. These programs created a cadre of ideologically aware activists and organizers, many of whom became academic intellectuals far removed form the communities that gave rise to the movement. However, they provided a framework that persists today in the political leadership that has risen from within the Chicano and Latino community in California. From Cruz Bustamante, the moderate Lieutenant Governor of California, to progressive Antonio Villaraigosa, the former speaker of the California state assembly and the city of Los Angeles council member, and many other men and women who serve in city councils, and school boards throughout the state, all were impacted by "Chicanismo." But the new identity was not without its contradictions, it was a counterracial narrative to the dominant, racist construction of Mexicans in the popular culture (Chavez, 2002). The lazy, indolent, oversexed Mexican in the racist white construction of Mexicans was confronted with a noble, indigenous, artistic, almost innate qualities of a new racial construction. Chicanos, who came in all sorts of colors and ancestries were now constructed as "brown," a new brown race was counterposed to the racist representation of Mexicans. A diverse ethnic group, in terms of ancestries, and class was now homogenized in a brown, working-class racialized representation. It was a racist counter-narrative that was still within the hegemonic racist discourse constructed by white supremacy.

While the image did not receive total acceptance in the community, almost half of Chicanos see themselves as "white" in the census, it was strong enough to lead the movement away from alliances, from being inclusive it became exclusive at a time when the movement was also being destroyed from within by surveillance programs like the FBI's Counter Intelligence Program (COINTELPRO). While the Chicano movement also contradictorily served as the leaven for the rise of Chicana feminism, it was strongly imbued by a construction of maleness that was also disempowering for women. Ironically, it is the syncretic relation between the influence of Marxism and nationalism in the cauldron

that the movement represented, which gave rise to a new Chicano and Latino politics for the twentieth century.

One of the contributions of organizations like CASA and HMN was not accepting the dichotomy between the various strands that make the Latino sense of self. Latinos are not only male or female, but also are working-class, middle-class, are Mexican, Puerto Rican, Salvadorean, are straight or gay, are religious or agnostic, all ways of being that are dialectically related in a complex matrix that we have yet to understand and pigeonhole. Most of the Latino leadership that has emerged today is petit bourgeois, isolated from the community and not accountable in any organized way to the aspirations of those communities. Nativo Lopez and his coalition avoided the petty ideological squabbles over ideological purity and focused on what worked and empowered the community. Without being radically feminist/*mujerista*, women developed leadership in the movement, without being exclusively a labor union movement, it aided the development of trade union cadres, and without being a partisan political party it trained numerous members and allies who now have become prominent and rising political leaders.

But the most important contribution that the movement initiated by the HMN was three-fold, an acknowledgment of a debt with history and its political ancestors (Bert Corona, Cesar Chavez, Dolores Huertas, Corky Gonzalez), its structured system of accountability (connecting HMN leadership with the grassroots) and its ideology and practice of organizing the most oppressed. Labor unions and community organizations all served as places that connected the interests of various constituencies without erasing the real differences of race, ethnicity, class, and gender but intersecting them in dynamic and creative ways. Ironically, the movement failed because it was effective in hitting white supremacy in its economic interest core. At the same time, the involvement of its leaders in the bureaucratic practice within the school district weakened the grassroots organizing and mobilization that was needed to fight the power. Contrary to previous campaigns, this time the mainstream political forces like the Democratic party, and elected political officers that the movement had earlier carried on its shoulders, decided to turn their backs because of short-term political expediency. There is not another social movement at the local level in California that came so close to transforming the institutional nature of white supremacy, and because of that it was temporarily delayed. For an antiracist social movement to be effective, it must follow this model and share the complex vision of the humanity of Latinos that emerged in this movement. This is essential in a society that daily questions the humanity of Latinos.

References ● ● ● ● ●

Acuña, R. 1988. *Occupied America*. New York: Harper Collins.

Amin, D. Phone Interview by Aline Winkler, December 4, 2001.

Applied Research Center. 2004. "Historical Timeline of Public Education in the US." http://www.arc.org/erase/history.html.

Avila, E. 2004. *Popular Culture in the Age of White Flight: Fear and Fantasy in Suburban Los Angeles*. Berkeley: University of California Press.

Bonilla, D. 2003. "Santa Ana School Board Rejects Abstinence-Only Curriculum" *Los Angeles Times*, May 15. 2003:B 3.

Bonilla-Silva, E. 2003. *Racism Without Racists: Color Blind Racism and the Persistence of Racial Inequality in the United States*. Oxford, UK: Rowman and Littlefield.

Chapman, J. I. 1998. "Proposition 13: Some Unintended Consequences." San Francisco: Public Policy Institute of California.

Chavez, E. 2002. *"¡Mi Raza Primero!": Nationalism, Identity, and Insurgency in the Chicano Movement in Los Angeles, 1966-1978.* Berkeley: University of California Press.

Citrin, J. and B. Highton. 2002. "How Race, Ethnicity and Immigration Shape the California Electorate." San Francisco: Public Policy Institute of California.

Cleeland, N. 1997. "Hermandad Seeks Apologies," *Los Angeles Times*, December 6, 1997: B1.

Cleeland, N. and, S. Martelle. 1998. "For Different Reasons, Few Celebrating" *Los Angeles Times*, Feb 4, 1998: 1.

Cheeseman Day, J. *Population Projections of the United States by Age, Sex, Race, and Hispanic Origin: 1995 to 2050*. U.S. Bureau of the Census, Current Population Reports, P25-1130, U.S. Government Printing Office, Washington, DC, 1996.

Corwin, M. and D. Yis. 2001. "Latino Nonprofit Agency Indicted Over Use of Funds" in *Los Angeles Times*, July 13, 2001:B 4.

Cruz Takash, P. 1999. "Remedying Racial and Ethnic Inequality in California Politics: Watsonville Before and After District Elections." *Chicano/Latino Policy Project* 1, (4) University of California, San Diego.

Dana, R.H. 2001. (1835). *Two Years Before the Mast: A Personal Narrative of Life at Sea*. New York: Modern Library.

de la Garza, R. O. Et al. 1992. *Latino Voices: Mexican, Puerto Rican and Cuban Perspectives on American Politics*. Boulder, CO: Westview Press.

DeSipio, L. 1996. "Making Citizens or Good Citizens? Naturalization as a Predictor of Organizational and Electoral Behavior Among Latino Immigrants," in *Hispanic Journal of Behavioral Sciences* Vol. 18 No. 2 (May): pp. 194-213.

Diaz, W. A. 1996. "Latino Participation in America: Associational and Political Roles" in *Hispanic Journal of Behavioral Sciences* Vol. 18 No. 2 (May): 154-174.

Durkheim, E. 1995 (1912). *The Elementary forms of Religious Life*. New York: Free Press.

Edsall, T. B., and M. D. Edsall. 1992. *Chain Reaction: The Impact of Race, Rights, and Taxes on American Politics*. New York: W.W. Norton.

EdSource Inc. 2003. "How California Ranks: The State's Expenditures for k-12 Education." Palo Alto, CA: EdSource Inc.

Fraga, Luis R., K. J. Meier, and R. E. England. 1997. "Hispanic Americans and Educational Policy: Limits to Equal Access" in *Pursuing Power: Latinos and the Political System*. F. C. Garcia, Ed. Notre Dame, IN: Notre Dame University Press.

Fraga, L. R. and R. Ramirez. "Latino Political Incorporation in California, 1990-2000" in D. Lopez, and A. Jimenez, Eds. *Latinos and Public Policy in California: An Agenda for Opportunity*. Berkeley, CA: Institute for Governmental Studies.

Garcia Bedolla, L. 2003. "The Identity Paradox: Latino Language, Politics and Selective Dissociation," in *Latino Studies* Vol. 1, No. 2 (July) pp. 204-283.

Garcia Bedolla, L. 2005. *Fluid Borders: Latino Power, Identity and Politics in Los Angeles* (University of California Press, forthcoming).

Garcia, J. A. 1997. "Political Participation: Resources and Involvement Among Latinos in the American Political System," in F. C. Garcia, Ed. *Pursuing Power: Latinos and the Political System*. Notre Dame, IN: University of Notre Dame Press.

Garcia, M. T. 1994. *Memories of Chicano History: The Life and Narrative of Bert Corona*. Berkeley: University of California Press.

Gomez Quiñones, J. 1990. *Chicano Politics: Reality and Promise, 1940-1990*. Alburquerque: University of New Mexico Press.

Gonzalez, G. G. 1990. *Chicano Education in the Era of Segregation*. Philadelphia: The Balch Institute Press.

Gonzalez, G. and R. Fernandez. 1998. "Chicano History: Transcending Cultural Models" in *The Latino Studies Reader: Culture, Economy and Society*. A. Darden & R. Torres Eds.: pp. 83-100. London: Blackwell Publishers.

Gonzalez, G. G. And R. A. Fernandez. 2003. *A Century of Chicano History: Empire, Nations and Migration.* New York: Routledge Press.

Gonzalez, M. G. 1999. *Mexicanos: A History of Mexicans in the United States.* Bloomington, IN: University of Indiana Press.

Gould, S. J. 1996 (1981). *The Mismeasure of Man.* New York: W. W. Norton & Company.

Griswold del Castillo, R. 1990. *The Treaty of Guadalupe Hidalgo: A Legacy of Conflict.* Norman, PK: University of Oklahoma Press.

Haberman, D. 1998. "Naturalized Latinos Surprise in '96 Polls, Report Says," in *Los Angeles Daily News,* August 18, 1998:3.

Hajnal, Z. L., P. G. Lewis and H. Louch. "Municipal Elections in California: Turnout, Timing and Competition." San Francisco: Public Policy Institute of California.

Handbook of Texas Online, s.v. Edgewood v. Kirby, http://www.tsha.utexas.edu/handbook/online/articles/view/EE/jre2.html (accessed December 29, 2004).

Haney Lopez, I. F. 1996. *White By Law: The Legal Construction of Race.* New York: New York University Press.

Haney Lopez, I. F. 2003. *Racism on Trial: The Chicano Fight for Justice.* Cambridge: Harvard University Press.

Harders, R. and M. N. Gomez. 1997. "Separate and Unequal: Mendez v. Westminster and Desegregation in California Schools" in Marjorie DeMartino, Ed. *A Family Changes History: Mendez v. Westminster.* University of California, Irvine, Division of Student Services, Office of the Chancellor.

Hayes-Bautista, D. E., P. Hsu, A. Perez, and M. I. Kharamanian. 2003. "The Latino Majority Has Emerged: Latinos Comprise 50 per cent of all births in California." Los Angeles: Center for the Study of Latino Health and Culture.

Hayes-Bautista, D. E. 2004. *La Nueva California: Latinos in the Golden State.* Berkeley: University of California Press.

Hill, L. E. and H. P. Johnson. 2000. "Understanding the Future of Californians' Fertility: The Role of Immigrants." San Francisco: Public Policy Institute of California.

Ibarra Lopez, M. R. 2004. Taped Interview by Sandra Contreras, April 4.

Karenga, M. "Race and Ethnic Relations: Concepts, Definitions and Perspectives," in *319 The Ethnic Experience* reader, CSULB, Spring 2002:1-19.

Kass, J. 1997. "Santa Ana; Lopez Is Reelected School Board Chief" *The Los Angeles Times.* Dec 12, 1997: 2.

Kochhar, R. 2004. "The Wealth of Hispanic Households: 1996-2002." Washington, D.C.: Pew Hispanic Center Report.

Logan, J. 2001. "Ethnic Diversity Grows, Neighborhood Integration Lags." Presented at National Press Club, April 3, 2001.

Lopez, D. and Andres Jimenez, Eds. 2003. *Latinos and Public Policy in California: An Agenda for Opportunity*. Berkeley: Institute of Governmental Studies.

Lopez, N. Taped Recordings from June 6, 2002 through May 23, 2003.

Lopez, N. 1998. Phone Interview, February 5.

Maharidge, D. 1996. *The Coming White Minority: California's Eruptions and America's Future*. New York: Random House.

Marques, B. 1997. "The Industrial Areas Foundation and the Mexican American Community in Texas: The Politics of Issue Mobilization," in F. C. Garcia, Ed. *Pursuing Power: Latinos and the Political System*. Notre Dame, IN: University of Notre Dame Press.

Marques, B. 2003. *Constructing Mexican Identities in Mexican American Political Organizations*. Austin, TX: University of Texas Press.

Marti-Orvella, J. 1997. "When the Latino Family Goes Hollywood." Paper read at the 1997 meeting of the Latin American Studies Association, Continental Plaza, Hotel, Guadalajara, Mexico, April 17-19, 1997. http://136.142.158.105/LASA97/martiolivella.pdf

Massey, D. S. and N. A. Denton. 1993. *American Apartheid: Segregation and the Making of the Underclass*. Cambridge: Harvard University Press.

Matthewson, D. J. 2003. "Cultural Conflict and School Board Recall Elections." Paper presented at the annual meeting of the American Political Science Association, Philadelphia, August 28-31.

Menchaca, M. 1995. *The Mexican Outsiders: A Community History of Marginalization and Discrimination in California*. Austin: University of Texas Press.

Mercer, J. 1973. *Labelling the mentally retarded*. Berkeley: University of California Press.

Moscoso, E. 2004. "Polls: Hispanic Votes for Bush Overestimated" *Cox News Service* December 3.

Myers, D., J. Pitkin and J. Park. 2000. *California Demographic Futures: Projections to 2030, by Immigrant Generations, Nativity, and Time of Arrival in U.S.* Los Angeles: School of Policy and Planning, University of Southern California.

Noriega, C. A. "Between a Weapon and a Formula: Chicano Cinema and Its Contexts" in Chon A. Noriega, ed: *Chicanos and Film. Representation and Resistance*. Minneapolis: University of Minnesota Press, 1992): 141-167.

Omi, M. and H. Winant. 1986. *Racial Formation in the United States*. New York: Routledge.

Orfield. G. and C. Lee. 2004. "*Brown* at 50: King's Dream or *Plessy's* Nightmare?" Cambridge, MA: The Civil Rights Project Harvard University.

Palacio, J. 2001. Survey "Santa Ana Politics Questionnaire" December 4, 2001.

Palacio, J. 2001. Taped recording, December 16, 2002.

Pardo, M. *Mexican American Women Activists: Identity and Resistance in Two Los Angeles Communities.* Philadelphia: Temple University Press, 1998.

Parrillo, V. 1990. *Strangers to these Shores: Race and Ethnic Relations in the United States.* New York: MacMillan Publishing Co.

Pulido, L. 2002. "Race, Class and Political Activism: Black, Chicana/o and Japanese-American Leftists in Southern California, 1968-1978" in *Antipode* 34 (4): 762-788.

Rodriguez, C. 2000. *Changing Race: Latinos, the Census, and the History of Ethnicity in the United States.* New York: New York University Press.

Rodríguez, V. M. 1999. "Boricuas, African Americans, and Chicanos in the 'Far West': Notes on the Puerto Rican Pro-Independence Movement in California" in Rodolfo Torres and George Katsiaficas *Latino Social Movements: Historical and Theoretical Perspectives.* New York: Routledge.

Rodríguez, V. M. 2002. "Internalized Racist Oppression and Racialization in Latino Politics in the United States." Manuscript. California State University, Long Beach.

Rodríguez, V. M. 2003. "Latinos and the Republican Strategy: Lessons from Santa Ana, CA." *Hispanic Vista* http://ww.hispanicvista.com/html3/022403bc.htm.

Rodríguez, V. M. 2003. "Latinos Lost Big in Santa Ana; After a short hiatus, this elite is back in control" *Los Angeles Times*. February 23, 2003:B.17

Rodríguez, V. M. 2004a. "Republicans Develop a Three-Pronged Latino Strategy; Democrats Practice Benign Neglect" *LatinoLa* http://www.latinola.com/story.php?story=1507.

Rodríguez, Victor M. 2004b. "Browning the Greens: Building the Long Term Incorporation of Latinos into the Political System." *LatinoLA* http://www.latinola.com/story.php?story=2042. Also *Hispanic Vista Opinion.* http://www.hispanicvista.com/html4/092004rodriguez.htm.

Rodríguez, V. M. 2005. "The Racialization of Mexican Americans and Puerto Ricans: 1890s-1930s" in *CENTRO* Journal XVII (1) (Spring):5-40.

Rosaldo, R. 1989. *Culture & Truth: The Remaking of Social Analysis.* Boston: Beacon Press.

Rosales, R. 2000. *The Illusion of Inclusion: The Untold Political Story of San Antonio*. University of Texas Press.

Rothstein, R. 1997. "Where's the Money Going: Changes in the Level and Composition of Education Spending, 1991-1996." Washington, D.C.: Economic Policy Institute.

Ryan, W. 1976 (1971). *Blaming the Victim*. New York: Vintage Books.

Schmitz, R. 2004. Taped Interview by Ibet Garibay, May 2.

Seymour, L. 1998. "Texas Tries to Lure Away Teachers" in *Los Angeles Times* June 5, 1998:3.

Skocpol, T. 2003. *Diminished Democracy: From Membership to Management in American Civic Life*. Norman, OK: University of Oklahoma Press.

Slavin, R. and A. Cheung. 2003. "Effective Reading Programs For English Language Learners: A Best-evidence Synthesis" Baltimore, MD: Center for Research on the Education of Students Placed At Risk (CRESPAR) (December).

Smith, L. 1963 (1949). *Killers of the Dream*. New York: Doubleday Anchor.

Social Science Data Analysis Network, University of Michigan. www.ssdan.net. www.CensusScope.org.

Sonstelie, J., E. Brunner, and K. Ardon. 2000. "For Better or Worse? School Finance Reform in California" San Francisco: Public Policy Institute.

State of California, Department of Finance, Population Projections by Race/Ethnicity, Gender and Age for California and Its Counties 2000-2050. Sacramento, California, May 2004.

Stoskopf, A. 2002. *Race and Membership in American History: The Eugenics Movement*. Brookline, MA: Facing History and Ourselves National Foundation Inc.

Turner, M. A., et al. 2002. "Discrimination in Metropolitan Housing Markets: National Results from Phase I HDS 2002." Washington, D.C.: Urban Institute

Union Hispana. 1997. "Now Register Attacks Hermandad" *Union Hispana* December 26, 1997:4.

Unz, R. "California and the End of White America" in *Commentary* (November) p. 1. Web accessed 2/4/2005 http://www.onenation.org/9911/110199.html

U.S. Census Bureau, Census 2000 of Population and Housing, Summary File 1. Produced by the California State Census Data Center.

U.S. Census Bureau. 2000. *Census 2000*. Washington, D.C.

U.S. Census Bureau. 1976. *Statistical Abstract of the United States: 1976*. Washington, D.C. Los Angeles Times

U.S. Department of Labor. Bureau of Labor Statistics. (2005) "Employment Status of the Hispanic or Latino Population by Sex, Age, and Detailed Ethnic Group," in: http://www.bls.gov/cps/cpsaat6.pdf.

Wagner, M. G. and N. Cleeland. 1997. "Orange County D.A. Ends Latino Voter Fraud Probe," *Los Angeles Times*. December 20, 1997:19.

Wallis, J. 2005. *God's Politics: Why the Right Gets it Wrong and the Left Doesn't Get It*. New York: Harper Collins.

Warren, P. and J. Wilgoren. 1997. "House Plans to Drop Dornan's Vote Challenge" *Los Angeles Times*. February 4, 1998:A1.

Warren, P. 1997. "'Unlawful' Votes Fail to Change Outcome" *Los Angeles Times* April 10, 1997:B1.

Warren, P. M. And J. Wilgoren. 1998. "House Plans to Drop Dornan's Vote Challenge" *Los Angeles Times*. Feb 4, 1998: 1.

Wilgoren, J. 1998. "House Gives Sanchez Reason for Celebration" *Los Angeles Times*. February 5, 1998:1

Williams, R. M. 1970. *American Society: A Sociological Interpretation*. New York: Knopf.

Wilson, W. J. 1996. *When Work Disappears*. New York: Norton.

Endnotes ● ● ● ● ●

1. I want to thank Nativo Lopez, John Palacio, Maria Rosa Ibarra, Reina Schmitz, Linda Sanchez, David Amin, and other anonymous informants for sharing their experiences in the Latino political movement in south Orange County. I also want to thank my research assistants Brenda Quintero, Ibet Garibay, Aline Winkler, and Sandra Contreras for supporting my efforts to gather and transcribe these grassroots perspectives of an important process of Latino empowerment.

2. White supremacy refers not to individuals but to a system created by the process of racialization (Rodriguez, 2005).

3. In the 2003 elections in California Latinos represented a good percentage, 31% of the voters, electing Gov. Arnold Schwarzenegger. More recently, in November 2004, according to exit polls, 40% of Latinos supported President Bush's electoral victory, which was less than originally estimated by exit polls but still five points higher than in 2000 (Moscoso, 2004).

4. In 1997, Maria Rosa Ibarra, wife of Nativo Lopez and her twelve-year old daughter had to leave for Guanajuato, Mexico for medical treatment and to escape the levels of stress on the family.

5. Since the Treaty of Guadalupe Hidalgo conferred U.S. citizenship to Mexican Americans, they became defacto "honorary whites" and

able to legally participate in the electoral process. In some areas of the nation, Mexicans were excluded from voting through polling taxes, literacy taxes, and coercion, in other areas they were able to vote through the manipulation of local political machines. These political machines, for example, paid the poll taxes for the voters and required their vote for particular white political candidates. In this fashion, the Mexican vote was "delivered" to a white candidate perpetuating white supremacy and thus not enabling the empowerment of Latinos.

6. Most of the early Anglo immigrants into the Southwest were men who sought new avenues of upward mobility. Many Anglos married into the Mexican elite by marrying their daughters. In Arizona, for example, between 1872 and 1899, intermarriage remained high, with 148 of 784, or 14% of all marriages, being between Anglo men and Mexican females; during the same period only six involved Mexican men and Anglo women (Acuña,1988:89). In California, a similar process occurred, in some ways it was a way, for the Anglo elite to assure an incontestable "white" status for their progeny (Acuña, 1988:116-118)

7. In 1964, after the Civil Rights Act was enacted, California voters passed, two against one, Proposition 14, which was designed to overturn federal housing anti discrimination laws. Eventually the courts found the proposition unconstitutional (Maharidge, 1996).

8. Recent studies indicate the extent of the racial gap between whites and Latinos. Latinos have 10 cents out of every dollar of wealth whites have (Rakesh, 2004), they still experience strong rates of housing discrimination (Turner, et al. 2002); residential segregation of Latinos has increased (Logan, 2001) and Latino children experience very high rates of segregation, particularly in the area where they are the largest ethnic group, the west (Orfield & Lee 2004).

9. Proposition 13, or the Jarvis-Gann proposition (name of the antitax proponents) was an initiative measure approved by California voters in 1978. The prices of homes had increased and a shift in the tax burden from business to individuals had strained many individual tax payers. Proposition 13 was thought to be just populist tax relief reform, limiting the property tax rate to 1% of the property value and keeping the property value at its 1975-1976 value, this would only change if the property was sold. But the eventual outcomes of this measure was far broader than expected, from facilitating gentrification measures, to raise property taxes to, development of other complex tax revenue measures like Mello-Roos Act 1886 and perhaps more strategically, shifting the power of rasing revenues from the local communities to the state. " Between Serrano and 1978, the state became more heavily involved in school finance and complex formulas considering both foundation support and revenue lim-

its. Although school districts did have limited ability to raise the property tax, it was clear that any property tax reform passed by the legislature would have to deal with a non-property tax school finance plan" (Chapman, 2000:18).

10. A recent study by Myers, Pitkin & Park (2005) also indicates that in addition to the slowing of Latino population growth, the relative weight of the foreign born population within the Latino community will also decline. They point at the increasing social (and political) weight of the rising second generation of Latinos. This will have important but yet unexplored consequences for the educational and the political system in California. The generation that engendered the Chicano Movement was predominantly second and third generation Mexican Americans, not foreign-born.

11. The La Raza Unida Party with Jose Angel Gutierrez (Texas and California), Rudolfo "Corky" Gonzalez Crusade for Justice (Colorado) and Reies Lopez Tijerina's Alianza Federal de las Mercedes (New Mexico) were efforts to create politically and culturally autonomous movements to develop Chicano leadership. Even Cesar Chavez' farm workers' movement in California was increasingly dependent on the Liberal white political structure and developed contradictory policies (initially failing to organize undocumented workers) because of its lack of autonomy.

12. In addition to CASA MeChA (Movimiento Estudiantil Chicano de Aztlan) was also active in Santa Ana and some arrests were made during 1970 and 1971 (Lopez, 2002-2003).

13. Today (2005), John Palacio sits on the Santa Ana School District Board, he was elected in 1998 and has been a close ally of Nativo Lopez and the Hermandad Mexicana Nacional efforts for Latino empowerment. He grew up in Arizona where he became involved in public policy issues and public service. He also was a participant in the drafting of a new Santa Ana city charter in the 1980s.

14. From 1950 through 1968, restricted covenants in Santa Ana maintained the northern part of Santa Ana white. Close to 60% of the residents in this area in 2002 were white and the remainder included a good number of conservative Republican, upper middle class Latinos.

15. According to Nativo Lopez and David Amin, there was a Latino, Rudy Montejano who sat on the School Board in the 1970s. This has not been confirmed by any official source.

16. Saul Alinski was a radical union organizer who founded the Industrial Areas Foundation (IAF), Chicago, the organization's goal was to train a generation of community organizers throughout the region. Alinski, who died in 1972 was also is a writer, one of his most well known books, *Rules for Radicals* became an organizers manual.

His organizing motto was "Agitate + Aggravate + Educate + Organize." He was strongly anticommunist and used Catholic parishes as organizing centers in working-class communities. He also tried to focus on class issues and not bring race into his organizing because he thought this would divide working people.

17. The Treaty of Guadalupe Hidalgo, which legally ended hostilities between the United States and Mexico in 1848, also granted U. S. citizenship to all of the approximately 100,000 Mexicans who remained in the newly conquered territories. This was an anomaly because the Naturalization Act of 1790 and the 1789 constitution had established "whiteness" as a precondition for full membership in the United States body politic. Only a small fraction of the Mexican population, the light skinned elite was able to fully enjoy the full benefits of U.S. citizenship. In fact, even some darker skinned members of the Californio elite, like Manuel Domínguez, one of the signers of the California constitution, lost his honorary status as white after a few years (Acuña, 1988).

18. CASA had a branch in Santa Ana that lasted approximately from 1973-1976, its leader was Alex Garza (Lopez, 2002-2003).

19. Despite its anticommunist history, the IAF's focus on class at the expense of race and ethnicity, led them to fall in the Marxist deterministic theory of looking at race as epiphenomenal, that is, with no independent life from economic interests or practice.

20. The Immigration Reform and Control Act of 1986 required that immigrants provide evidence of their continued residence in the United States until 1982, those who came after that date would not be eligible. HMN lobbied to bring the date until 1986 but was unable to get congress to agree to that date. Since 1976, there was a long waiting list of people wanting to migrate legally to the United States but were held back by a change in U.S. law that did not allow United States' born children the right to bring their parents until they were twenty-one years of age. This created a very huge backlog of Mexican parents wanting to rejoin their U.S.-born children.

21. The author has an archive of racist flyers and propaganda distributed during this electoral process.

22. The author has an archive with examples of the racist flyers. To contrast the Chicano children photo they used a color photo of white children who are shown engaging in normal activities, and a black and white photo of Chicano children brandishing weapons is used with a caption saying these might be future gangsters.

23. These demographic factors are not universal determinants for electoral participation, even when they operate as such in the U. S. electoral process. For example, in Puerto Rico, an unincorporated territory of the United States, 80% of registered voters participate in the electoral process irrespective of class, education and race.

24. Agustin Gurza, a *Los Angeles Times* columnist and observer of Latino politics coined this term.

25. According to Fraga and Ramirez (2003) from 1994 to 2000, close to 1,084 Latinos, or close to 46% of all Latinos voters in the state became registered, 44% were born outside of the United States. This indicates the importance of the process of naturalization and the mobilization of these voters. The majority of these voters registered as Democrats, close to 42% registered in Los Angeles County alone and one third had incomes less than $20,000. Southern California, San Francisco's Bay Area, and the Central Valley experienced the highest regional Latino voter turnout.

26. The apartheid system in Santa Ana functioned through the segregated nature of the small number of fundamental schools, these schools, which had the best resources and offered best education was where the majority of the 3% white enrollment in SAUS attended school.

27. The State of California has a three tier-system of higher education, beginning with the community colleges where vocational and college preparation for four-year universities is provided, the California State University system with 26 campuses which prepares students in education, Liberal Arts and where students can achieve a master degree in many fields to the University of California system which are the research institutions and the only ones to independently provide doctoral programs in a variety of fields.

28. According to John Palacio (2002) less than 1% of the 350 million dollars in business contracts created by the district were received by Latino entrepreneurs. Superintendent Al Mijares, hired a consultant 1998-1999 to study the district's contracting system and found a lack of diversity in the system.

29. The racial disparities in the voting patterns between whites and Latinos was clear also on Proposition 209 (to dismantle Affirmative Action) and Proposition 187 (to exclude undocumented immigrants from receiving social services from the state). In all of these initiatives Latinos voted overwhelmingly against them while whites voted overwhelmingly in favor of them.

30. This organization is considered a hate group by the Intelligence Project of the Southern Poverty Law Center, their link http://www.americanpatrol.com/ includes strident anti-Mexican propaganda and conspiracy theories.

31. Recently, Jim Wallis (2005), a left wing Evangelical theologian, has called for liberal and leftist Christians to reclaim the contested terrain of public discourse on social issues and has chastised the secularism that pervades much of liberal and left politics. He harshly criticizes the Democratic party for failing to argue on moral and ethi-

cal grounds issues of economic justice and antiwar issues around the recent war in Iraq.

32. Dr. John Stanton, former president of U.S. English made these racist statements that were revealed in an *Arizona Republic* article on a confidential memo he wrote: "Gobernar es poblar translates 'to govern is to populate.' In this society where the majority rules, does this hold? Will the present majority peaceably hand over its political power to a group that is simply more fertile?... Can homo contraceptivus compete with homo progenitiva [sic] if borders aren't controlled? Or is advice to limit one's family simply advice to move over and let someone else with greater reproductive powers occupy the space?... Perhaps this is the first instance in which those with their pants up are going to get caught by those with their pants down!..."

● ● ● ● ● ● ● ● ● ● ● ● ● ● ● ● ● ●

¡Ni Una Bomba Más!: Racialization and Memory in the Vieques Social Movement[1]

Abstract

Despite decades of colonialism, racialization and oppression, the Viequense social movement developed a series of collective tactics, alliances and a collective memory of the experience of colonial oppression and resistance that aided the movement in capturing the imagination of thousands of people all over the world. Through its combination of creative nonviolent tactics and other forms of resistance it was able to reveal the violence of the U. S. armed forces, and enabled the movement to gain the high moral ground versus the U. S. Navy. Unlike any previous Puerto Rican liberation movement it was able to help the coalescence of civil society in support of its goals. The movement brought together, for the first time in Puerto Rico's political history, religious leaders, federal employees, socialists, lawyers, teachers, artists, congress-persons, retired persons, liberal and conservatives, pro-statehood supporters, and nationalists, all of whom found themselves together, marching, protesting, and willing to be arrested in acts of nonviolent civil disobedience. This essay places the  Viequense struggle to end naval bombardment in their island within a transnational theory of racialization. It will explore the role of race, class and gender in the development of the movement and will describe the

process by which Puerto Rico and Vieques were colonized and racialized within the context of U.S. imperial expansion. Finally, with the use of primary and secondary materials it will explore the formation of a narrative of oppression that resonated with a variety of sectors and how this recollection of the past led to the development of a new sense of self that challenges racialization and colonization.

> "The reality is quite plain, the "end of the era of nationalism," so long prophesied, is not remotely in sight. Indeed, nation-ness is the most universally legitimate value in the political life of our time."
>
> Benedict Anderson, *Imagined Communities*, (1991)

Introduction

On May 1, 2003, after decades of naval bombardment, environmental degradation, accidental deaths, rising rates of cancer in the local population, decades of struggle and pain, the people of Vieques, and the social movement they constructed, forced the most powerful navy in the world to end the military use of their island. Most of the two thirds of Vieques controlled by the U.S. Navy since the 1940s was transferred to the U.S. Fish and Wildlife Service, a bureau of the U.S. Department of the Interior.

Since 1941, Viequenses experienced the intensification of a gradual process of marginalization and intense racialization that expanded the dispersion of the Viequenses through the Caribbean and the United States creating an echo of the Puerto Rican diaspora. The occupation of Vieques by the U.S. Navy and the expropriation of two-thirds of the land led to the confinement of the population to a small slice of land, representing one-third of the island's area. The "civilian area" where the Viequenses were allowed to live was bookended on the east by land used for target practice by airplanes, artillery, and sharpshooters and in the west, by bunkers where ordnance and chemical weapons were stored. Despite an experience of racialization and subordination, a powerful grassroots community social movement became globalized and thus able to challenge the ideological might of the last remaining modern empire. Viequenses, were able to remember who they were and were able to affirm their own humanity and politically challenge, not only military institutions but also their own notion of who they were, and in the process developed a new sense of self. Presently, they are using this new identity to rebuild the "imagined community" they dreamed of, in a concrete way.

"Lo peor de todo era la memoria y el sentirse tan insignificante, hambriento y llagado en una isla de tantas que Dios debió de hacer una de esas noches en que discutía con el Diablo." ("The worst of it all was remembering and feeling so insignificant, hungry and injured in one of those islands God must have created one of those nights when he argued with the Devil.")

Viequense Novel, *USMAÍL*, Pedro Juan Soto

Racialization, Ideology and Imperialism

Empires are built and maintained not only through might and power but also by the power of myth and signification. The nature of empire and colonization have experienced a significant shift since the nineteenth century British model of an empire. Today, empires are not only built through military might, they are also constructed through economic external control (through debt or external investment) and by creating cultures that legitimize subordination and external control. Empires have always relied on ideology to justify their conquests, whether through a civilizing project like the Roman and the British empire building processes, that included a moral responsibility, the "white man's burden" in the British case, or "manifest destiny" in the United States' historical experience. The notion that populations outside of the metropolis were chaos in need of order, provides a philanthropic veneer to imperialism, after all, like British D'Israeli's said in 1872, this is done "not for our glory, but for their happiness." However, what has not been thoroughly examined until the work of Fannon (1986), Memmi (1991) and Cesaire (2000) is how the process of modern empire building is also a process of racialization. The content of colonization as it developed in modern imperialism is a process of racialization that internalizes in the colonized a racial, stigmatized sense of self that contributes to the perpetuation of imperial control. From Hobson to Lenin and other classic Marxists and non-Marxists alike, including Magdoff (1969), the focus was on the economic basis of imperialism. With the development of the antiracist movement in the United States from the 1960s until today, the focus shifted away from imperialism and onto domestic racism. Some, like Aronowitz (1991) and Gitlin (1996) have incorrectly called the antiracist movement "identity politics" when in fact most antiracists are neo-marxists and see imperialism as the foreign policy of a racist state (Rodriguez, 2005).

As Magdoff (2003) noted, the word imperialism disappeared from polite discourse and is returning into political analysis not from the left but from the right. From Zbigniew Brzezinski to Henry Kissinger, main-

stream conservative political analysts don't fret about using the term empire in the same sentence together with the United States. But imperialism disappeared from political discourse after the decline of the new left, when many of its members disappeared from the streets and ended in the ivory tower of academia or ensconced in middle-class and upper-middle-class niches. This meant that they were, for the most part, relatively disconnected from popular struggles, so that empire and imperialism became the work of ivory tower academicians and not the praxis connected work of non-academic intellectuals (Jacoby, 2000). A significant segment of the contemporary work of "post-colonial" theorists, so popular in academic today, has focused on some of these processes but in many instances with no theoretical continuity to the important work done by Marxists. In their total rejection of Marxism's closed system and economic determinism, a body of significant work in the area of imperialism was not brought to bear on contemporary analyses of imperialism. Also, unfortunately, much post-colonial theory is written in a language that excludes, obfuscates, and therefore cannot connect with social movements and their intellectuals.

One important contribution of the work of these classical Marxists, beginning with Lenin (1969), who argued that not only was capitalism and imperialism linked but that imperialism *was* capitalism in the period under analysis. Lenin contrasted monopoly capitalism with the competitive capitalism that has created powerful nations such as Great Britain and the United States and the kind of socio-economic formation that was leading to underdevelopment and subordination in the colonies beginning in the late nineteenth century (Rodriguez, 1987). Recent historical and theoretical work is developing a more nuanced description of the mechanisms of imperialism (Gonzalez & Fernandez, 2003). One of the ways in which capitalism began to operate outside of its economic and political borders in this qualitatively different phase was through what Gonzalez & Fernandez (2003) call the 'transnational mode of imperial control." Instead of direct control of the colonized nations (classic colonialism) more subtle yet effective methods of control were used. One of the first instances of this new and evolving mode of imperial control was exercised in Mexico under the dictatorship of Porfirio Diaz (1876-1911). This new transnational mode of imperial control follows the description of U.S. Secretary of State John Foster Dulles: "there are two ways of dominating a foreign nation: invading it militarily or controlling it financially" (Gonzalez & Fernandez, 2003:30). But one aspect that needs to be highlighted in this new form of empire-building process is the role of institutional arrangements which lead to cultural transformations in the colonized spaces. The British in India were not interested in changing Indian culture and traditions, or in transferring

"democratic" institutions, their interest was control and economic exploitation. The new forms of transnational imperial control use a variety of means that include military, financial and ideological control. Puerto Rico and Vieques are current models of the level of development of this new mode of empire building in the twentieth century. Although in political terms Puerto Rico is a "classic" colony, its relative degree of economic and political development, albeit colonial, fits more into the category of a nation where the classic colonial mode of control coexists with a transnational mode of imperial control. The principal means of control of Puerto Rico today is not brutal force, but through the subtle mechanisms of financial and economic control and the development of a consumeristic society tied to United States aspirations and culture. But it is in Vieques where the classic colonial nature of imperial control was more salient. For this reason, the struggle in Vieques had a double character: an anti-colonial struggle (to expand the realm of choice and political and economic freedom) and antiracist (challenging the racialization of Viequenses).

But racialization is not merely a process of economic and political subordination; it is also a process of signification. The construction of meaning is used to create and legitimize racially stratified systems which perpetuate the control of colonized and racialized populations. To achieve this level of control, the colonizer creates institutional arrangements that reproduce imperial power by internalizing in its subjects its own self-congratulatory narratives and substituting those for their own memory and history. These institutions socialize the colonized to question its own self-worth and human value and lead them to contribute to their own dehumanization. The dynamics of imperial power and control in the colonized space becomes submerged in an ideological fog, which masks how it serves the empire; the structure and the objective of domination seem opaque to the colonized. Passivity, acquiescence, and adaptation, vis a vis the colonizer, flow out as a response to a failure to recognize and discern the final objective of domination and of a magnified perception of the power of the colonizer. Fatalism, while not inherent to the colonized, is taught and reinforced by structures designed to perpetuate domination and control. Vieques, as the Viequense novelist Pedro Juan Soto describes in the epigraph, was not envisioned as the object of U.S. military oppression but as a people condemned by God and destiny to a life of wretchedness and pain. A racially stigmatized sense of self is super-imposed on the sense of self of the racialized subject and his sense of powerlessness is magnified as is the power of the oppressor. This process of internalization leads to the perpetuation of white supremacy.

While the ideological underpinnings of colonization and racialization have been described as crucial for colonial domination, the way in which anti-colonial, anti-oppressive social movements create meaning to challenge these ideologies needs further analysis (Cesaire, 2000; Fannon, 1986; Rodriguez, 2005). It is through a praxis that involves memory and self definition that allows social movements to challenge the cultures of empire and domination. This analysis becomes both a scholarly and a political task given the resurgence and legitimacy of ideological notions of empire and global uni polarity. As we begin another century, a new phase in U.S. empire building is being revealed to the world. The United States has unveiled a new "calling" to defend peace and extend its civilization and the "blessings of liberty" by waging war. In order to achieve that objective in a multiracial society it has refined its ideological efforts to subsume racialized groups like Latinos in order to further strengthen white supremacy (Bonilla-Silva & Glover, 2003). Some of the ideological tools were utilized with some success in colonial spaces like Puerto Rico and Vieques.

At the beginning of the twentieth century, the United States waged another war, the Cuban-Spanish American War of 1898, to purportedly bring the benefits of democracy and civilization to the new possessions: Puerto Rico, Cuba, and the Phillippines. Just like in contemporary imperial adventures, there were the underdogs that were marketed to the North American public just as Somalia, Bosnia and Iraq were recently represented as nations that needed to be rescued. In flyers reminiscent of the propaganda distributed over the skies of Iraq before the 2003 war, another general, General Nelson Miles, told the people of Puerto Rico:

> " We have not come to make war upon the people of a country that for centuries has been oppressed but on the contrary to bring you protection...to promote your prosperity, and to bestow upon you the immunities and blessings of the liberal institutions of our government" (Rivero, 1972:502).

While history does not necessarily repeat itself, in the *18ᵗʰ Brumaire of Louis Bonaparte*, Karl Marx says, "Hegel remarks somewhere that all great world-historic facts and personages appear, so to speak, twice. He forgot to add: the first time as tragedy, the second time as farce." However, this time around, the farce has no comedic content. In the Caribbean, where modern empires began 500 years ago, a new page in a new century is being written. The 10,000 citizens of Vieques defeated the mighty U.S. Navy and won the first stage in their struggle for peace and their right to define themselves. David did defeat Goliath in what is another chapter of anti-empire movements that have a long history in this part of the Americas.

The Caribbean for centuries was the stage for many historical events that have shaped the world as we know it. The first major encounter between the two civilizations that shaped America, took place as Christopher Columbus, lost on his journey to India, was discovered by the indigenous people of Guanahani, in what today are the Bahamas. Columbus, in a second trip to the Americas, landed on the shores of Puerto Rico in 1493. The Tainos, the indigenous people of the Caribbean, initially thought the Europeans were deities. In that epic of conquest, the Spaniards also represented their war of domination as an endeavor to uplift the "savages" from ignorance and heathenism. But the Spanish were to eventually "liberate" the Tainos of their gold, their land, and even their lives using symbolic tools like the "Requerimiento" to provide a legitimate facade to a war of conquest and pillage.[2] In exchange, the indigenous people would be Christianized and placed in "encomiendas," a system of indentured servanthood much akin to slavery. They would be deprived of their liberty on earth but they would be promised their eternal freedom in heaven.

The cruelty of the Spanish served to challenge any notion that they were godly emissaries. It was also in the Caribbean, where the first anti-imperialist mass movement began. But this effort could not have been conducted if the Spaniards were thought of as supernatural beings. On November 1510, in the Guaorabo River of Puerto Rico, the Tainos set about to carry out the first empirical test of an ideology held in the Americas. The Tainos wanted to know if, in fact, the Spanish were immortal (Scarano, 1993:177-178). That day, the Tainos drowned a Spanish soldier called Diego de Salcedo. The news of the death of the Spaniard spread across the island like a wildfire. Later next year, in 1511, Agueybana II, Taino leader of Puerto Rico, led a rebellion against Ponce de Leon, the Spanish governor. While the Tainos were eventually defeated, they learned that the Spaniards were mortals like them. But the Spanish empire lasted 500 years more until, during the Cuban-Spanish-American War, the United States, a more technologically advanced nation, representing itself as the "liberators" of Puerto Ricans from Spanish oppression, defeated Spain.

Also on May 1, 2003, another chapter in the democratization of Puerto Rico was begun while another myth was shattered: the invincibility of the "hegemon." Since the Cuban-Spanish-American War, Puerto Ricans have lived in a political limbo. Contrary to the experience of other territories conquered by the United States in the nineteenth century, Puerto Rico and the Phillippines were relegated to a classic colonial status. While Arizona and New Mexico became territories, which is the first stage in the process of acquiring statehood and full political rights, Puerto Rico and the Phillippines were placed in a a different political track

(Rodriguez, 2005). Congress did not want to place either of these newly conquered territories as possible states because of their "mongrelized" populations.

The Supreme Court, in a number of decisions to clarify the island's political relationship with the United States, called the "Insular Cases" at the beginning of the twentieth century, determined that Puerto Rico was an "unincorporated territory" of the United States. That meant that the Puerto Rican archipelago (which includes Vieques, Culebra, Mona, and other neighboring islands) "belongs to, but it is not a part of" the United States. In many ways, Puerto Ricans became a "possession" of the U.S. empire. They could have a "resident commissioner" in Congress, with voice, but no vote. While the position has been enhanced in the last decades, this delegate is dependent on the generosity of Congress. Since 1917, when U.S. citizenship was imposed on Puerto Ricans, Puerto Ricans can be drafted in U.S. wars of conquest, yet can't vote for the commander-in-chief, the president of the United States. Ironically, the conquest of Puerto Rico transformed the United States into a formal empire, like the anti-imperialist and Walt Whitman had argued. Democracies do not have colonies, and the United States colonized Puerto Rico until today and the Phillippines until 1946.

Puerto Ricans and Viequenses in the twenty-first century live under an anachronistic colonial system that has attempted to legitimate itself through the internalization of an ideology of invincibility and reasonableness. For many years, anything labeled as "federal" led to the raising of eyebrows among Puerto Ricans because it meant something so frightening and powerful that it almost seemed sacred and transcendent. But in Vieques, the "federal" lost its aura of sacredness and it became a symbol of what was wrong and needed to be challenged. In fact, the "federal" became a symbol of what needed to be transgressed if the Viequenses were going to regain their sense of self and build their life and gain humanity for themselves and future generations.

While most of the lands expropriated by the Navy were returned to some form of civilian use in 2003, the U.S. military still controls a radar system used for monitoring of drug traffic in the region, the ROTHR (Relocatable Over the Horizon Radar) is located on Monte Pirata in the western part of Vieques. Since most of the land is held by the Department of the Interior there is still no permanent assurance that the lands will not be used for military exercises and the decontamination process has not begun yet. The Viequenses want to develop their economy and have a sustainable development plan that includes organic agriculture, ecotourism, and a zoning plan that will maintain the pristine quality of one of the most beautiful islands in the Caribbean. But despite the uncertainties that Viequenses face, the residents of this island have writ-

ten another chapter in the expansion of democracy in the Americas, and have provided a model that works and that builds on the best of human beings. They also were able to build an "imagined community" based on a common, collective memory that provided the grounding for a new sense of collective identity that served as a shield against the empire's effort to in effect erase Vieques' past from future generations of Viequenses. In fact, Viequenses developed a myth to challenge the imperial myth.

Constructing "Subjects":
Racialization of Puerto Rico and Vieques

To make sense of the Vieques social movement's development of a "narrative of oppression and resistance" that served as a tool for the construction of an "imagined community" it is important to contextualize and situate this movement in the historical process of racialization in Puerto Rico. "Racialization," in the sense that Omi and Winant use it means "to signify the extension of racial meaning to a previously racially unclassified relationship, social practice or group" (1986:64). Racialization is also an ideological process, and a historically specific one that assigns ethnic groups a racial identity and status. "Racial ideology is constructed from pre-existing conceptual (or if one prefers, "discursive") elements and emerges from the struggles of competing political projects and ideas seeking to articulate similar elements differently" (1986:64). A more descriptive way of talking about racialization is:

> "Racialization is the social and historical process of assigning individuals and groups a socially constructed racial identity and status. As populations compete for land, status and resources they build hierarchies based on clusters of phenotypical biological factors which are then assumed to represent archetypes for members of a particular racial group. Those who become the dominant group interpret those presumed phenotypical biological differences as indicators of essential differences and assign a negative meaning to them, subordinating the contending group and limiting their access to those things their society values. The process of racialization in modern societies, is historically specific, and is carried out by its basic social institutions: economy, education, family, religion, government, criminal justice system, media, etc." (Rodriguez, 2002:7).

The historical context of this process of racialization occurs as the United States becomes an empire and its economy transitions from competitive capitalism to the capitalism of trusts and corporations, monopoly capitalism. During this period, at the end of the nineteenth century, the U.S. popular sense of "Manifest Destiny" clearly becomes global in character and projection (Rodriguez, 1988). Racialization, then, occurs within a nation defining itself politically and economically as an empire, and racialization, domestically and abroad, becomes a way of managing the "natives" and/or "subalterns," foreign and domestic, by placing them within racialized hierarchies of power. Modern empire as racialized states whose foreign policies lead to both colonizing and racializing their colonies and subjects. Colonization and racialization are parallel processes, one focusing on the exploitation of the colonial resources and subordinating the ethnic or national group (Puerto Rico's case) and the other reproducing in the colonial sphere the racial stratification system and ideology prevalent in the empire (Rodriguez, 2005). This process occurred earlier in the continental United States, after the Mexican American War, which ended in 1848 as the conquered populations of the Southwest were constructed as racialized subjects.

Historical Processes of Racialization

There are at least four identifiable processes or "moments" in the racialization process (Rodriguez, 2002:9). The four moments of racialization:

○ Limiting access and control of the land

○ Use of ideology and cultural racism

○ Negotiation and contestation of racialization

○ Assimilation

For Puerto Ricans, this first stage in the process of racialization or limiting access and control of the land under United States hegemony, occurs later, when 400 years of Spanish colonial rule is defeated during the Spanish-American War. In the island, the colonization process (economic, political, social, cultural) of Puerto Rico by the United States, was led by sugar, tobacco, textile, and other U.S. corporate interests. This led to a gradual process by which a significant section of the peasantry were expropriated and either became proletarianized in the growing agricultural enterprises or migrated, initially to Hawaii and later to the industrial hubs of the United States. It is within this historical context that Puerto Ricans are racialized in this first stage. These forces and interests also gave rise to the forces that created the process of migration and the large scale beginning of the Puerto Rican diaspora.

Limiting Access and Control of Land in Vieques

While Vieques in many ways represents a microcosm of Puerto Rican society and its historical experience of racialization, these processes in Vieques were more intense because Vieques was colonized by Spain, later by the United States and also the island experienced significant marginalization from the *Isla Grande* institutions.[3] The more stable European colonization of Vieques begins in 1832, before this time the island was a contested terrain where Tainos, and Europeans struggled unsuccessfully to establish a permanent presence. The geopolitical role of Vieques began early when the Danes, French, Dutch, and North Americans struggled to gain a foothold in Vieques. During this period, John Adams, the United States' future second president, staunchly opposed in 1783, independence for Cuba, Puerto Rico, and Vieques, although proposing the annexation of these territories to the United States (Cruz Monclova, 1957). Four years later, Thomas Jefferson stated that the United States should be the "nest" from which the rest of the Americas should be populated, but given the relative weakness of the nation that it would have to wait until it was stronger and more numerous and then take those countries away "piece by piece" (Cruz Monclova, 1957:224).

According to Melèndez Lopez (1982) after the visit of Latin American liberator Simon Bolivar to Vieques in 1816, the United States' opposition to Puerto Rican and Cuban independence mostly centered on Vieques. Ironically, just like Puerto Rico, its geopolitical importance shaped its history and the intensity of racialization in Vieques. The United States, concerned about Bolivar's efforts on behalf of the Hispanic Antilles and of the Spanish efforts to recuperate its empire, monitored and intervened, through back-door diplomatic channels and military efforts, to assure future access to Cuba and Puerto Rico. A mili-

tary expedition on the Puerto Rican archipelago, organized by D. Holstein and Irvine in 1822, was supported by the United States (Melèndez Lopez, 1982:14-15).

But despite Spain's desire to maintain its empire it was not until 1832 that Vieques had a formally constituted government; in that year, Teofilo Leguillou was named the island's first governor. Leguillou was a military hero who had helped defeat the British and this assured that Vieques' future was aligned with Puerto Rico and its Hispanic culture. His policies until his death in 1843 not only created the infrastructure for the economic development of Vieques but also laid the basis for a process of land concentration. The development of sugar production in Vieques became the most important source of economic momentum and labor for its population. It also created the conditions for the importation of enslaved Africans for work in the sugar industry. Because of labor scarcity in Vieques, its sugar economy depended on the importation of labor from the British Caribbean. This became even more necessary after the abolition of slavery in 1873, when many freed slaves initially tended to avoid work in sugar plantations.

As the sugar industry began to depend on wage workers the space for contesting the sugar elite expanded. The proletarianized sugar workers developed modes of resistance to exploitation that were not available to the enslaved African workers. These workers were the center of a labor conflict that led to a bloody clash between workers and the Spanish Civil Guard in 1874. Puerto Rico's governor, General Sanz, wanted to deal harshly with the workers but since many were British subjects the British consul intervened and General Sanz gave amnesty to the workers (Melèndez Lopez, 1982). Labor strife and dependence on the importation of sugar workers from the Caribbean would extend themselves into the twentieth century.

According to Melèndez Lopez (1982), Vieques also experienced more intensely the consequences of the U. S. military campaign against Puerto Rico during the Spanish-American War. In fact, Vieques was the only island of the Puerto Rican archipelago to suffer an extensive naval blockade by the U.S. Navy. The steamship Yale blockaded Vieques for four months, creating so much hunger and anxiety among the Viequenses that the Viequense began to believe that the Yankee soldiers were savages who would cut the throats of the islanders when they landed. As soon as the North American troops landed, the geopolitical importance of Vieques was highlighted and numerous scientific, military, and economic studies were conducted about Vieques.

The sugar industry in Vieques continued to develop under U.S. hegemony and the process of land concentration in a small elite continued unabated. The sugar proletariat continued to develop its resistance of wage exploitation and joined Puerto Rico's growing labor movement. Labor strife in Vieques led to the killing of three Viequense workers in

1915, and others were injured and suffered mutilation because of the injuries caused by a police assault on the protestors. During the 1920s, Vieques had five sugar mills and instead of being a net exporter of labor like today (the island of Culebra is now a major recipient of Viequense labor migration) it was the recipient of migrant workers from Puerto Rico and the Caribbean who were attracted to the growing Viequense sugar economy. Many of these workers were of African descent, which increased the black presence in Vieques.

Early in the U.S. domination of Vieques, the United States was interested in the establishment of a naval base. According to Meléndez Lopez (1982) the daily newspaper *El Mundo* revealed on January 31, 1926 the Navy's interest in using the island of Vieques to build a large naval base. On May 31, 1939, Admiral William D. Leahy, was appointed by President Franklin Delano Roosevelt as governor of Puerto Rico. Admiral Leahy was close to President Roosevelt and as former chief of naval operations had been to Vieques observing Navy maneuvers in the region with the president. Admiral Leahy's mandate was to build naval and air bases in Puerto Rico, eliminate the political challenge represented by the nationalist movement and supervise the 1940s elections. During the 1930s, the nationalist movement had developed an aggressive anti-imperialist and militant campaign against U. S. colonialism. At times, the conflict resulted in armed confrontation with colonial forces. On Palm Sunday 1937, in the southern city of Ponce, twenty-one nationalists were massacred by the colonial police during a peaceful demonstration. In June of that same year, Pedro Albizu Campos, the charismatic leader of the Nationalist Party was jailed and flown to a federal penitentiary in Atlanta, Georgia. Admiral Leahy was to insure the hegemony of the United States over Puerto Rico by eliminating the remnants of political dissent and perpetuate the control of the island by establishing the naval base while helping build a facade for a pseudo-democratic regime in the island (Rodriguez Beruff, 2001:8).

The process of excluding Viequenses from access and control to the land was led by the economic process of centralization of production and then the concentration of ownership over the land in Vieques. This process left masses of Viequenses at the mercy of the landed elite and began another qualitatively different phase in Vieques social development. During this period, Vieques experienced one of the highest levels of land concentration in Puerto Rico. In 1940, 78% of the land in Vieques was under the control of the Benítez family and Eastern Sugar Associates. The population of the island was entirely dependent on the sugar industry and the agricultural elite who controlled the industry (Ayala & Carro, 2002).

Beginning in 1942, a large-scale land expropriation process began in Vieques. In this process, Viequenses not only were to be again excluded from control of the land but also would be excluded from any

form of access to the land. This process occurred at the same time the
armed forces were accumulating large amounts of land in Puerto Rico
for the purpose of building military installations. These "land grabs" by
the military, which continued after World War II, was a source of conflict
between the United States and Puerto Rico's colonial government. The
first Puerto Rican governor appointed by the United States, Jesus T.
Piñeiro, advocated the reversal of the land takeovers with the representatives of the United States military. Admiral Leahy, a representative of
Truman in 1948 clearly states to Gov. Piñeiro that:

> "I don't think I can do anything about Vieques except tell
> Washington what you want. There is not much purpose in my
> talking about that to you. The island is strategically valuable.
> I think nowhere they can get a better one of higher value.
> This is a very important military training area. It is a key in
> the overall Navy defenses" (Rodriguez Beruff, 2001:47).

The rights of the Viequenses were obscured in this discourse where
Vieques, like Puerto Rico is "chattel," "belongs to but is not part of" the
United States. Its inhabitants become objectified and seen as burdens,
obstacles in the way of protecting national defense. These were the same
justifications that were used for sixty-two years later to justify the military presence in Vieques and the expropriation of Viequense land in the
name of "national security." The wave of land expropriations took place
in Vieques in two waves, one in 1942-1943 and another in the period
from 1947-1950 (Ayala & Carro, 2002:3). These land expropriations carried out by the Navy were facilitated by the intense concentration of
land that was pervasive in the island.[4] One family, the Benitez' owned
one-half of all the land of Vieques in the late 1930s. Another owner, Eastern Sugar Associates owned 11,000 acres of land in an island with close
to 33,000 acres of land. In sum, 78% of all the land in Vieques was in the
hands of these two major landholding entities. In the shadows of this
land tenure system lived the *agregados* who were agricultural workers
and their families who in exchange for usufruct rights over some land
provided labor for the sugar plantations. Most of the Viequense population lived in *agrego* relations to the small landowning class. Access to
small plots of land provided the rural worker with a way of subsidizing
his survival with food that he grew and animals he grazed on the land he
had access to. The sugar plantation system was able to survive because
at times of labor scarcity the *agrego* system provided cheap and accessible labor during times of high labor demand.

Unfortunately, the *agregados* were not indemnified in any way for
their loss of access to land and the homes they had built on the landown-

ers plot. These semi-feudal forms of access to land were completely destroyed since the workers and their families were completely removed from the land they had called home. During the two periods of exploitation 89% of the population ended up residing in one-fifth of the area they populated in 1940 (Ayala & Carro, 2002). In ways that are reminiscent of the removal of the "civilized tribes" during the 1830s Indian Removal Act process, the *agregados* were forced to immediately gather what they could of their meager belongings and were then relocated to other relocation sites in the island. This process of exclusion from access to land was rooted, particularly during this period, in satisfying the "national security" needs of the United States (Santiago Caraballo, 1997). Many Puerto Ricans in the *Isla Grande* also experienced these forced relocations, but it is in Vieques where its impact was much more intense.

The colonial government was deeply involved in facilitating the process and mediating between the conflict of imperial and local needs. The process, in many cases was done with little care for the evicted. According to Ayala and Carro (2002) in an analysis of a survey conducted by the Proyecto Caribeño de Justicia y Paz (Caribbean Project for Justice and Peace, (CPJP, 1979)), 74% of the workers were given ten days to leave the property and move elsewhere, the remainder, received between forty-eight and twenty-four hours notice to move (CPJP, 1979). They were relocated to a plot of land chosen by the Navy, and were coerced into signing a paper where they relinquished all their rights to future claims. They also were forbidden from building any permanent structure, a way of telling them they could be relocated anytime the Navy felt it was expedient. Almost instantaneously, thousands of Viequenses became homeless, uprooted and without access to the land that was their place of memory and birth. While it is a fact that 95% of the Viequenses were landless, the *agrego* system, with all its contradictions (a semi-feudal relationship to the land in a capitalist economy), provided Viequenses with a sense of rootedness in their Viequense homeland (McCaffrey, 2002). The history of this process was partially hidden from future Viequense generations like a family secret, a secret that was kept hidden like a shameful event. Racialization involves internalizing shame for one's tragedies as if caused by personal volition. Shame, leads to isolation and self-doubt and to passivity and demobilization. One of the strategies of the Viequense social movement was to bring to the public sphere the memory of these events and build a new sense of identity rooted in a common experience of oppression and resistance.

"Se me cayó el mundo" ("My whole world collapsed") (Anonymous Viequense after expropriations, CPJP, 1979)

Resistance to "Expropriation"

Resistance to this process of "expropriation" of access to land did not assume any organized fashion. According to the survey carried out by the CPJP besides the limited number of cases where civil litigations were carried out by the property owners, among the *agregados* there were small instances of individual resistance. Their resistance included some who refused to leave their lands forcing the Navy to physically evict them. Some effort to inform the evicted of what was happening occurred when community leaders like Carlos Vélez Rickehoff, Felipe Benítez, Luisa Guadalupe and Ángel Pérez set up a podium at the entrance of the Casa Grande Sugar mill in the western part of the island and spoke to the *agregados*. Some *agregados* said "they had to be killed first" before leaving their land (CPJP, 1979). In the Mosquitos neighborhood many resisted but were also some of the first to emigrate from Vieques. Many had to be physically removed from their homes. Some refused the place they were assigned to live because of fear they would again be evicted and found another home.

But in general, the resistance was subtle and muted. The overwhelming power of the United States, the "federal" power led to a sense of despair and disempowerment. Some of the reasons for not resisting included: "the government and all the big people were Americans," and "we did not have any support, we did not understand our rights. We were slaves"(CPJP, 1979). The "hegemon" was coded in popular language by the term "lo federal." One of the Viequenses, when asked why there was no resistance to the evictions said: "the people had a lot of respect for anything 'federal'" (CPJP, 1979).

The main obstacle to resistance was not the threat of violence or the military weaponry, the power of the military was represented in the notion that anything federal could not be questioned or challenged. The lack of organization and the lack of institutions that could agitate, educate and mobilize the *agregados* facilitated the process of "expropriation." The ideology of control that became common sense among the Viequense population became the means by which the Navy was able to perpetuate its presence in Vieques with very little resistance. This is precisely the expected outcome that takes place when a people are "expropriated" and the myth of invincibility receives empirical validation.

To sum, limiting the access and control of a people to land is essential for instituting a process of subordination and of cultural change. Most of the island's political, economic institutions were in the hands of the military (1898-1901) and later, of U.S.-appointed and U.S.-monitored civilian authorities. The process of subordination is aided because lack of access and control to the land places limits and shapes contestation of the racialization process. However, despite the political repression led by the state apparatus, those oppressive spaces were also grounds for

resistance. The resistance, as it has occurred historically, did not emerge from the elites, it emerged from the working classes and their allies. While the Puerto Rican landed elite had some economic power, its economic foundation was based on the fact that the United States included Puerto Rico within its tariff structure. Its ability to sell its product, sugar, was dependent on the state policies of the empire. Former peasants and small agricultural producers become integrated into the growing and expanding sugar plantation complex under the hegemony of U.S. capitalist investment and their local intermediaries. Later in places like Vieques they are completely excluded from having access and control of the land and become almost totally dependent on the U.S. Navy just like before they were dependent at one point on the sugar elites.

Ideology and Institutional Arrangements

Ideologies need institutions that reproduce and expand their realm of influence beyond the immediate presence. One important outcome of these institutionalized practices is the normalization of power and subordination. The reality and experience of subordination become enmeshed in the culture as "commonsense" knowledge. This is achieved in this second process of racialization by implementing the creation of what Karenga (2002) calls "institutional arrangements," which are constructed and supported with an ideology that gives legitimacy, stability, and continuity to a system of exploitation based on class, race, ethnicity, and gender. These institutional arrangements are the systems and social institutions that ensure the continued subordination of the racialized subjects. They contribute to perpetuate subordination but without the same degree of coercion that marks the first stage. The arrangements include clusters of norms such as slavery and Jim Crow Laws in the African American experience, reservations and federal laws in the American Indian experience, and dual wage systems, school segregation, and "Americanization" programs in the Chicano and Boricua experience. For example, "Americanization" as an ideology legitimates institutional arrangements that lead to a process of cultural racism that distorts, trivializes the indigenous culture, and imposes a different way of life on the subjects. The idea that there is a superior culture and a superior race becomes a "commonsense" idea that is internalized by the colonialized subjects.[5]

But more important, the educational system, among the most strategic institutional arrangements, is the place where the organization of production and the ideologies that support their role and function takes place. Its most enduring and powerful consequence is the erasure of a people's collective memory, or history. A conqueror needs to substitute the life-giving, "social fabric-creating common memory of experiences,"

which is history, with its own self-congratulatory narrative (Karenga, 2002). The conquered person begins to "disappear" as a historical subject with agency and becomes a colonized subject, dependent, powerless, with self-doubt and connected to the imperial hegemonic world view.[6] The people of Vieques just like Puerto Ricans in general, were taught not to trust or affirm their memory, their historical experience as a people, but in the process of liberation they reaffirmed and began to trust their memory by re-membering and re-calling those hidden secrets, those "shameful" events that once were only spoken in a whisper and now were shared, shouted, and perpetuated as printed texts.

In the educational system in Puerto Rico, racialization through "Americanization" took its course. English became the medium of instruction, North American textbooks were utilized, including Puerto Rican history textbooks written by North Americans, which degraded the collective memory of Puerto Ricans and painted a racialized representation of Puerto Ricans. In Vieques, the subject of the expropriations of Viequense land, the hardships endured by the Viequenses were not the object of any intellectual reflection in the educational system (Guadalupe, 2004). It was like a whole period of Viequense history had never happened, the United States Navy was in Vieques as almost a "natural" event, not as the consequence of a violent act of conquest and subordination. This lack of reference to the violence of the expropriation led to a "normalization" of the contemporary experience of subordination and control. The naval presence just like the *tinglar* (sea turtle) was part of the natural environment of Vieques. The ideological outcome of the absence of a critical historical account of the forceful removal of the Viequense from the Navy's path reinforced the dehumanization of the Viequense and the sense of powerlessness and fatalism that became pervasive among significant sectors of the population.

The only frontal challenge of the act of colonization came from the nationalists, who early on condemned what was happening in Vieques as a microcosm of what had happened to Puerto Rico. Pedro Albizu Campos, during the 1940s said: "In Vieques the United States is carrying out the vivisection of our nation." But, the voice of the nationalists had also been muffled by repression and ideology and not heard or transformed into human praxis, it was more of a lament, an expression of grief rather than a battle cry.

Meanwhile, the United States attempt to "Americanize" the entire Puerto Rican population presented some obstacles. In this case, since Puerto Ricans were the numerical majority in the island, there was no need to segregate them as were in the United States. However, white teachers were brought in from the United States to teach "American" cultural norms and folkways to domesticate Puerto Ricans and instill the kind of loyalty the United States required to maintain its colonial

domination. Martin G. Brumbaugh, Commissioner of Education (1900-1901) said that "Under wise and conservative officers, the people of Puerto Rico have turned to this Republic with a patriotism, a zeal, and enthusiasm that is perhaps without parallel" (Negron de Montilla, 1970:37).

Also, like in other areas of the United States, the process of subordinating Puerto Ricans included a dual-wage system. According to Negron de Montilla (1970) a newspaper article said in 1900:

> "The American teachers enjoy a better salary than the Puerto Rican teachers, yet instructions are given to the School Boards in the official newspaper, *La Gaceta*, that all American teachers must sign their contract for next year. No mention is made of Puerto Rican teachers, who are in more need because they earn lower salaries" (1970:55).

This dual wage system taught "American" teachers they were superior and taught Puerto Rican teachers that they were inferior. This institutional arrangement was part of the process to socialize the Puerto Rican population into acceptance of its new inferior status vis a vis the white "Americans."

The implementation of this educational system included the use of English as the medium of instruction and relegating Spanish to a subordinate status within the curriculum. The Puerto Rican was being domesticated into accepting its proper place within a racial hierarchy that had whites as the archetype of what Puerto Ricans should aspire to be.[7] In Vieques, particularly, the "yankee" soldiers became the model of what Viequenses should aspire to be despite the daily humiliating experiences they endured with the sailors.[8] In fact, marrying an "American" sailor was considered a symbol of status, it was the Viequense version of the Puerto Rican saying "mejorar la raza" (improving the race), which meant that marrying a white sailor would provide the woman a higher step in social and racial status (Conde, 2004).

But the educational system had the reinforcement of the daily presence of the U.S. Navy whose power was feared and admired. One way they developed admiration was by engaging in civic actions like taking school children in buses to participate in events sponsored by the Navy and eat hamburgers and soda, sailors painting the schools, and also sponsoring militarized youth organizations which instilled military values (Guadalupe, 2004). These civic efforts were combined with the repression of faculty and students who expressed anti militaristic values or participated in anti-navy protests (Guadalupe, 2004).

Also, the internalization of a stigmatized identity was firming up the years of institutionalized and individual racial prejudice that existed

against people of African descent. The processes of internalization in Vieques use the pre-existing memories of racialization under the Spanish colonial system, a racialized system similar to the one that developed in the United States where blacks are considered less human, the more socially distant they are perceived to be from the white racial paradigm. In Pedro Juan Soto's *USMail* (2003) he details the racial dynamics, that the colonial and military institutions work and develop even further. His main character represents the Viequenses tragedy, which also includes how racialization led Viequenses to be divided amongst them on the basis of race. *USMail* 's name, used by Soto because of a story he heard about a Puerto Rican who named her child after reading those letters on a mail truck, indicates the ambivalence of Viequenses about their own sense of self (Berrocal, 2000). As a consequence of cultural racism even a logo in English is better and has a higher status than a name in Spanish for one's child. But the character, not only has ambivalence about his colonial status he also has ambivalence about his status as a mulatto, half white, half black. The dynamics of "colorism" or pigmentocracy are very prevalent in Vieques as an outcome of the process of racialization in a population which has a higher percentage of people of African descent. Contrary to the Isla Grande where 80.5% of Puerto Ricans chose "white" as their racial identity, 72.7% of Viequenses chose that category in the 2000 census. Also, only 8% of Puerto Ricans identified as black while 13.8% of Viequenses chose black as their race. Even in an island with a significant African ancestry, most Viequenses choose to negate their blackness. This paradigmatic character reflects some of the racialization dynamics in Vieques as Viequenses endure the construction and perpetuation of the ideology of white supremacy in their midst.

This internalization could have been expected to be smooth, particularly since Puerto Ricans already were constructed in the American mind as a malleable and peaceful people. Victor S. Clark's representation of Puerto Ricans: "The great mass of Puerto Ricans are as yet passive and plastic... Their ideals are in our hands to create and mold. We shall be responsible for the work when it is done, and it is our solemn duty to consider carefully and thoughtfully today, the character we wish to give the finished product of our influence and effort" (Negron de Montilla, 1970:13). However this malleable character that Clark refers to is not malleable enough to shape a population of free citizens in either an independent republic or a state of the union. Just like in the experience of Mexican Americans, the shaping and forming of the subjects is directed to create effective workers and docile subalterns.

North Americans had learned these representations from travelers, academics and businessmen, who had begun to shape in the U.S. popular mind, the notion of Puerto Ricans as children, products of miscege-

nation, who needed the strong paternal hand of the master in order to learn their proper role in a racialized relationship, that between colonizer and colonized. As historian Matos Rodriguez (1999) explains in his article how U.S. writers (in similar ways as Mexicans were represented) represented Puerto Rico and Puerto Ricans as a "problem":

> "Racial stereotypes in the U.S. also reinforced the vision that Puerto Ricans were intellectually inferior people given the high incidence of "mestizaje." U.S. writers and government officials constructed a perfect justification for colonialism: a disorder in need of intervention, an able United States willing to serve as problem solver, and an anxious Puerto Rican people striving to improve under U.S. guidance" (1999:42).

However, this "disorder" that needs reorganization was one that had the potential for achieving a higher yet subordinate status vis a vis the United States. Thompson (1995), in his reading of *Our Islands and their People* finds that some U.S. observers believed that Puerto Ricans were somewhat redeemable:

> "[The Puerto Ricans] are a different race from the sodden populations of the Orient and the humbled and degraded masses of many European countries. When one looks into the intelligent faces of the Porto Rican girls or boys employed in the various little factories that exist in the island, he realizes that they have souls... Spanish tyranny, during the three hundred years of its iron rule, did all it could to crush the spirit of the people but the benign climate and fructifying soil counteracted the poison of official repression, and the masses of the Porto Rican are today nearer the high standard of American thought and intelligence than the common people of any other country" (1995:55-57).

These racialized stereotypes were reproduced within the very heart of the Viequenses community by the North American colony in Vieques. While many North Americans were involved in the Vieques social movement, in fact, one of the principal leaders is Robert Rabin, of the *Comite* (Committee for the Rescue and Development of Vieques) many other North Americans performed the role of a settler class. Imbued with racist stereotypes they intensified the racialization and dehumanization of Viequense within the Viequense society. They forbid workers in their business establishments to speak Spanish, they describe the Viequenses as lazy, they support the navy's stance and today ironically they have been economically rewarded by the real estate boom (Conde, 2004).

Larger numbers of tourists are coming to a peaceful Vieques and a large number of properties and businesses catering to tourists have been established by North Americans in the island. However, for many years the local North American colony did not learn Spanish, kept mostly to itself and shared a racist culture that despised the Viequenses (McCaffrey, 2002).

North Americans control, for example, the Vieques Conservation and Historic Trust (VCHT), which has taken an environmental position that blames the Viequenses for environmental problems and ascribes to the Navy the preservation of the island's ecosystem. They also control the island tourist trade and the access to the island's unique bioluminescent lagoon, an international environmental treasure. They also negate the memory of oppression of the Viequenses and reduce them to "squatters." Frank Jones, president of the Navy League, an organization supporting the Navy:

> "They claim that the navy stole their land—they bought it. Bought it from the sugar plantation owners who were more than happy to get rid of it. There were people squatting on the land and the army built them houses" (McCaffrey, 2002:107)

These institutionalized arrangements, supported by a racist ideology spread through the economy, the educational system, criminal justice system, religion etc. and helped maintain the stability of the system of racialization, while at the same time it integrated sectors of the subordinated groups as "gate keepers." These gate keepers were Viequenses who had married navy personnel, or who benefitted from the few jobs created by the naval presence and who served as a Navy Trojan horse with a Puerto Rican face within the community. These institutional arrangements perpetuated white supremacy and simultaneously undermined resistance of other sectors of the racialized communities. "Whiteness" became a value internalized by the Viequenses while their African racial ancestry became a weakness that Puerto Ricans and particularly Viequenses had to endure and somehow transcend. But no racialization process is so homogeneous that it does not offer spaces for resistance. However, this structural organization of racialization sets the stage for another process.

Placement in the Racial Hierarchy

During this third phase the racialized group is assigned a racial status within the racial system of stratification. This process is led by how communities of color participate in what Clara Rodriguez (2000) calls "the

acceptance of and participation in discrimination against people of color" (2000:17). This process leads into what Clara Rodriguez describes as the "negotiations regarding the group's placement in the U.S. racial ethnic queue" (2000:18). It is within this phase that the racial "others" are constituted in the culture of the dominant and the dominated group. Since racial categories are comparative taxonomical systems a process of categorization includes a process of comparison. The comparison and categorization not only occurs between whites and the racialized "other" but this process of comparison may include other racialized subjects. This fluid process is shaped by historically specific correlations of power and the nature of social and economic changes taking place within the United States, or the colonial spaces of racialization.

Precisely because the system is based on comparative taxonomies, new groups entering the racialized system begin to internalize the norms that guide and maintain the racial hierarchy (Haney Lopez, 1996). As these groups are being socialized and assimilated, they attempt to gain leverage by discriminating against the group immediately below or close to their own standing in the racial ladder. The Irish discriminated against blacks to establish their "whiteness" or more accurately, their "non-blackness," and assure a better placement in the racial ranking (Ignatiev, 1995). Blacks became the "other" that whitened them. Boricuas and Chicanos in various degrees attempt to distance themselves from African Americans or other Latinos. This distancing also takes place within racialized groups, particularly in terms of colorism and pigmentocracy and also in terms of the native versus the foreign-born which in the United States and Puerto Rico become quasi-racial categories.[9]

During the early representations of Puerto Ricans in the United States the Filipinos became the racial "other" that mediated the racial status of Puerto Ricans in the public imagination. In 1917, all Puerto Ricans were granted U.S. citizenship, an anomalous act given that a significant proportion of the population was, in the U.S. racial system, "non-white." There were a number of factors involved, one is geopolitical, the United States wanted to assure control over Puerto Rico for strategic reasons. Or, like Pedro Albizu Campos, the nationalist leader said, "The U.S. wants the cage, not the birds." Secondly, many members of congress perceived the island as the "whitest" of the Antilles.[10] But this process that enabled Puerto Ricans to be granted U.S. citizenship in 1917 included the comparative perception that they were less socially distant than Filipinos in U. S. popular culture (Cabranes, 1979:17-18). Sectors of the U.S. Congress were concerned about opening the doors to a nation of "Orientals" if Puerto Rico became a precedent for the Philippines. It was not until it was clear the Philippines would not be annexed that enabled congress to grant statutory U.S. citizenship to all Puerto Ricans. This process of racialized comparison vis a vis Filipinos

is also present in museum representations of Puerto Ricans and Filipinos during the early twentieth century (Duany, 2002).

In Vieques, this process leads to internal divisions among Viequenses on the basis of race. However, in Puerto Rico, race is always part of a background, hidden conversation, rarely entering the public sphere. The practices of "marrying up" or *mejorando la raza* (improving race) were ways of negotiating a lighter skin status in a society where racial differences were less dichotomized than in the United States. In the United States, race is defined along a polarized system based on the "drop of blood rule," which places any person with some degree of African ancestry in the non-white cell of the polarity.

In Puerto Rico, having white ancestry contributes, especially if the child born of an interracial relationship is of lighter skin, to that person's higher status. So the racial system in Puerto Rico mostly pivots on a cluster of physical characteristics, especially skin color, which tends to add those products of miscegenation to the white side of the continuum. In other words, lightness of skin could grant white status in the island's racial hierarchy (albeit many Puerto Rican whites would be considered non-whites in the U.S. racial system), however, even in a system based on a continuum of color rather than on the stark polarity of the U.S. racial system, "whites" would always feel ambivalent of their status vis a vis other whites. Therefore, race is a conversation better ignored or left to the sphere of humor and literature (Rodriguez, 2000; Rodriguez, 2002b).

This conspiracy of silence is particularly more salient among mixed race Puerto Ricans, whom while they have distinguishable "black" features still "pass" as whites in the islands.[11] This system of color classification and the "bleaching process" is presented in Puerto Rican literature but still there is a silent consensus among Puerto Ricans not to speak about it because it is considered impolite (not racist, but improper). *La cuarterona* (a play based on the story of a person who has one-fourth black ancestry) of Alejandro Tapia y Rivera during the nineteenth century and *La mascara* of Francisco Arriví during the twentieth century deals with these issues in an explicit way. Strong criticism has arisen against this theme when these theater pieces were presented to the public (Rodriguez, 1997). However, the process of "whitening" remains unabated, both in the *Isla grande* and Vieques.

Although the sailors were at times feared, especially when they were on shore leave, in other safer social environments some sailors or naval personnel were considered bridges into a higher, whiter social status. Some of the naval personnel were stationed in Vieques for six months to a year. These men were considered different since they occasionally became part of the Viequense daily routine. They attended religious services, participated in community events, dances and some ended marrying local women (McCaffrey, 2002). But the relationship was still

ambivalent, one time young people would throw rocks at the marines while the parents invited some for dinner at their homes (McCaffrey, 2002:57).

But the sailors and marines were symbols of power, when they broke the law the local system was lenient with them or never engaged them because they were quickly frisked away by naval authorities before local courts could intervene. Fernando Torres, a Viequense, described the local judge as favoring the navy and treating the sailors with a soft glove, the judge would say "Oh well, they are only here for a short time" (McCaffrey 2002:57). There were instances of rapes, fights, and murders that went unpunished during the Navy's tenure in the island (Guadalupe, 2004). The message for Viequenses was these are superior people who deserve the acquiescence of the Viequenses. The ambivalence about the Navy presence impeded the development of an anti imperialist and nationalist response to the military domination of their homeland. But the Viequenses were not always submissive; in 1943, hundreds of Viequense workers marched down the streets of Vieques with black flags protesting their situation of economic and social oppression. But these short bursts of protests did not withstand the power of the navy over their lives. They felt torn between the Navy and their daily lives. This ambivalence was rooted in a magnification of the power of the military institutions because internalized racist oppression led Viequenses to see themselves as less worthy than the white soldiers. In some sense, they contributed to their own placement in the racial hierarchy, and their challenge of racialization and domination would have to wait a few decades.

Crystallization of a Racial Identity

The fourth and final stage in racialization is the "crystallization of a racialized identity," this process of individuation takes place through the systemic processes of assimilation, "Americanization" and homogenization. During this phase, the internalization of racist oppression becomes a signifying characteristic of being that jointly, with institutional arrangements, serves to reinforce the systems at the individual level and limit the process of contestation at the systemic level (Rodriguez, 2002a). Internalization is a major factor limiting resistance, and as developed by Franz Fannon (1986) and later described by Pan-Africanist Steve Biko, as "the most powerful weapon of the oppressor is the mind of the oppressed." It is within this process where the racial system finds its strategic mechanism toward self-perpetuation.

The internalization of racist oppression becomes the "carimbo" or branding that marks the racialized subject. A mark that is not physical but sociopsychological. The power of the changes in culture and iden-

tity that take place in this process, is that these new forms of being and behaving do not appear as the products of coercion, they are perceived as innate to the individual and the culture. A racialized culture and identity, either "Mexican American," "Boricua" or "Viequense" is created in response to and in contestation of the process of racialization. Therefore, the individual and groups that arise as racial groups, Mexican Americans, "Boricuas" and Viequenses, not only are racialized by the institutions and systems of white supremacy, they are also racialized by colonized and racialized cultural practices. They are colonized from within the cultural spaces of these communities. These new racialized cultures are constructed by oppressed communities using, in these cases, Viequense, Mexican, and Puerto Rican cultural elements together with these new cultural traits that arise out of an experience of oppression.

However, at times these new learned behaviors are divisive and self-destructive. The sense of self that is constructed in this stage of racialization is one imbued with a sense of powerlessness. It is the mode by which "race," in its political sense, becomes a lived reality. Subordination becomes embedded in the culture in subtle and powerful ways. "Parejeria" and "pochismo" in the Puerto Rican and Mexican American context don't lead to liberation, yet provide the means to survive in hostile environments.[12] Yet, people can begin to "decolonize" their minds from the effects of colonialism as Cesaire described (2000). That is precisely what the Viequenses did, and in the process, defeated the most powerful naval institution in the world.

Challenging Racialization

In order to challenge racialization effectively, a new worldview must be constructed to challenge the "common sense" and unexamined assumptions that permeate colonized cultures. The most powerful way that racialized thinking works is by operating as "commonsense," as that unexamined part of our conscience that leads us to operate in a world where racial hierarchies seem natural (Haney Lopez, 2003). How to develop an identity that is rooted in a culture that sustains and affirms a people? How to challenge a process of subordination when oppression is not only expressed in military and political terms but is rooted in its internalizing in the colonized and racialized subject of a sense of self that perpetuates domination? How to develop a social movement that sustains itself for the long term?

Just like the Tainos centuries before, Puerto Ricans and Viequenses also believed the ideology that was internalized into them. Decades of military presence, decades of neglect by the colonial government and their manipulation by external forces, who while motivated by justice concerns, were unable to engage Viequenses where they were and in-

stead used their plight to advance their cause. Don Pedro Albizu was the first to call attention to the Viequense tragedy but Nationalists were unable, like most leftist and progressive forces after him to create a critical mass of Viequenses who would place themselves in clear contradiction with the empire in Vieques.

The Viequenses, while oppressed were imbricated with the oppressor. They had developed social relationships with the military, and were dependent on some economic support from the military and even had some of their children serving in the armed forces. Their sense of rootedness was bifurcated and ambivalent given these circumstances. They did not have a clear sense of identity and even being "Viequense" was not a clear and uncontested place in which to be. The history, or collective memory that serves as a foundation for a collective platform for resistance was hidden, or spoken about softly, most often whispered among a few or held in secret from the young. In order for Viequenses to challenge their racialization and provide the critical mass for a social movement for liberation they had to recover the rudiments of a Viequense culture and identity. The externally led efforts had failed to achieve that, and the local efforts were unable to break through their ideological constraints in order to develop a mass based social movement.

The problem was not that the Viequenses were passive, they had shown clear signs of resistance to oppression, from the worker protests in 1943 to the large scale riot that occurred in the late 1950s and later in 1967 (McCaffrey, 2002:58). It was not the lack of organized efforts that precluded Viequenses from achieving liberation, many organizations had been formed, from the Crusade to Rescue the Land, late 1960s (mostly pro independence and leftists), United Viequenses, late 1970s (members of all political parties), the Crusade for the Rescue of Vieques (with a strong constituency of fishermen) and finally, with the Crusade for the Rescue and Development of Vieques that continues to this day (Guadalupe, 2004). It was not the lack of courageous actions by Viequenses and their supporters, fishermen, and anti-imperialist activists had been picketing, marching and engaging in various forms of social struggles (Zenón, 2001). There was not lack of martyrdom before the death of David Sanes, who was killed by a bomb from a navy airplane, in 1979 twenty-one activists, including Ismael Guadalupe, Angel Rodriguez Cristobal, and other were arrested on federal charges.[13] In fact, Angel Rodriguez Cristobal, a Socialist League activist from Ciales, Puerto Rico was found hanged in his federal prison cell in mysterious circumstances. The problem is that until the last efforts of the Committee for the Rescue and Development of Vieques (Comite Para Rescate y Desarrollo de Vieques, CPRDV), which was founded in 1993, most groups had been unable to sustain a long term effort of resistance to the Navy

and build a pro-liberation majority among the island's residents. These efforts also took place amidst significant repression and surveillance by various intelligence agencies (Guadalupe, 2004).

In order for a successful, long-term social movement for liberation to succeed a number of obstacles had to be transcended. First, a clear sense of identity as Viequenses, rooted in a collective memory, sense of place, had to develop; second, the spaces for the broader participation of larger sectors of the Viequense population needed to be expanded (this includes a larger role for women and broader forms of participation and the issue of the movement's ideology); third, neutralization of the power and influence of the small colony of North Americans; fourth, the fear of anything "federal," fear of the "hegemon" had to be surpassed.

Construction of a Viequense Cultural Identity

"Those who do not remember their past are condemned to repeat it."

George Santayana

McCaffrey (2002:45) points out that "memories of the past are often colored by understanding of the present." One must add to this that also memories of the past lead to interpretations of the present which expand or contract the sense of potential and future possibilities. The Viequenses built a "collective narrative of oppression and resistance" that served as an anchor for a Viequense identity that could imagine itself free and sovereign. There are a number of themes that are clearly discernible in the emerging history of Vieques: the nature and implications of the expropriations, the navy abuses of the Viequenses, the nostalgia for an imagined past that represented "better times." Another theme that is also beginning to emerge is that of the hidden history of people of African ancestry in Vieques.

There are aspects of the Vieques past that remain hidden in the consciousness of older Viequenses; some of these memories bring shame, anger and a sense of victimization. A number of Viequense women were raped by U.S. sailors and Marines and yet, despite the obvious markers of those events, there is no public conversation about the consequences of these acts (Conde, 2004). Some Viequenses who have Anglo last names are either the children of rape or the offspring of furtive sexual affairs between naval personnel and Viequense women (Conde, 2004). Some people remember how naval personnel placed Viequenses in a *chiquero* (literally a pig pen) while naval bombing took place in nearby proximity (Conde, 2004). These incidents remind present-day activists of the time when after engaging in a year of civil disobedience after the death of

David Sanes in 1999, hundreds of protestors were placed in dog cages inside Camp Garcia in Vieques. In 1939, a few Viequenses remember how naval ships got close to the shore of Vieques and dropped boxes of food and other materials for the Viequenses. Some recall feeling like animals who are fed in a zoo. This feeling is enhanced by the reality that Viequenses live between two large fences, one on the east and another on the west side of their community. On occasions where there were conflicts between Navy personnel and Viequenses, sailors furtively brought boxes of food and other gifts and placed them at the door of the Viequenses homes (Conde, 2004). Many Viequenses remember the *hoyo* (hole) a place used as a dumping ground by naval personnel (Guadalupe, 2004). Viequenses went to this place to remove usable items that they found while rummaging through the garbage. Another woman describes this period of relationships with the Navy as "All they gave us were bombs and dirty clothing" (Valentin, 2001). This referred to the bombings carried out by the navy and to the fact that many women survived by doing the laundry for the naval personnel.

All of these experiences had remained hidden because they had been experiences of dehumanization. The most dehumanizing experience was the process of being evicted and relocated from their land of birth and work. In fact, according to a letter discovered in President Lyndon Baines Johnson library, written in 1961, the Secretary of Defense, Robert McNamara, wanted all Viequense to be expelled from their homeland, including taking all the mortal remains in Viequense cemeteries (Fernandez, 1996:201). It was believed that this measure would not provide any motivation for Viequenses to ever return to Vieques and the Navy could retain the use of the island in perpetuity. Not only would the history be erased, even the place where the memories were rooted would be unaccessible to the Viequenses.

The trauma of these processes of dehumanization (racialization) were not only individual but were in fact a collectively experienced process. Many Viequenses still use the term *me expropriaron* (they expropriated me) not in its technical term, but in the collective sense of being robbed, not of a property title (which most of them as *agregos* did not have) but of their land of birth and memory and of their humanity. The fact that they were thrown into resettlement places that contrasted with their original homes, brought a lot of pain to the Viequenses. Justo Pastor Ruiz contrasts the settlement tract where they were settled and their original site: "Those with garden plots lived happily on the landowners land surrounded by farmland and fruit trees, live today in overcrowded conditions and lack even air to breathe" (Pastor Ruiz, 1947:206). Their new spaces of settlement were instant slums full of squalor and blight.

The process of eviction included the expeditious destruction of their former homes. Ayala & Carro (2002:18) quote a *Newsday* article where seventy-four-year old Severina Guadalupe, who was only thirteen years

of age when her home was destroyed, described how her home was razed down by a bulldozer, and while they were not *agregos* because they owned their land, they too ended up in the squalor of the Santa Maria resettlement tract. The scale of the dislocation was intense, in an island of 10,000 inhabitants between 4,250 and 5,000 persons were relocated according to the Navy's estimate (Ayala & Carro, 2002:19). Many Viequenses recall not being able to take all their farm animals, having to leave them on the new expropriated lands. Many of the evicted had to sleep in the open because the Navy did not bring immediately the materials to build their homes, some women gave birth out in the open field, covered only by a zinc board, and some fell sick and had to be carried in hammocks to the hospital (2002:21). The power of these traumatic memories is quite instructive given that people hardly recall the good times when the navy was building mosquito pier and other naval installations, which was a time of relative prosperity in Vieques following the expropriations (Ayala & Bolivar, 2004).

In the 1990s, Viequense activists, aware of the importance of the cultural realm for the development of a social movement for the liberation of Vieques, had become active in the Vieques Cultural Center. The center, sponsored by the government of Puerto Rico's Institute of Puerto Rican Culture, sponsored a historical excursion to the ruins of the *Playa Grande* and *Resolución* sugar mills, which were in the Navy sector (McCaffrey 2002:132). The important consequence of this excursion is that unexpectedly, hundreds of Viequenses participated, above and beyond the organizer's expectations. Inside of the Navy base and while visiting the sites people began to spontaneously share their oral history of how things were before the expropriations. The emotions of the participants were very high as many were seeing the places of their birth for the first time in decades. Rivera, a leader of the Cultural Center encouraged people to share their experiences and urged the children to hear their elders tell their stories. The event ended with a fiery speech by Rivera where he said: "This is not just a historic tour of our past, but a visit to our present and future" (McCaffrey, 2002:134).

This event marked the beginning of the creation of a collective memory of oppression that was "safe" and did not entail taking an anti-U.S. radical perspective. The narrative of the expropriations became part of the public discourse and the event was widely covered in the local press. These memories began to evoke a nostalgia of a better past and created a concrete, rather than an abstract sense of loss. The issue was not "imperialism" but how concretely Viequenses had lost access to their place of memory and birth. The massive participation in this event and the positive and broad repercussions contrasted with the more militant pickets in front of Camp Garcia that had been conducted a few months before by the Committee for the rescue of Vieques when a botched naval bombing a year before had placed the community at risk (McCaffrey,

2002). On October 24, 1993, an F-18 pilot had accidentally dumped five 500-pound bombs at the edge of the town. Mayor Manuela Santiago received a phone call from Commander Hilera, who "apologized for the noise" (Mullenneaux, 2000). Despite the danger caused by the botched bombing to the Viequenses, this last event was still seen through ideological lenses as an anti-U.S. event and while receiving good press coverage did not move the movement to a qualitatively higher level of activism.

The re-membering of the way things were and the re-connecting to the land where many were born, was crucial in shifting the Viequense sense of self. Very often leaders of the movement talked about how they felt when with all the U.S. concern for endangered species in Vieques, very little focus was placed by the U. S. Navy on one species on the verge of extinction: Viequenses (Conde, 2004). This is related to the decline in the population of Vieques as a result of underdevelopment; young people went to college in the *Isla Grande* and never returned. Others migrated to St. Croix or the United States. But it was the concrete fact that Viequenses no longer were being born on the island that led many to fear the possibility of actual extinction. For many, being born in Vieques was the symbolic marker of being a Viequense.

Vieques was not only marginalized by the Navy, it was also marginalized by the colonial government of Puerto Rico. It policies had a negative effect in the more precarious and smaller island society. For example, since the 1980s, the colonial government began a process of privatization of health services and their regionalization, this led to the closing of prenatal care and child-birth facilities in the island's small hospital (McCaffrey 2002:120-121). One informant in McCaffrey's study, Marganita, told sadly about the fact that her daughter Maria was born in Fajardo, in the eastern region of the *Isla Grande* and where Viequenses went for medical attention. "She's from Fajardo, not Vieques. Little by little, soon, there will be no one from Vieques" said Maria's mother (2002:121). The process of limiting access and control of the land had led to a total disconnect between the Viequenses and their homeland. The connection between no Viequense being born and the navy was not seen as a coincidence, it was more like a conspiracy for some: "I believe there is some subtle hand at work. It's like there is a plan—it's like some hidden hand is orchestrating this (no births in Vieques)" says Rosa, another informant (McCaffrey 2002:122). That vital, sacred connection to the homeland was being tenuously cut by forces that seemed beyond the control of the Viequenses. Only a strongly defined identity, rooted in a connection to the land, would lead the Viequenses to in turn expel the cause of their own uprootedness: the U.S. Navy.

One of the strategic decisions made by a newly formed organization, the *Comite* (CPRDV) was to break out of the narrow ideological confines of pro-independence, antiimperialist and left-wing ideology and

begin to draw in centrists and moderates including leaders of the local religious organizations. While the core organizers were pro-independence and leftists, they were able to bring into the organization a more broad perspective that did not include an explicit pro-independence platform. They expanded the environmental focus; they developed a discourse about sustainable development that indicated awareness that a new paradigm for community grassroots organization was necessary. Advocacy in Congress, while not a favorite activity of the militants, enabled many with scientific skills and legal and cultural perspectives to engage and feel a sense of place in the developing new movement. Non partisanship became the way of bringing together disparate individuals and groups into an evolving and growing struggle to free Vieques (Guadalupe, 2004).

There were still ideological struggles about what to do and how militant Viequenses needed to be to challenge and confront the navy but there was a clear attempt not to become an isolated vanguard like in previous waves of the Vieques social movement. There was awareness that not everyone could afford going to jail or being arrested in militant actions against the Navy. The formation of the *Alianza de Mujeres Viequenses* (Viequense Women's Alliance) added another layer to the social movement in Vieques. Women like Mercedes Soba, Carmen Valentin and Judith Conde tried to figure out how to provide women with a voice and a place in the movement. Ordinary women, with household responsibilities and children, in a local culture steeped in patriarchy were not given to engage in public events that might place them at risk of public criticism. Many of the women who began participating in these meetings were connected to the group by activities that promoted the re-membering of the history of Vieques. Not the congealed, frozen history that is printed in texts, but the oral histories of the elderly women who remembered the old Vieques.

The sharing by these women of the oral histories of Vieques began to develop a common, collective historical consciousness about the loss of a connectedness to the homeland. These stories also widened the distance between the Viequenses and the navy by recalling the injustices and shames caused by the sailors. One of the women recalls that one young man went to the beach to fish for some crabs and was stunned when he noticed what was hanging from bushes and strewn all around the beach. It seems that Navy airplanes used the wild cattle and other animals left behind by the *agregados* as targets in their exercises. The remains of the animals were spread across the beautiful beach scene like a surreal nightmare (Conde, 2004).

While many have learned about the Vieques struggle by the images of fishermen facing navy battleships like David facing Goliath, the fishermen's struggle, while courageous, represented a small segment of the Viequense social movement. This is particularly true in the last stages

of the struggle. The fishermen, as autonomous producers in a very individualistic culture were unable to sustain the long-term struggle of Vieques. Their contribution was more in the reinforcement of a centrist ideology that helped the movement maintain itself and not isolate itself with a purely leftist perspective that would have divided and weakened the movement.

> "Aquello era una tierra muerta, muerta, pero muerta." ("That land was dead, dead very dead.")
>
> Judith Conde, leader *Alianza de Mujeres Viequenses*
> (Conde, 2001)

Women in the Vieques Social Movement

The *Alianza de Mujeres Viequenses* was formed on May 14, 1999 after the death of David Sanes (Conde, 2001). One of the motivating factors for this organizing drive was a desire to understand why, despite all that had happened to the Viequenses after decades, the participation of women in the social movement was so small. Not that it was nonexistent, there were courageous women like Norma Guadalupe, Lucy Carambot, Aleida Encarnación, Luisa Guadalupe from Vieques, Isabel Rosado, and Lolita Lebrón from Puerto Rico who were at the forefront of the struggle. But the core leadership fo the movement was always male and the strategy and dynamics was shaped by patriarchal values.

The lead organizers of the *Alianza*, Mercedes Sobá, a social worker and Judith Conde, a teacher, were pleasantly surprised to find twenty-five women at their first gathering. They saw this organizational effort in very modest terms, they wanted to "create a space where women could speak to each other" (Conde, 2001).

> "We all felt concerned with what the military presence in Vieques represented for our families, but for many reasons we had not...we did not dare express ourselves because of fear, fear of losing our jobs, fear of political persecution, many people grew up in a culture where the navy was not challenged, fear of being labeled as communist or subversives in a small society where we interacted with each other very often in public spaces" (Conde, 2001).

The range of perspectives present among the women was not monolithic. Some expressed ire and righteous indignation at the pain and suffering endured from the Navy. Some women spoke in terms of "I have been hit in the face for so long that I am tired" (Conde, 2001). The Navy's

relationship with the Viequenses was analogous to the dysfunctional relation between a victim of domestic violence and her/his abuser. The political issue was personalized in terms of the world view of women in Vieques:

> "...the navy tells you what you want to hear, kind words, they offer you jobs, a memorandum of understanding in 1983, they fake you out and then they hit you even harder with more severe naval bombardment. I caress you, I touch you softly with my hand and then I hit you again" (Conde, 2001).

The range of concerns and perspectives gathered from the women of Vieques leads to a reflection about how women can be provided a space within the social movement. From the early 1970 through the 1980s, fishermen had a prominent role in the social movement. The overwhelming majority of the fishermen are men, and their tactics of confrontation on the sea were more in tune with maleness as defined in Vieques. There was no space for women to participate in a struggle dominated by men and the kinds of tactics utilized. The site of struggle after the death of David Sanes clearly shifted from the ocean to the land. One activist described it as "we have gone from *pescadores* (fishermen) to *rescatadores* (land rescuers)" (McCaffrey, 2002:152). From April 22, 1999 Monte David camp was erected in the east side of the island, inside the naval base. This first camp, mostly organized by the Zenón family was the first direct confrontation after the killing with the naval authorities (Zenón, 2001). The Navy had ended naval bombardment while it investigated the accident, the Viequenses had decided to end, once and for all, bombing in their island. Their motto was "¡Ni una bomba más!" (Not one more bomb!).

However, it was difficult to break through decades of racialization and domination, Viequense women would not automatically jump into the camps in droves. There was a need to connect local women with the struggle in a way that made sense to their world view. In the following months various organizations from the *Isla Grande*, in solidarity with the Vieques social movement created camps all over the contested Navy territory. From the Federation of Teachers to the Catholic Diocese of Caguas, people came in droves to place their bodies as shields against naval bombardment. One outcome of this land invasion was that people saw with their own eyes the environmental damage caused by the Navy, but they also saw the incredible beauty of Vieques. Many Viequenses, just like when they went on the Cultural Center Tour of the west side of the island were moved by the experience of visiting a forbidden land, their own land. Most of the encampments avoided becoming ideologically partisan, just like Monte David camp they emphasized the sym-

bolic nature of the cultural connection to the land. The organizers built a *casita* (small house), which had become a way of establishing stewardship over their homeland (McCaffrey, 2002). Puerto Ricans in the United States had constructed these small models of Puerto Rican homes throughout the cold empty lots in the northeast. These *casitas* were a way of re-membering better days and of re-creating Puerto Rican culture in the diasporic space.

In the area around Monte David, white crosses had been placed around the hill in such a way that they framed the view of the ocean and the lagoon destroyed by naval bombardment. The cross, as a multivalenced symbol allowed multiple connections with a diversity of audiences. For international observers, it was a symbol of peace and religiosity; it brought in and legitimated the increasing role of religious organization in the Vieques social movement. For the Viequenses, it also symbolized the victims of the naval presence, and later they stood for the cancer victims of the environmental degradation and pollution ascribed to the naval presence. As Medina (2000) argued "the only polluting element (in Vieques) is the Navy." Both the *Comité* and the *Alianza* were able to develop this theme effectively and this allowed them to transcend the partisan ideological divide and develop empathy for the Viequense plight. Also, there were continued references to the children who were afflicted with cancer as empirical validation for the damaging effects of the naval presence (Medina, 2000).

But the use of the religious symbol of the cross, at many levels provided a way to morally challenge militarism, not only on ideologic grounds but also on moral and religious grounds. This additional meaning added another space for another constituency in the Viequense social movement. Viequenses then felt emboldened to do pilgrimages to place crosses for their lost loved ones. Rituals full of transcendent meaning gave legitimacy to the resistance against militarism and to the struggle for peace in Vieques. The ideological terrain of the Vieques social movement had shifted from the nationalist, militant, and militaristic content of the 1970s and 1980s, including the role of the various movements of the Puerto Rican *independentista* armed resistance, to a more pacifist and universalistic content.[14] It is within this context that the role of nonviolent civil disobedience became one of the primary tools for confronting the navy, one tactic that allowed a broader participation of people.

However, while women increasingly felt emboldened to visit the forbidden zone, they still found themselves ensconced in traditional roles. Women manned the kitchens that fed the *rescatadores* in the camps. Even in the midst of powerful cultural resistance to the Navy, women were being constructed in domestic roles and men were the primary spokesmen and symbols of the struggle. The polarity of the domestic and the public sphere were still being reproduced in the midst of the

contested site of the camps. Patriarchy had managed to reproduce itself in the context of struggle for liberation. But the change in the content of the struggle provided a space for a more public, visible and broad role for women.

Very few women, like Nilda Medina, a leader of the *Comité* found themselves in positions as public spokespersons for their organizations of the Vieques struggle in general (Medina, 2001). The crosses, as McCaffrey (2002:160-161) contends, fused to important symbols and/or themes for the movement: a struggle for life (peace) and a struggle for health. In doing this, they enabled another constituency to be organically and symbolically connected to the social movement, environmentalists and public health advocates and human rights activists throughout the world. Also the cross as a symbol had a powerful message of martyrdom, which resonated among Christian organizations in Puerto Rico and throughout the world. The death of an innocent victim like David Sanes (his working for the Navy made him even more innocent) and the likeness to the crucifixion of Christ did not escape religious activists. A significant number of Catholic religious orders, their members, bishops, priests and ministers developed a discourse rooted in the idea of martyrdom and justice. This enabled the movement to occupy a higher moral ground than the Navy, which was at times compared with the biblical "principalities and potentates" in religious discourse.

In June 1999, the group of Viequense women who had met to dialogue carried out their first public event. They tied ribbons in the form of crosses along the fence surrounding Camp Garcia (Conde, 2004). The purpose of the event was to claim a space for women's concern for health, peace, and family in the midst of the navy's violence. The event was a great success with scores of women participating in the placement of crosses on the fence. The ritual of placing the crosses was continued until the fence was bristling with white cloth as far as the eye could see. People liked the image of the cross because it was innocent, positive, and identified with peace and spirituality (Conde, 2004).

Another characteristic of the *Alianza* was that it did not identify itself as a "feminist" organization, although many middle and upper middle class feminist organizations supported them on the basis of feminist principles. The women of the *Alianza* wanted to represent the average, ordinary woman of Vieques, they did not want to become ideological or "political" but their positions were more tactical than ideological (McCaffrey, 2002:164-165). Conde (2004) described how different women middle-class organizations in Puerto Rico were from their own group in Vieques, she also talks about these organizations as organizations of white Puerto Rican women. Valentin (2001) highlights that one of their achievements was to enable a broader participation of the entire family in the Vieques struggle. So rather than articulating their struggle as mainstream middle-class white women struggle vis a vis men, it was a

way of incorporating the entire *familia* into the liberating praxis. Mercedes Sobá (2001) explained how Judith Conde carried her child and breastfed him while participating in events supporting the ending of the naval presence in Vieques. Their ability to tell stories about life and daily struggle rather than fiery speeches about imperialism and militant confrontation with the empire, captivated broader audiences and expanded the connections with broader constituencies. They became popular in the liberal and activist lecture circuit in the United States in which they moved audiences with the stories of ordinary people facing extraordinary circumstances and facing the most powerful Navy in the world.

The increasing role of the women of Vieques in the struggle also forced other organizations in the social movement to address the role of women and to provide women a more public and visible role. Today, the main organizations involved in maintaining the pressure on the United States to decontaminate the pollution in Vieques have a significant number of experienced and skilled women in positions of leadership and influence. Also, women have extended their involvement in other areas, a home for victims of domestic violence is part of the Viequense project, and a support group for women surviving cancer. In sum, women have expanded their involvement in everyday issues impacting the women of Vieques. This includes their involvement in a recent project, *Africa en Tu Piel* an effort to recall and re-member the African cultural and historical memory of the black women in Vieques (Conde, 2004). Just like the hidden history of Vieques, women respond to this project with amazement at how much they did not know about their African heritage.

Women had to struggle against racialization as Viequenses and also struggle against patriarchy with the social movement. In this process they expanded and broadened the movement and contributed to the long-lasting changes that marked the struggle of Vieques. They also have begun to find themselves amidst the opaqueness of memory and ideology.

The "Federal" Is Transgressed

In order for the Viequense social movement to succeed, a clearly defined "Viequense" identity had to be created, rooted in a collective memory of oppression. This identity had to be shared by increasing sectors of the Viequense population. This identity needed to be claimed by a critical mass of the Vieques population. But also, creative tactics had to be implemented that broadened participation and motivated the movement so that the momentum of the struggle would not be lost. The July 29, 2001 referendum in Vieques, when 68% of the population told the Navy to immediately leave their homeland was a barometer of how

this identity had spread across a majority of the population. The Navy, not used to being told "No" continued its efforts to demoralize the Viequense people by continuing the bombings. The Viequenses, who had lost fear of anything labeled "federal," were ready and emboldened to make their refusal to be oppressed, a concrete reality. With a broad coalition, both in Vieques and in *Isla Grande,* where a year before more than 150,000 people marched with white flags down the streets of San Juan in a peaceful and powerful expression of support for Vieques, the social movement never let their guards down. Now that much of the fear was gone, now that the influence of the local North American colony had been neutralized, now that the Navy was being forced to leave the island by May 1, 2003 the leaders of the movement continued their pressure. The cutting down of the fences surrounding the naval base as a symbolic representation of expanding the realm of freedom for Viequenses, the continued trespassing of the Vieques territory still controlled by the Navy was all designed to challenge the ideological control the Navy exerted for decades (Guadalupe, 2004). But also, more importantly the Viequenses did not trust the navy any more; they knew that in the military mindset Viequenses were less important than the ability of the United States to hold onto this land for military purposes. As Admiral Ernest Christensen said in hearings to Congress in 1994:

> "...whether the ammunition which is stored on the western side is worth more than the municipality of Vieques to this Nation than to the Nation in its national defense. It is my firm conviction it is worth more to the United States Nation and to the national defense (McCaffrey, 2002:137).

But the Viequenses already were familiar with the previous plans to permanently evacuate Viequenses from their island. Under President Kennedy, the "Dracula Plan" in 1961 included even the transfer of their cemetery remains so that Viequenses would not have any connection to their homeland. A community would have been totally erased from existence by the Navy in the name of national security. The Viequenses movement kept the pressure and devised novel and creative forms of resistance, which included hiding water and food buried in strategic spots inside the naval base so that those engaging in civil disobedience could survive for longer periods of time (Guadalupe, 2004). They created "tools" like the "jueyitos," (little crabs) which pierced the tires of the navy's vehicles, they used brigades of young men and women who wore a hood over their faces and cut the fences so the civil disobedients could enter Navy territory (Guadalupe, 2004). These young Puerto Ricans became known as the *"encapuchados"* and were the object of much speculation and interest. They knew the terrain and were able to elude Navy personnel when inside of the Navy territory. The consistent training of

the peaceful disobedients became a normal aspect of the movement, a practice not used this broadly in Puerto Rican movements for peace and justice. These tactics are an example of what McAdams (1983: 752) call "tactical innovation" which were the outcome of "tactical interaction" between the movement and their opponents. Since they "lacked institutional power, challenges must devise protest techniques that offset their powerlessness" (1983: 752). These new tactics which broadened participation and challenged the image of Navy invincibility also bolstered the moral of the movement and cemented an identity of resistance.

Allies in the Media

The shift in tactics, ideology, the broadening of the movement, the construction of a victimized image of Vieques and the increasing sense of self-assurance of the Viequenses began to create a representation of the Vieques people that acquired epic proportions. The Viequenses were described as heroic; the island was "feminized" in its representation in the media. Juan Gonzalez, a Puerto Rican writer from New York, and an ardent supporter of the Vieques struggle describes the Navy-Vieques relationship as "The Navy reminds me of a man who desperately wants a beautiful woman... The woman keeps saying 'no' and you keep insisting you have to have her..." (Jiménez, 2001:66). This feminine view of Vieques fit quite well with how the Caribbean islands and its people have been racialized historically, not only in terms of race but also in terms of gender. Cuban novelist Antonio Benítez Rojo has argued that the Caribbean is painted with sensuality, as *"nativa," "india pintorezca"* (picturesque Indian woman) or *"negra jacarandosa"* (self-assured black woman) (Jiménez, 2001:63).

This feminization of the image of Vieques and its struggle blunted the dangerous revolutionary model that potentially the social movement could have if emulated. But hardly ever Vieques was seen through its own lenses, just like the Navy in the eyes of the colonized Vieques was also magnified. Elements in the gay movement supported the Vieques struggle as theirs, "If you're queer and Viequense (sic) you'll probably need a good lawyer" wrote two writers in the electronic magazine, *The Gully*, seeking to develop empathy for the Viequense plight with its gay readers (Jiménez, 2001:43). In France, according to Jiménez (2001:41-42) some depicted the struggle of the Viequense women as a feminist vanguard, the new subaltern who before struggling against the Navy empowered themselves in their homes. In general, the press, especially the Puerto Rican press painted a positive image of the Viequense struggle, this allowed the Viequenses to see themselves in a positive light and to feel that their struggle was followed by the entire world. Whether

or not this was true the reality is that it served to construct a myth that gave the Viequenses the motivation and validation that their struggle was fair and just.

> Both (myth and gospel) involve stories foundational to culture, but myth is from the perspective of the perpetrators of founding violence and Gospel is from the perspective of the victims. The Resurrection of Christ represents the permanent establishment of the victim's perspective in history.
>
> Paul Nuechterlein, *The Anthropology of Rene Girard*

Conclusions

In Plato's Republic the term *poiesis* is used to describe something that is constructed for its own sake (poetry is derived from this notion). But sometimes, there can be poetry without a poet. Because *poiesis* is also a place of truth, a space that can help reveal hidden meanings. *Praxis,* however, is human action whose purpose exists outside of itself. Political behavior as praxis, seeks the empowerment of the actor or actors; it is not behavior which has its meaning within itself but outside of the action. Social movements engage in praxis, however, since they also operate within a culture, they cannot avoid the construction of meanings or of benefitting from poetical events. Some human events can be considered poiesis within a social struggle, but just like in Plato's Republic they become subversive and dangerous for the status quo, more for what they are than for what they say. The Viequense social movement developed a foundational story that served as a tool for its liberation. This "gospel," in girardian terms, included the poetical act of the death of David Sanes, which served as a moment of insight into the truth and deeper meaning of the naval presence in Vieques. As McCaffrey argues, it is precisely the innocence of the victim that gives his death a power and meaning beyond that of earlier victims of the military use of the island. The process of struggle in which the death occurs, which had been full of uncertainty and a measure of chaos, then begins to achieve a measure of certainty and life-giving force as it develops in response to the symbol. It is at this moment when the social movement becomes invincible, the cry of "¡Ni una bomba más!" is not a cry of a victim but the statement of an oppressed whose worldview has become dominant. A social movement does not need to include 100% of a community, it only needs to have that "tipping point" critical mass that will provide momentum and legitimacy. But also, its discourse must become dominant as the anti-Navy discourse became so dominant that even within the traditional pro-American forces of the New Progressive Party, a party that supports statehood, powerful voices from former Governor of Puerto

Rico Pedro Rossello (who negotiated the initial withdrawal of the Navy) to Senator Norma Burgos, took strong positions in support of the Viequenses.

The world view and narrative of the Viequenses in struggle became the dominant narrative in Vieques, in the *Isla Grande* and was reflected by the media and legitimated by Puerto Rican colonial institutions, institutions that where originally designed to perpetuate the hegemony of the empire but that for a brief moment allied themselves with the subalterns. From the Catholic Bishop to the Lutheran Bishop, to the evangelical movement, all supported, for moral and justice reasons, the struggle of the Viequenses. The new governor in 2000, Sila Nazario, main leaders of the legislative branches of the colonial government, and the resident commissioner Anibal Acevedo Vila (who became in 2004 governor of Puerto Rico) all were in unison supporting the Viequense demands for liberation.

It is ironic that this outcome occurred in the context of a colony of the most powerful empire in recent human history and while the empire was preparing for another war of domination in Iraq. This speaks to the power of the oppressed in wresting power for them, in the midst of challenging global and local conditions. It is also meaningful that this struggle, led by a group of people that were colonized by the United States, and for many years marginalized by their brethren from the big island, was successful because it was able to defeat the empire in producing meaning that clarified their journey.

The process of liberation in Vieques developed a new discourse of struggle that can be replicated elsewhere. It is a model that acknowledges the diversity of its participants and the diversity of the forms of struggles that can liberate a people. But also it is a model that taps into the deepest cultural and creative recesses in order to maintain the authenticity and humanity of its users. The Viequenses where not epic heroes, the people of Vieques and their supporters were ordinary people achieving extraordinary things.

References ● ● ● ●

Aronowitz, S. 1991. *The Politics of Identity: Class, Culture and Social Movements*. New York: Routledge.

Ayala, C. J. 2001a. "From Sugar Plantations to Military Bases: The U.S. Navy's Expropriations in Vieques, Puerto Rico, 1940-45," *CENTRO Journal*. XIII (1).

Ayala, C. J. and V. Carro. 2002. "Expropriation and Displacement of Civilians in Vieques, 1940-1950," Manuscript.

Ayala, C. J. and L. W. Bergad. 2001. "Rural Puerto Rico in the early twentieth century reconsidered: Land and Society, 1899-1915" *Latin American Research Review* 37 (20:65-97).

Ayala, C. 2001b. "From sugar plantations to military bases: The U.S. Navy's expropriations in Vieques, Puerto Rico, 1940-45." *CENTRO Journal* 13(1): 22-44.

Ayala. C. and J. Bolívar, "Entre dos aguas: economía, sociedad, e intervención estatal en Vieques, 1942-1948." Paper read at Puerto Rican Studies Association Meeting, Hunter College, New York, October 22, 2004. (Manuscript)

Barreto, A. A. 2002. *Vieques, the Navy and Puerto Rican Politics.* Gainesville, FL: The University Press of Florida.

Berrocal, Beatriz. 2000. "US Mail: Epopeya de un pueblo" *Exegesis.* 13, (37 / 38). http://cuhwww.upr.clu.edu/exegesis/37/Exeg-37-15-18.pdf .

Bonilla-Silva, E. and K. S. Glover. 2005. "'We Are All Americans': The Latin Americanization of Race Relations in the U.S." Manuscript.

Cabranes, J. A. 1979. *Citizenship and the American Empire.* New Haven, CN: Yale University Press.

Cesaire, A. 2000. *Discourse on Colonialism.* New York: New York University Press.

Conde, J. 2001. "Origins of *Alianza de Mujeres Viequenses*" personal interview. July 14.

Conde, J. 2004. "Memories of Viequense History" personal interview. October 14.

Cruz Monclova, L. *Historia de Puerto Rico (Siglo XIX).* Rio Piedras, P.R.: Editorial Universitaria, 1957.

De Montilla, A. N. 1971. *Americanization in Puerto Rico and the Public School System: 1900-1930.* Rio Piedras: Editorial Edil.

Duany, J. 2002. *The Puerto Rican Nation on the Move: Identities on the Island and in the United States.* Chapel Hill, NC: University of North Carolina Press.

Falcon, A. 2004. *Atlas of Stateside Puerto Ricans.* Washington, DC: Puerto Rican Federal Affairs Administration.

Fannon, Franz. 1986. *The Wretched of the Earth.* New York: Grove Press.

Fernandez, R. 1996. *The Disenchanted Island: Puerto Rico and the United States in the Twentieth Century.* Westport, CN: Praeger Publishers.

Foster, J. B. 2003. "Introduction to Essays on Imperialism and Globalization" in H. Magdoff *Imperialism Without Colonies.* New York: Monthly Review Press.

Gitlin, T. 1996. *The Twilight of Common Dreams: Why America Is Wracked by Culture Wars.* New York: Henry Holt & Company

Gonzalez, G. G. And R. A. Fernandez. 2003. *A Century of Chicano History: Empire, Nations and Migration*. New York: Rouledge.

Gonzalez, G. G. 2004. *Culture of Empire: American Writers, Mexico and Mexican Immigrants*. Austin: University of Texas Press.

Gonzalez, M.G. 1999. *Mexicanos: A History of Mexicans in the U.S.* Bloomington, IN: Indiana University Press.

Guadalupe, I. 2004. Personal Interviews. July.

Haney Lopez, I. F. 1996. *White by Law: The Legal Construction of Race*. New York: New York University.

Haney Lopez, I. F. 2003. *Racism on Trial: The Chicano Struggle for Justice*. New Haven: Harvard University Press.

Ignatiev, N. I. 1995. *How the Irish Became White*. New York, Routledge.

Jacoby, R. 1987. *The Last Intellectuals: American Culture in the Age of Academe*. New York: Basic Books.

Jiménez, F. 2001. *Vieques y la Prensa: El idilio fragmentado*. San Juan, P.R.: Editorial Plaza Mayor.

Karenga, M. 2002. *Introduction to Black Studies*. Los Angeles, CA: University of Sankore Press.

Lenin, V.I. 1969. Imperialism: The Highest Stage of Capitalism. New York: International Publishing Co.

Magdoff, H. 1969. *The Age of Imperialism: The Economics of U.S. Foreign Policy*. New York: Monthly Review Press.

Magdoff. H. 2003. *Imperialism Without Colonies*. New York: Monthly Review Press.

Maldonado, E. 1979. "Contract Labor and the Origins of Puerto Rican Communities in the United States." *International Migration Review* 13(!): 103-21.

Matos Rodriguez, F. V. 1999. "Their Islands and Our People: U.S. Writing About Puerto Rico, 1898-1920." in *CENTRO* Vol. XI, No. 1: pp. 33-49.

McAdam, D. 1983. "Tactical Innovation and the Pace of Insurgency" *American Sociological Review* 48:735-754.

McCaffrey, K. T. 2002. *Military Power and Popular Protest: The U.S. Navy in Vieques, Puerto Rico*. New Brunswick, NJ: Rutgers University Press.

Medina, N. 2000. "El Comite Pro Rescate y Desarrollo de Vieques" personal interview. August 3.

Melèndez Lopez, A.1982. *La Batalla de Vieques*. Morelos, Mexico: COPEC-CECOPE.

Memmi, A. 1991. *The Colonizer and the Colonized*. Boston: Beacon Press.

Mullenneaux, L. 2000. *"¡Ni una bomba más! Vieques vs. U.S. Navy*. New York: Penington Press.

Murillo, M. 2001. *Islands of Resistance: Puerto Rico, Vieques and U.S. Policy*. New York: Seven Stories Press.

Omi, M. and H. Winant. 1986. *Racial Formation in the United States*. New York: Routledge.

Pastor Ruiz, J. 1947. *Vieques antiguo y moderno*. Yauco, P.R.: Tipografia Rodriguez Lugo. 1947.

Perez, Gina. "Puertorriqueñas rencorosas y Mejicanas sufridas: Constructing Self and Others in Chicago's Latino Communities" *CENTRO Talks*. http://www.prdream.com/patria/centro/02_26/perez.html.

Proyecto Caribeño de Justicia y Paz. 1979. "Entrevistas a los Expropiados de Vieques. Vieques, Puerto Rico," Archivo del Fuerte del Conde de Mirasol, Vieques.

Rivero, A. 1972. *Cronica de la Guerra Hispano Americana en Puerto Rico*. New York: Plus Ultra Educational Publishers.

Rodriguez Beruff, J. Ed. *Las Memorias de Leahy: Los Relatos del Admirante Leahy Sobre su Gobernacion de Puerto Rico (1939-1940)*. San Juan, P.R. Red de Geopolitica, Relaciones Internacionales y Seguridad Regional, 2001.

Rodriguez, C. 2000. *Changing Race: Latinos, the Census and the History of Ethnicity in the United States*. New York: New York University Press.

Rodríguez, V. M. 1988. *External and Internal Factors in the Organization of Production and Labor in the Sugar Industry of Puerto Rico, 1860-1934*. Unpublished Dissertation. Ann Arbor, MI: University Microfilm International.

Rodriguez, V. M. 1997. "The Racialization of Puerto Rican Ethnicity" in Aaron Ramos and Juan Manuel Carrion, Eds. *Ethnicity, Race and Nationality in the Caribbean*. Rio Piedras: Institute for Caribbean Studies.

Rodriguez, V. M. 2000. "Censo 2000: Nacion, raza y el discurso independentista" in two parts in *Claridad* (Puerto Rico) January 7-13, 2000 pp. 14 & 31 and January 14-20, 2000 p. 14 & 31.

Rodriguez, V. M. 2002a. "Internalized Racist Oppression and Racialization in Latino Politics in the United States." Manuscript. California State University, Long Beach.

Rodriguez, V. M. 2002b. "Racism and identity in Puerto Rico" paper read in panel "Census 2000 Says We Are White: Racism and Identity in Puerto Rico" at the biennial meeting of the Puerto Rican Studies Association Conference, Congress Plaza Hotel, Chicago October 5, 2002.

Rodriguez, V. M. 2005. "The Racialization of Mexican Americans and Puerto Ricans: 1890s-1930s". *CENTRO Journal* XVI (3):5-40.

Santiago Caraballo, J. 1997. "Algunas observaciones en torno a la colaboración del PPD y Muñoz con el auge de la militarización en Puerto Rico" *Exegesis* 11 (31). http://cuhwww.upr.clu.edu/exegesis/31/santiago.html.

Scarano, F. A. 1993. *Puerto Rico: Cinco Siglos de Historia*. Bogota, Colombia: McGraw Hill Interamericana.

Sobá, M. 2001. "Origins of the *Alianza de las Mujeres Viequenses*" July 14.

Soto, P. J. 2003. *USMail*. San Juan: Editorial Cultural.

Souza, B.C. 1984. "Trabajo y Tristeza—'Work and Sorrow': The Puerto Ricans of Hawaii, 1900-1902" *Hawaiian Journal of History* 18: 156-73.

Spring, J. 1997. *Deculturization and the Struggle for Equality: A Brief History of the Education of Dominated Cultures in the United States*. New York: McGraw-Hill.

Stewart, A. 2000. "Internalized Racist Oppression, IRO." Manuscript. Crossroads Institute Core Training Manual, Chicago, IL.

Thompson, L. 1995. *Nuestra isla y su gente: La construccion del "otro" puertorriqueño en* Our Islands and their People. Rio Piedras, PR: Centro de Investigaciones Sociales y Departamento de Historia, U.P.R.

Valentin, C. 2001. "Role of the Alianza de Mujeres Viequenses" July 14.

Zenon, C. 2001. "Vieques Fishermen in the Vieques Struggle" personal interview July 19.

Endnotes ● ● ● ● ●

1. Politically, as it is used in this essay, "race" is "a social category used to assign human worth and social status using Europeans as a paradigm." (Karenga 2002). This social category also leads to a process of internalization, called internalized racist oppression (IRO) which leads the racialized subject to develop a stigmatized sense of self. White supremacy refers to both the system of white supremacy and the ideology that is used to legitimate this historically based, institutionally perpetuated system of exploitation and oppression of continents, nations, and peoples of color by white peoples and nations of the European continent, for the purpose of maintaining and defending a system of wealth, power, and privilege.

2. Beginning in 1510 a document written by jurist Palacios Rubios, of the Council of Castille was read in Spanish to the indigenous people of the Americas as a way of legitimizing their dispossession. The document was read to the conquered groups as a way of making the conquest a legal, orderly event with a final mention that a notary would attest to the legality of the process.

3. Viequenses refer to Vieques as *Isla Nena* and to Puerto Rico as *Isla Grande*.

4. Technically, only a limited number of land owners were legally expropriated, because of the intense concentration of land these

amounted to approximately a few hundred expropriations and the overwhelming majority of the Viequenses who lived in agrego relationships experienced what could technically be labeled as an eviction. However, in the narratives that Viequenses use to describe their experience they use the term "me expropriaron" ("I was expropriated") which signifies a deeper sense of loss than a mere eviction.

5. In the Mexican American experience, for example, the "Americanization" program's content was informed by an ideology of the "Mexican Problem." Mexicans, in Mexico and the United States were seen as innately unable to be assimilated and therefore were trained for menial labor in the structure of the United States economy (Gonzalez, 2004).

6. The educational system has a major role in providing an intellectual character to the process that internalizes internalized racist oppression (IRO) in communities of color. IRO is defined as "complex, multigenerational process of socialization that teaches people of color to believe, accept and/or live out a negative societal definition of self. These behaviors contribute to the perpetuation of the race construct. (Anne Stewart 2000)

7. A process of subordination that was utilized in various shapes and forms in the racialization of Native Americans/Indians, African Americans see J. Spring (1997) who provides a good synopsis of the impact of imperial education on the subaltern.

8. Many women in Vieques remember that when the white sailors came to Vieques on shore pass women were "Guardadas a las 6:00 p.m." ("Put away at 6:00 p.m.") Hidden from the drunken sailors who sexually harassed the town's women calling them "Margaritas" (Conde, 2004).

9. In Arizona and California native-born and foreign-born Mexicans have been recently involved in fights, hurling racial epithets at each other. In Puerto Rico many Puerto Ricans born and/or raised in the United States experience a significant amount of prejudice that borders on race prejudice.

10. The perception that most Puerto Rican were "white" in the eyes of congress was crucial to conferring citizenship to Puerto Ricans. Since the 1790 Naturalization Act, only whites could become U.S. citizens. This did not change until the 1951 Walter-McCarren Act which opened the door to "non-whites" being able to become U.S. citizens.

11. During the course of interviews carried out on the race questions in Puerto Rico, I interviewed a number of pro-independence leaders about their perspective on race and racism in Puerto Rico (Rodriguez, 2000). The mulatto, intermediate, pro-independence leaders were the most adamant in rejecting even the raising of the racial question in Puerto Rico. Obviously, the racial advantage offered to darker skinned Puerto Ricans by the "mulatto escape hatch"

in the racial system of Puerto Rico, meant there was more to lose by injecting race into political and social discourse (Rodriguez, 1997).

12. "Parejeria" is one way of individually challenging dominant groups or individuals without outright confrontation. "Pochismo" is a culture that arises out of being rejected in the mainstream for not being fully "American" and from rejection in the Mexican culture for not being "Mexican" enough. Other racialized coping mechanisms are gendered. Gina Perez in her lecture "Puertorriqueñas rencorosas y Mejicanas sufridas: Constructing Self and Others in Chicago's Latino Communities" at the CENTRO of Puerto Rican Studies explains the use of gender based coping mechanisms where stereotypes are then presented as positive traits that while they do not challenge racialization, they help survival. Web published by CENTRO Talks at http://www.prdream.com/patria/centro/02_26/perez.html.

13. Around 6:49 p.m. on April 19, 1999, the pilot of a FA-1BC Hornet, flying at 400 miles an hour was cleared to drop two Mark-82 500-pound bombs by the range office at the Observation Post 1 (OP1), The payload missed its target by a mile and a half killing David Sanes, A 35 year old civilian security guard and injuring four other in the OP1. This was not the first incident, all the way back in 1946, when Culebra was part of the Atlantic Weapons Training Facility (AFWTF) a similar accident killed nine navy personnel (Mullenneaux, 2000, 16-17).

14. On December 4, 1979 a group of naval personnel travelling in a van near the Naval Station of Sabana Seca, Puerto Rico were ambushed by a contingent of members of the Machetero-Ejercito Popular Boricua and other Puerto Rican armed resistance organizations. Two sailors were killed and 10 others were wounded in reprisal for the alleged killing of Angel Rodriguez Cristobal, a Socialist league activist who was arrested with 20 others when they trespassed into the naval base in a protest. A number of the trespassers were arrested and condemned to federal prison in the United States, Rodriguez Cristobal was found dead in his cell in Tallahassee, Florida with suspicious marks on his body. Federal authorities claimed he committed suicide, activists claimed he was murdered.

• • • Index • • •

D

English, as second language, 137
English language
  among California Puerto
    Ricans, 77
  Los Angeles and, 49
  as medium of instruction, 24
  in Puerto Rico, 17
English language proficiency
  (LEP), 113, 141
English Only politics, 67n4
English Only proposition (1986),
  125
Enslavement, and racialization,
  1890-1930, 4
Espinosa, Paul, 32
Esther (pseudonym), 80
Ethnic divisions, between
  workers, 22
Ethnic identity, in California,
  1960-1980, 75
Ethnic Quilt (Allen & Turner),
  95n14-15, 17-21
*Ethnicity, Race and Nationality in
  the Caribbean* (Carrion, ed.),
  95n11
Ethnographies, 11
Europe, as paradigm, 104
European immmigrants, and
  racialization, 4
Evangelical Lutheran Church,
  66n1
Exodo Puertorriqueño (Natal),
  94n7
Expropriation, resistance to,
  Vieques, 186-87

F

Factories in the Field
  (McWilliams), 74
Faculty firings and, La Lucha, in
  Bay Area, 84
Fannon, Franz, 46n27, 195
Farm workers movement, 166n11

Fausto, Tomas Ybarra, 46n26
FBI, 48, 83
"Fear and Loathing in Los
  Angeles?" (article), 63
Federación Libre de Trabajo
  (FLT), 22
Federal, as term, 198, 207-9
Federal Emergency Management
  Agency (FEMA), 62
Federation of Teachers to the
  Catholic Diocese of Caguas,
  204
Feliciano, Carlos, 86
Feminism. *See* Women
Feminist analysis, of PSP, 91
Fernandez, Raul A., x
FHA, 36
Figueroa, Father Allan (Peck),
  131, 134
Filipino. *See also* Philippines
  labor, 34
  Mexican vs., 22
  as racial"other," 26
  workers, strikes and, 21
Films, Latino, 121
Findlay, E.J. Suarez, 23, 30
Flores, Juan, 8, 107
Flow of labor, in California,
  1960-1980, 72
FLT (Federacion Libre de
  Trabajo), 22
Foothill Sentry, 144, 149
Forced migration, of colonial
  peoples, 17
Frank (pseudonym), 85
Franklin, Benjamin, 146
Free Labor Federation (FLT), 22
French Revolution, 67n8
Friedman, Milton, 148

G

Galan, Hector, 32
Galician cultural club, 27

I

IAF (Industrial Areas Foundation), 131-32, 166n16, 167n19
Ibarra, Maria Rosa, 131-32, 138, 164n1, 4
Ideology
    education and, 115-22
    racialization, 1890-1930, 18-25
    Vieques social movement, 173-79, 187-92
Iglesias, Cesar Andreu, vii
Iglesias Pantin, Santiago, 22
Illiberal Education (D'Souza), 69n20
Imagined Communities (Anderson), 172
Immigration and Naturalization Services (INS), 48
Immigration Reform and Control Act (IRCA), 134, 139, 167n20
Imperialism, and Vieques social movement, 172-79
Imposition, processes of, 13-16, 106-9
Independence activists, alliances of, 93n1
Independentista armed resistance, 205
Industrial Areas Foundation (IAF), 131-32, 166n16, 167n19
Inner cities, economics of, 57-60
Institute of Puerto Rican Culture, 200
Institutional arrangements, of racialization, 18-25, 187-92
Insular Cases, 178
Intelligence Project of the Southern Poverty Law Center, 168n30
Intermarriage, 76, 97n46, 165n6
Internalized Racist Oppression (IRO), 31, 46n25, 215n1, 216n6
International Conference of the Americas, 86

International Conference on Hispanic Cultures in the U.S., 66n1
International Report, 67n1
Invention of the White Race (Allen), 95n12
Invisibility, Puerto Rican, 74
IRCA (Immigration Reform and Control Act), 134, 139, 167n20
Iron Law of Oligarchy (Michels), 60
Isla Grande
    institutions, 181
    relationship with Vieques, 185, 194, 201, 204, 208
    term for Puerto Rico, 215n3
Isla Nena, term for Vieques, 215n3

J

Jacobs, Jane, 69n17
Japanese
    labor, 34
    racialization and, 21
    unions and, 22
Japanese-Mexican Labor Association (JMLA), 20-22
Jarvis-Gann proposition, 165n9
Jibaro, 28-29
Jim Crow Laws, 18, 116, 187
JMLA (Japanese-Mexican Labor Association), 20-22
John Birchers, 125
Johns Hopkins University, 152
Johnson, Lyndon Baines, 199
Jones, Bill, 100
Jones, Chester Lloyd, 19
Jones, Frank, 192

K

Kant, Immanuel, 10
Katz, Michael, B., 56

educational achievement in, 76-77

endnotes, 93-97

ethnic identity and, 75

Factories in the Field, 74

flow of labor, 72

hegemony of Latino culture in, 77

household income for, 76

intermarriage, 76

invisibility in west, 74

La Lucha, 78-90

Lenin and, 73

Marxism and, 73

McWilliams, Carey, 74

mexican Americans and, 74-75

models outdates, 72

Nuestra Señora de Los Angeles, 73

political organizations of, 73

Raza Unida Party, 73

references, 92-93

socioeconomic experience in, 75

sugar plantations and, 74

Treaty of Guadalupe Hidalgo, 73

U.S. Commission on Civil Rights, 77

Virgin of Guadalupe, 75

Puerto Rican Socialist Party (PSP), 73, 78-87

Puerto Ricans, racialization of, 1890-1930, 5, 16-18

Puerto Ricans Born in the USA (Rodriguez), 35

Puerto Rico and Its Problems (Clark), 19

Puerto Rico Solidarity Committee (PRSC), 79

Puerto Rico, as classic colonial model, 16

Pulido, Miguel, 128, 136, 154

Q

Quayle, Dan, 49

Quintero, Brenda, 164n1

R

Rabin, Robert

Race and Angelazo of 1992, 56-57

Race, definitions of, 44n14

Racial categoires, in U.S., 3

Racial grid, 4

Racial hierarchy, placement in, 25-30, 192-95

Racial identity, crystallization of, 20-35, 195-98

Racial system, in Puerto Rico, 5

Racialization

through Americanization, 188

challenge to, in Puerto Rico, 6-7

challenge to, in Vieques, 196

contested, 21

defined, 11-12

demystifying of, 3

process, historical, 12, 105-9, 180

process, of Mexicans, 7

process, of Puerto Ricans, 16

resistance, 109

of U.S. Census Bureau, 5

of Vieques social movement, 173-79

Racism, scientific, 9

Racist flyers, 167n21-22

Railroad, arrival of, 7

Ramirez, Alex, 80

Ramirez, Pedro, 85

Ramos, Paco, vii

Raza Unida Party, 73

Reagan, Ronald, 36, 54, 91, 112, 125, 133

Rebuild L.A. Foundation, 61-62, 69n18

••• Citation Index •••

E

Edsall, M.D., 148
Edsall, T.B., 148
EdSource Inc., 113, 114
Ehrenreich, Barbara, 57
England, R.E., 124

F

Fannon, Franz, 173, 176, 195
Fernandez, R.A., 107, 111, 174, 199
Fernandez, Raul, 7, 14, 15, 16
Fernandez, Ronald, 96n25
Flores, Juan, 2, 27
Flores, William V., 3
Fraga, Luis R., 124, 168n25

G

Garcia, I.M., 94n5
Garcia, J.A., 132
Garcia, M.T., 94n5, 97n39-40, 129
Gitlin, T., 173
Glasser, Ruth, 27
Glover, K.S., 176
Godinez, V., 43n5
Gomez Quiñones, J., 104
Gonzalez 2004, 216n5
Gonzalez, G., 7, 14, 15, 16, 18,
    19, 20
Gonzalez, G.G., 103, 107, 111,
    122, 174
Gonzalez, Gilbert, 14, 21, 44n15
Gonzalez, Jose Luis, 29, 31
Gonzalez, M.G., 7, 8
Gould, Stephen Jay, 116
Griswold del Castillo, R., 14,
    46n26, 107
Guadalupe, I., 189, 195, 197, 198,
    199, 202, 208
Guerra, Lillian, 5, 28, 29, 31, 32
Gutierrez, I, 97n47

H

Haberman, D., 140
Hajnal, Z.L., 137
Haney Lopez, I.F., 4, 42n2, 95n12,
    108, 112, 118, 119-20, 193, 196
Hanson, Victor Davis, 69
Harris, M., 44n10
Harrison, Bennett, 68n13
Hart, S., 93n1
Hayes-Bautista, D.E., 114
Haynes, K., 45n20
Hernandez, E., Jr., 94n9
Highton, B., 137
Hill, L.E., 114, 115
Hobsbawn, E., 67n2
Hubler, Shawn, 51, 69n18
Huntington, Samuel, 69n20

I

Ibarra Lopez, M.R., 131, 32
Ignatiev, N., 42n2, N., 95n12
IUPLR, 5

J

Jacobs, Jane, 69n16
Jiménez, F., 209
Johnson, H.P., 114, 115

K

Karenga, M., 18, 44n14, 104, 187,
    188, 215n1
Katz, Michael B., 56
Keen, B., 45n20
Klor de Alva, J.J., 5
Kloss, R.M., 94n2
Kugel, S., 43n5

L

Laila, R., 53, 68n9
Le Bon, Gustave, 50, 67n6
Lea, Clarence F., 117-18
Lee, C., 123, 165n8
Lenin, V.I., 174
Levins-Morales, Aurora, 81, 96n27, 96n29, 96n31-32
Lewis, P.G., 137
Logan, J., 165n8
Lopez, N., 97n41-44, 133, 134, 135, 140, 166n12, 167n18
Louch, H., 137

M

Magdoff, H., 173
Maharidge, D., 113, 125, 126, 165n7
Makowski, M., 10
Maldonado, E., 45n22, 94n6, 96n28
Marmor, T., 68n12
Marques, B., 130, 132
Marti-Orvella, J., 121
Marx, Karl, 176
Massey, D.S., 124
Matthewson, D.J., 147, 148, 149
McAdams, D., 209
McCaffrey, K.T., 185, 192, 194, 195, 197, 198, 185, 200-201, 204, 205, 206, 208
Medina, N., 205, 206
Meier, K.J., 124
Melendez Lopez, A., 181, 182, 183
Melendez, Hector, 96n30
Memmi, A., 173
Menchaca, Martha, 14, 108
Mercer, J., 122
Michels, Robert, 59
Miles, Nelson, 176
Mirande, Alfredo, 45n19
Montilla, A. Negron de, 24, 189, 190
Moscoso, E., 164n3
Mullenneaux, L., 201, 217n13
Myers, D., 166n10

N

Natal, Carmelo Rosario, 74, 94n7-8
Negron de Montilla, A., 24, 189, 190
Nieto-Phillips, J., 8, 43n8
Noriega, C.A., 121
Nuechterlein, Paul, 210

O

Oboler, Suzanne, 43n3, 43n4
Omi, M., 11, 12, 42n1, 104, 179
Orfield, G., 123, 165n8

P

Palacio, John, 126, 127, 135, 143, 168n28
Pardo, M., 128
Park, J., 166n10
Parrillo, V., 146
Perez, Gina, 217n12
Phelan, J., 43n3
Pitkin, J., 166n10
Pulido, L., 94n5

R

Ramirez, R., 168n25
Reisler, Mark, 33, 34
Rivero, A., 176
Roberts, R., 94n2
Rodriguez Beruff, J., 183, 184
Rodriguez, Clara, 2, 9, 25-26, 35, 130, 192, 193

Rodriguez, G., 96n26, 32-35, 97n36
Rodriguez, Matos, 11, 25, 191
Rodriguez, P., 97n45, 52
Rodriguez, R., 21, 28
Rodriguez, Victor M., 12, 22, 30,
    43n7, 44n13, 46n27, 50, 95n11,
    105, 140, 141, 164n2, 173, 176,
    177-78, 179, 180, 194, 195, 216-
    17n11
Roediger, D.R., 42n2, 95
Rosaldo, Renato, 3, 11, 13,
    45n17, 106
Rosales, R., 101, 102, 130, 140
Rosario Natal, Carmelo, 74,
    94n7-8
Rosenblatt, R.A., 68n9
Rothmiller, Mike, 68n10
Rothstein, R., 113
Rowe, Leo Stanton, 34
Rude, George, 67n8
Ruiz, Vicky, 33

S

Santiago-Valles, K.A., 29
Scarano, F.A., 177
Schlesinger, Arthur, 69n20
Schmitz, Reina, 2004, 138, 139
Seymour, L., 145
Skocpol, T., 149
Slavin, Robert, 152
Smelzer, Neil J., 67n7
Smith, Lillian, 116-117
Sonstelie, J., 111, 112
Soto, Pedro Juan, 173, 175, 190
Souza, B.C., 45n22, 94n6
Spring, J., 45n23, 216n7
State of California, Department
    of Finance, 110

Stein, K., 53, 68n9
Stewart, Anne, 46n25, 216n6
Stoskopf, A., 116, 117-18
Suarez Findlay, E.J., 30

T

Taylor Haizlip, S., 44n11
Thompson, L., 25, 29, 191, 215
Turner, E., 95n14-15, 17-21
Turner, John Kenneth, 15
Turner, M.A., 53, 165n8

U

U.S. Bureau of Census, 44n12,
    44n14, 95n13, 95n16, 96n22,
    114, 125
U.S. Department of Labor, 110
Unz, Ron, 146, 147, 150
Utley, G., 69n21

V

Valentin, C., 206
Vega, B., 17

W

Wallis, Jim, 168n31
Williams, R.M., 145
Wilson, W.J., 110
Winant, H., 11, 12, 42n1, 104, 179

Z

Zenon, C., 197
Zentella, Ana Ceilia, 95n10